Theology,
Politics, and
Peace

Theology, Politics, and Peace

Edited by
Theodore Runyon

ORBIS BOOKS

Maryknoll, New York 10545

The Catholic Foreign Mission Society of America (Maryknoll) recruits and trains people for overseas missionary service. Through Orbis Books, Maryknoll aims to foster the international dialogue that is essential to mission. The books published, however, reflect the opinions of their authors and are not meant to represent the official position of the society.

Library of Congress Cataloguing-in-Publication Data

Theology, politics, and peace/edited by Theodore Runyon.
    p. cm.
    "Based on lectures delivered at a conference . . . held at Candler
School of Theology and the Carter Center of Emory University . . . in
April of 1988"—Pref.
  Includes bibliographies and index.
  ISBN 0-88344-598-0
  1. Peace—Religious aspects—Christianity—Congresses.
2. Christianity and politics—Congresses. 3. Peace—Religious
aspects—Judaism—Congresses. 4. Judaism and politics—Congresses.
5. Judaism—Doctrines—Congresses. I. Runyon, Theodore.
II. Candler School of Theology. III. Emory University. Carter
Center.
BT736.4.T54 1989
261.8'73—dc20
                                89-15977
                                    CIP

Table of Contents

Preface

Based on lectures delivered at a conference on the theme "Theology, Politics, and Peace," this book brings together theologians and political leaders from three continents—Europe, Latin America, and North America—for dialogue around a common concern for peace. The conference, which was held at Candler School of Theology and at the Carter Center of Emory University, was keynoted by former President Jimmy Carter and attracted theologians, politicians, and laypersons from across the country in April of 1988, for three days of presentations and discussion. Both audio and videotapes of many of the lectures are available from the Media Center, Bishops Hall, Emory University, Atlanta, Georgia 30322.

Support for the conference was provided by the Candler School of Theology and the Carter Center, with assistance from the Georgia Humanities Council and Goeth-Institute Atlanta. Our appreciation goes to them for helping to make this event possible. We are also grateful to Susan Johnson for her expertise in preparing the manuscript for publication.

We are pleased to join forces with Orbis Press to make the results of the conference available to a wider audience.

THEODORE RUNYON

Introduction:
Theology, Politics, and Peace

THEODORE RUNYON

The conference which gave rise to this book was a unique event. It brought together for the first time *theologians*, representing three different approaches to "political theology," with practicing *politicians* from three continents. The result is a lively exchange that reflects the diverse views not only of the theologians from Europe, Latin America, and the United States, but also of the politicians whose task it is to reflect on the usefulness of theological perspectives to the political quest for peace.

First, a word concerning the three theological approaches represented here. European political theology has sought to overcome the compliant establishment role of European Christianity by making the church a critical force in society, pointing to the Christian vision of the kingdom of God as the hope for justice in a transformed society. Latin American liberation theologies have turned the church from an ally of the wealthy into an advocate of the poor and of those without a voice, not only in Latin America but in much of the Third World. In the United States "Christian realism" owes its theoretical base to Reinhold Niebuhr, who made use of the traditional Christian doctrine of sin to analyze the forces of power and self-interest and the constraints due to persistent tendencies in human nature which have to be taken into account in any political system. His analysis influenced political theory and the formulation of policy in this country during and after World War II. It is still influential today. How are these diverse approaches viewed by working politicians, charged with the task of responding not only to the inevitable day-to-day challenges but of thinking about long-range public policies and the goal of peace?

In Europe and Latin America, where the presence of Christian political parties makes the discussion of theological factors an accepted part of the political process, theology plays a more direct and open role. In the United States, the "wall of separation" between church and state tends to obscure the extent to which theological presuppositions are operative in political analysis and in the values out of which politicians approach public issues.

Although former President **Jimmy Carter** has been more willing than most chief executives to make his own religious convictions public, he has always done so with the proviso that these are privately held values within the pluralistic context of American democracy, where no one theological orientation has the right to impose its values on others. Religiously grounded values are thus privately held, but can be publicly invoked when in accord with a broad public consensus. Although the politician must avoid any hint of sectarianism, an appeal to the "civil religion" is an appropriate way to carry out one's Christian witness in public office.

Speaking out of the Chilean situation, where church and state institutionally interrelate, **Manuel Antonio Garretón**, a member of the Central Committee of the Chilean Socialist Party, views cooperation between politicians and the church as appropriate where they share common goals, as they have in recent years in opposition to the Chilean dictatorship. Thus he welcomes theological arguments that support the cause of democracy. Nevertheless, he anticipates a day when the church's conservatism will make further cooperation impossible, if the church follows a reactionary moral policy as set by the Vatican.

Kurt Biedenkopf, a member of the West German Parliament and former general secretary of the ruling Christian Democratic Party, recognizes that the issue is not to be understood on the institutional level alone—the role of the church in politics—but rather in terms of the role played by religion in the political consciousness of the people. Only religious convictions are powerful enough, claims Biedenkopf, to motivate freely willed self-sacrifice and to call forth from the populace the kind of behavior that rises above self-interest. Given the ecological and financial world crises, Biedenkopf sees no peaceful way into the future which does not entail for Western democracies a heightened sense of worldwide economic justice and ecological self-discipline. Yet democracies exist by the support of the people. And this means that public support must be mobilized for policies that predictably will not be popular in industrial democracies whose citizens are addicted to ever-increasing material wealth, consumption and comfort. "We will have to rely on the strength of religion . . . to make the kind of sacrifices and exercise the self-discipline that will be demanded." Human rationality and enlightened self-interest are not sufficient, if at a more profound level there is not a "covenant" of solidarity with, and justice toward, both the disadvantaged and exploited peoples of the world and the disadvantaged and exploited environment. This covenant must be "stable enough to continue even in the face of substantial conflict." Such a covenant "requires God as the institutor, as the guarantor," i.e., a source which can command loyalty sufficient to sustain a reorientation of such fundamental proportions that it could not ordinarily be attained without coercive and oppressive power. Nothing less than this kind of shared internalized goal of responsible transformation can lead toward a peaceful future. For in a world of injustice and selfishly squandered resources there can be no peace.

Biedenkopf's more explicitly theological stance sets the stage for the theologians to share their own visions of the theological contribution to peace with justice. According to **José Míguez Bonino**, former dean of the Protestant Institute for Advanced Theological Studies in Buenos Aires, theology provides a hermeneutic, a perspective from which the politician can view the political situation. All judgments are made from value perspectives, argues Míguez, whether this bias is recognized or not. Middle-class politicians tend to view things through middle-class glasses. A theological corrective must be added, therefore, if issues are to be analyzed in terms of their impact on the impoverished majority. This corrective is what the Latin American bishops mean by their "preferential option for the poor." The church is called to be an advocate of those without political and economic power, and politicians are called to view legislation and governmental policies in the light of their impact on the disadvantaged. This theological stance is not restricted to a single issue but defines an angle of vision that can be implemented in a variety of ways, but always with the interests of the poor in mind. Such a perspective does not dictate a single possibility in concrete cases. One could argue for more socialist or more capitalist economic policies, for example. But the argument would have to demonstrate how the rights of the poor are to be advanced through any given policy. This option for the poor is grounded, notes Míguez, in Christ's suffering and his mission to bring "good news to the poor, release to the captives, and to set at liberty the oppressed." Such a theologically informed bias cannot be ignored by those who would claim Christian identity—i.e., identity with Christ and his mission—and it functions to press constantly for new solutions that have as their goal to approximate more concretely the justice and love of the kingdom of God. Such an argument is intrinsic to Christian theology. It follows from the nature of the gospel itself.

A different kind of intrinsic argument is advanced by **Theodore Weber**, professor of social ethics at Emory. He spells out in some detail the approach of Reinhold Niebuhr, whose thought, often termed "Christian realism," is appealed to frequently in these pages by theologians and politicians alike. Niebuhr took as his task, in his significant and influential publications of the 'thirties, 'forties, and 'fifties, to apply insights derived from traditional Christian doctrines to the political life of the nation. He claimed that the truth inherent in biblical and historical Christian interpretations of human existence showed more insight into the practical human situation, both as to its possibilities and limits, than did the Enlightenment rationalistic sources at the root of much American political thought. Human nature is the *given*, according to Niebuhr, with which all efforts toward peace must come to terms. His own method is *dialectical* because it is rooted in the ambiguity of human nature. The human creature is both flesh and spirit, both finite and, by virtue of the power to transcend self, a participant in the infinite. The Christian vision of the kingdom of God calls for an ever more complete realization of justice and serves both as a prophetic criticism of the present order and the imaginative source of new possibilities which transcend the present. The Christian doctrine of "original sin," however, points to the constant tendency of human beings — especially when they are seeking good ends — to underestimate the ambiguity of all human enterprises, an ambiguity attendant to the fact that power is both necessary and dangerous. From this follows Niebuhr's positive evaluation of the "balance of power" as a self-limiting principle and his call for built-in measures against human pride, such as provisions for self-criticism and regularized means of review and revision.

To turn to **Jürgen Moltmann**, professor of systematic theology at the University of Tübingen, is to turn to a side of Niebuhr often neglected in the presentation of his views, namely, the role which utopian thinking plays in opening up new possibilities for the human spirit. Conservative interpreters of Niebuhr, for instance, point to his reminders of the seeds of corruption at work in the human condition due to human pride and selfishness. But Niebuhr also identifies the sin of sloth, of failing to seize the possibilities present in the self-transcendent qualities of human existence. Utopian thought, for example, though it can never be actualized in its fullness in history, nevertheless provides a vision of what is possible beyond the present and moves history forward toward those new possibilities.

In Moltmann this becomes even more pronounced, because he takes New Testament eschatological thought as normative for the Christian gospel. Moltmann does not derive self-transcendent possibilities from the capacities of the human spirit but from the call of a transcendent God. Because there are no limits on the divine Spirit who is the constant source of creativity in the faithful, Moltmann does not set the same limits to human possibilities that Niebuhr assumes. Trusting that God is working in history to create "a new heaven and a new earth," as revealed in Jesus' message of the kingdom, Christians are called to "take seriously the possibilities with which all reality is fraught. [Christian faith] does not take things as they happen to stand or lie, but as progressing, moving things with possibilities of change."[1] Therefore, Moltmann is not willing to let past political impasses, which he sees as caused by past insecurities, determine the future. This is not to ignore the weight of the past, for Moltmann gives attention to the "vicious circles" that plague human existence and drag it down into despair. The vicious circles of poverty, arbitrary force, racial and cultural alienation, and increasing pollution, cannot be overcome by wishing them away, or even by throwing money at them. For the deeper problem to which they contribute is a fundamental uncertainty and despair about the future which undermines all positive efforts. Confidence that things can be different must come from beyond the protracted lines drawn from our present dilemmas. This confidence is the gift of the God who beckons us into an uncertain future with the promise of divine faithfulness. Confidence requires a transcendent source, but it is then implemented practically through concrete efforts to extend economic and political democracy, guarantee human rights, and cooperate with nature, all of which can serve to break through the vicious circles and furnish signs of hope in the midst of hope-lessness.[2]

In the chapters that follow, other contributors provide further examples of theological wrestling with political issues in the cause of peace.

Andrew Young, mayor of Atlanta and former U.S. Ambassador to the United Nations, traces the theological development of Martin Luther King, Jr., and the biblical images and theological ideas that informed King's thought and action. Young then shows how the courageous steps which King took, and the pressures which he brought to bear on the political system, opened up possibilities for increased justice, not just for African-Americans but for the nation as a whole.

The continuing resources for political responsibility to be found in the thought of Reinhold Niebuhr is the subject of **Gordon Harland**, professor of theology and ethics at the University of Manitoba. Recognizing that "self interest is a fundamental datum of all collective life," creative and sensitive leaders will use this fact positively to seek out "the points of coincidence between the group or national interest and the needs and interests of the wider human community." Harland sees Abraham Lincoln as such a leader, one who was resolute in his cause and convinced of its justice, but who had a keen sense of the ambiguity of even the best of causes, which preserved him from the human tendency toward self-congratulation, self-righteous-ness, and pride.

Marc Ellis, Jewish faculty member and director of the Peace and Justice Institute at Maryknoll School of Theology, examines the anguish raised for Jewish thinking—given the history of activism and commitment of Ameri-can Jews to justice for minorities—by the Palestinian uprisings and the measures taken by the Israeli government against them. Not only a political but a theological transformation is necessary, claims Ellis, to move the troubled Middle East toward a more permanent solution. Fears for the survival of Israel cause authentic Jewish theological perspectives on justice and peace to be silenced or simply lost from sight, and the future is ap-proached on the basis of a harsh *Realpolitik*. Such a policy is finally self-defeating, Ellis believes, and will in fact bring the very results Jews fear most. The only viable way ahead is one that builds on common interests in a common destiny for both Jews and Palestinians.

Dennis P. McCann, director of the Center for the Study of Values, DePaul University, approaches the issue of peace from the standpoint of the U.S. Catholic bishops' pastoral letter, "Economic Justice for All: Cath-olic Social Teaching and the U.S. Economy." According to the bishops, the developing interdependence of the world economy is forcing a rethinking of "national interest." A case is made for restructuring the international economic system. The distorted patterns of global economic development, the debt burdens of Third-World nations and the patterns of exploitation are all destabilizing. Peace is therefore an impossibility unless a greater degree of justice becomes the foundation stone and goal of an international economic policy.

Analyzing the Religious Right, which has been a potent force in U.S. politics over the past decade, **Gabriel Fackre**, professor of theology at Andover-Newton Theological School, sorts out the varieties of fundamentalists and clarifies their different commitments and agendas. Although fundamentalists assert the absolute authority of Scripture, they tend to fall into an "us and them" approach that distorts the Bible's understanding of both sin and grace, and promotes a nationalist mentality that ascribes evil to "them" while assuming virtue for our side. Hence the holy war against sin is all too easily projected into the arena of international conflict. Because this fundamentalist mentality will remain a constant on the American scene into the foreseeable future, efforts toward peace need more realistically to take it into consideration.

African Americans have consistently demonstrated their patriotism in wartime, according to **Riggins R. Earl**, professor of ethics at Interdenominational Theological Center, who traces the participation of African Americans in the Civil War, World Wars I and II, and the Vietnam War. Often blacks believed that by fighting for their country they could win the acceptance and equality which they had sought in vain as civilians. Once the wars were over, however, they were most often disillusioned and disappointed. In his criticism of the Vietnam War, Martin Luther King, Jr., broke with the traditional support given the nation in time of war by black clergy. He called upon blacks and whites alike to recognize that both international and domestic conflict are rooted in injustice, and that poverty, violence and racism are not removed but rather exacerbated by war. The commandment to love one's enemies takes precedence over an uncritical patriotism. Justice at home and justice abroad are interrelated realities. In neither place are they likely to be guaranteed by the methods of destructive violence.

Gonzalo Castillo-Cardenas, professor of Third-World studies at Pittsburgh Theological Seminary, raises the question of the implications of liberation theology for indigenous peoples such as the Indians of Latin America. They have been displaced by Western "civilization," robbed of their land and resources, and their cultures and community structures have been broken down. If the goal of liberation theology is both solidarity with the poor and the right to autonomous development under conditions of justice, it should campaign for guaranteed rights for indigenous minorities as well as the preservation of their cultures and traditional ways. Castillo-Cardenas points to the new constitution of Nicaragua as a model in this regard.

Contrasting the establishment "center" with the "margin," **Rebecca Chopp**, professor of theology at Emory University, sees feminist theologies as carrying out a more radical critique from the margin of the establishment than European political theologies (as represented by Moltmann) and Niebuhrian realism (as represented by Weber) can do from the center. Feminist theologies call for a transformation not just of political and economic structures but also of the basic patterning of language, subjectivity, and relationships, in order to eradicate often unconscious and unrecognized underlying forms of oppression imbedded in the cultural structures that maintain them. The feminist contribution is not limited, however, to the struggle for equality. What are the special gifts and unique contributions that women can bring to public life? It is these to which Chopp wishes to draw attention, for they can benefit both the margin and the center.

Delwin Brown, professor of theology at Iliff School of Theology, argues that if three of the most influential theologies in America today—Niebuhrian realism, liberation theologies, and process theology—could speak with one voice concerning the necessity and possibility of social change, they would find a hearing and begin to influence policy. Therefore Brown, who himself represents the process orientation, seeks to demonstrate the compatibility of the three by extending the vectors he perceives in each until they converge in mutually affirmative positions.

After reviewing the debate over the nature of Dietrich Bonhoeffer's "pacifism," **G. Clarke Chapman**, professor of religion at Moravian College, traces the German theologian and martyr's peacemaking activity to his Christocentric view of human existence. "In Christ we are offered the possibility of partaking in the reality of God and in the reality of the world, but not in one without the other." The authority of Christ sets limits to the authority of any worldly power. Therefore Bonhoeffer found himself in opposition to the "totalism" of the rising Nazi state in the 'thirties, which he called upon the church to oppose as an idolatrous challenge to the authority of Christ. The parallel in our time, Chapman contends, is "nuclearism," the claim of a new technological deity to contain evil forces and guarantee peace by its overwhelming power. This deity demands to be given priority and authority above all else, for it can preserve life or take it away. It is this theological heresy which Chapman claims that Bonhoeffer, consistent with his stance in the 'thirties, would attack today.

The just-war theory is often lifted up as informing U.S. military policy. **John Howard Yoder**, professor of theology and ethics at Notre Dame University, argues—on the basis of a lecture course on "The Legality and Morality of War," which he has regularly team-taught at Notre Dame with a military instructor, a law professor, and a philosopher—that the just-war tradition which, in principle, could restrain and moderate wars and conflicts, is in actuality undercut by the reluctance of the military to endanger the efficiency and uncritical solidarity ("team spirit") so important to a fighting force. Thus any theological approval given to the just-war theory would have to ask whether "the military enterprise as a whole, as presently structured," can adequately implement the self-discipline for which the theory calls. If not, does the tradition serve simply as moral window dressing for an immoral system?

In the concluding chapter, **James E. Will**, director of the Peace Institute,

Garrett-Evangelical Theological Seminary, examines the relationship of peace to salvation in the Judeo-Christian tradition. The universalistic themes in the wisdom literature of Hebrew Scriptures and the Logos of the New Testament are in tension with the cultural particularity of these or any other religions as they are appropriated and lived out in specific cultural contexts. Concreteness is necessary (e.g., the Jewishness of Jesus) if religion is to be authentic. Christianity affirms this in its doctrine of the Incarnation. But a culture reads its own particularity into its religion, which in turn leads to conflicts with the religions of other cultures and even with different cultural appropriations of the same religion. Thus a religion which, on the basis of its fundamental principles, should promote unity and peace, results instead in conflict and strife. National particularism leads to similar divisiveness as the nation defines peace in terms of its own particular security and inviolability. Anything that threatens it, threatens "peace." Over against this seemingly inevitable human particularism is Jesus' command to "Love your enemies and pray for those who persecute you." The threat to any particular peace is a perceived "enemy," but the universal threat to peace is *enmity* as such. Therefore, "it is precisely the love of all enemies that finally vanquishes enmity." The ministry of Christ is effective wherever God's power is active through him to "reconcile to himself all things, whether on earth or in heaven, making peace by the blood of his cross" (Colossians 1:20). This becomes concrete as we participate spiritually and politically in "transforming the conflictual social reality of which we are a part" by dissolving enmity through removing the threatening nature of the enemy, both in ourselves and for others. And this is the task of love.

Areas of Consensus

Many conclusions could be drawn from these chapters, but let me suggest just four, which represent a kind of consensus emerging from these pages.

No stable peace is possible without an increase in justice. The search for justice is universal in the hearts of humanity wherever the awareness of injustice has been raised. Traditionally, religion has contributed to the acceptance of the status quo as God-ordained, an arrangement that one-sidedly benefitted those in power. This is no longer the case. Most religions include among their chief tenets standards for justice and for the treatment of the poor, and these have now become the source of the questioning of unjust arrangements and structures worldwide. As President Carter pointed out, however, "justice" is defined differently depending upon one's cultural location and the primary concerns of the culture. Nevertheless, there are common forms which the universal quest for justice takes in our own time, and they are political, economic, and ecological.

Political justice. The yearning of the people for participation in the political order that governs them is found everywhere, although the degree of participation obviously varies from culture to culture. "Democracy" is the universal cry, East and West, North and South, in Communist as well as capitalist and mixed societies. The political and human rights necessary for democratic institutions would therefore seem to be a necessity if a more peaceful world is to be achieved.

Economic justice. Equally necessary is the right to economic democracy. The Judeo-Christian religious tradition places, if anything, more emphasis upon the basic economic rights of the poor and economically disenfranchised—"the widows, the orphans, and the foreigner in your midst"—than upon the political. God is seen as siding with those who have no one else to defend their interests. Hence the Latin American bishops' "preferential option for the poor." As some of the early church fathers claimed, "the rights of the poor" become the hermeneutic principle for determining priorities. What kind of order—political and economic—is capable of assuring the poor their right to justice?[3] Moreover, there is a rising theological concern for the generational injustice caused by mounting debts which benefit the present generation at the expense of future generations. This is especially onerous in the Third World, where often debts have been incurred by previous governments and military regimes without regard to viable, long-term economic improvement. And present governments are saddled with inherited debts that make new and more responsible programs impossible.

Ecological justice. The resources of the earth are finite and the balance of the planet's ecosystem is fragile, but until recently these resources have been exploited without regard to the "rights" of the earth and the claims of future generations. Thus we are forced to expand our concept of justice to include nature and the future, and to recall the original covenant of God with Adam to care for the earth and its inhabitants, nonhuman as well as human. The biblical concept of peace, *shalom*, encompasses all of these factors in a holistic understanding of all things working together in mutual respect and for mutual benefit. Justice will inevitably involve balancing some rights claims against others. Rights are not absolute but are always in relation to the wholeness of society and the wholeness of history, future as well as past and present. And such wholeness has now become a necessity as never before. The vision of the kingdom of God, the "peaceable Kingdom," is no longer a utopian dream but a prescription for the survival of the planet.

Anthropological presuppositions play a key role in efforts to achieve and maintain peace with justice. The understanding of human nature, its limits and possibilities, will inevitably affect the ways in which political institutions are shaped, power is channeled, and checks and balances are applied. Here some of the sharpest differences between the three main theological orientations presented in this book become visible. As theologies of hope, both European political theology and Latin American liberation theology are persuaded that there are divine resources to enable humans to transcend the limitations of their present condition. According to Moltmann, humanity is constantly in the process of "being brought into being by the calling, coaxing, compelling word of God."[4] Therefore human nature is not a fixed entity and individuals and society are not completely determined by past conditioning or by the constraints of the present situation. When new alternatives are opened up, new responses are made possible. Thus unilateral steps toward peace, taken by nations genuinely desirous of overcoming present stalemates, can have the effect of "opening a way where there was no way" and redefining the situation in new and more flexible terms. European and Latin American theologians would like to see political leaders venture forth on more creative paths to justice.

Although it is aware of the importance of self-transcendence in the Christian understanding of humanity, Niebuhrian realism relies more on an interpretation of the classic Christian doctrine of original sin to inform its understanding of human nature and its basic political approach. It assumes that human beings will continue to be insecure and therefore defensive, both as individuals and as groups, in the future as they have been in the past. This means that self-interest will remain a powerful factor to be taken into consideration in any political system. This does not imply that it is impossible for human beings to rise above self-interest, and even to sacrifice self-interest to a higher cause when a crisis demands it. Political strategies, however, should not rely on these occasional moments of altruism and transcendence, but should be formulated on the basis of the predominant pattern of human behavior.

Realism also reminds us of the ambiguity and constraints of the political process. In order to achieve desirable ends, compromises have to be made and deals struck which often sully the goal when it is finally reached. Only by relying on divine grace and forgiveness can politicians face honestly the ambiguity of the process and their own guilt, and continue to pursue goals that may be relatively better but are never ideal. The human tendency toward pride and corruption in any situation that involves power and influence makes necessary a system of checks and balances and self-critical review to counteract the temptations of power. Realism's greatest contribution may be to the post-revolutionary situation, therefore, when high aims and bright goals prove elusive and yet politicians must be sustained in commitment to the slow process of perfecting a state and society that in fact will never be perfect.

The differing doctrines of humanity held by these theological dialogue partners may prove *complementary*, therefore, rather than contradictory. The one serves as the constant resource for change, and the other guarantees the modesty and yet steady moral persistence of the political enterprise. Thus both have their contribution to make to the self-understanding and sense of vocation of the politician.

The third point of consensus that can be drawn from these chapters is that there is no peace without *mutual* security. It is habitual for humans to think, as individuals and as nations, that security is based on power: the more power, the more security. With the advent of nuclear weapons that truism not only no longer obtains, it is highly dangerous. The nuclear threat is a real threat—but always to *both* sides. There is no longer any superiority of power that can guarantee national interests and objectives. Yet the "national security doctrine" continues to see the primary purpose of the state as securing the interests of the nation by the power to defend those interests and, inevitably, to impose those interests on other nations. Issues of power are not irrelevant and have to be taken into account in any realistic policy. But a new maxim is gaining more and more converts: a nation can no longer increase its own security by increasing the insecurity of other nations. As Mikhail Gorbachev has formulated it, the basic principle of "an all-embracing system of international security" is the fact that "one's own security cannot be ensured at the expense of others'."[5] This proposition offers the possibility of building down world armaments, which are undermining the economies of wealthy and poor nations alike. The balance-of-power doctrine remains relevant because this building down can only succeed as confidence is built up on both sides, a process possible only when each is assured that the other will not take advantage of any perceived imbalance. Unilateral moves by the Soviets have not only signaled their commitment to peace and their willingness to take the initiative to move negotiations off dead center, but also their awareness of psychological factors and the necessity to provide an objective basis for trust by Western nations. The West stands under a similar obligation.

Finally, this new approach of mutuality is based on the recognition of *mutual self-interest*. This is a page out of Niebuhrian realism. Peacemaking requires attending to the self-interests of the various parties. Normally we think in terms of *conflicts* of interest. But today the *self* in self-interest is the *world* in its interrelatedness and its essential need for peace if it is to survive. Self-interests have converged to become *mutual*. No nation can survive the destruction of its own environment or the destruction of the environment of other nations with which it is interrelated and on which it is dependent. Ecology is truly a problem of mutual self-interest, and serves therefore as a paradigm for the kind and quality of solutions that must be sought. Drugs and terrorism are other examples. Not only the major powers recognize them as threatening their self-interests. Even drug-producing nations and exporters of terrorism are discovering that these inevitably contribute to internal instability and external sanctions, and hence are not in their self-interest. Proxy wars, the use of local conflicts by the major powers to extend their influence or combat the influence of a rival, are also proving not only costly abroad but divisive at home. Self-interest is beginning to question their usefulness as well.

To be sure, the restraining nature of self-interests can very quickly be dissipated and become inconsequential if incidents occur which arouse ideological loyalties. Ideological passions can quickly overrule the cost-benefit reasoning of cooler heads and make individuals and nations willing to make any sacrifice, including self-sacrifice, in devotion to a cause deemed larger than self-interest. This is why peacemaking involves cultivating the recognition that any ideology, to survive and grow, requires a planet in which it can demonstrate its truth. Hence the ultimate self-interest *and* ideological commitment of all require the survival and viability of the earth. The recognition of long-range interests as mutual provides a stronger and stronger basis for accords and peace-promoting structures.

At the same time, mutual self-interest requires justice. Liberation theologians fear that major powers, with an eye to their own interests, will divide up the world into mutually recognized spheres of influence in which the control of each will be unquestioned by the other. This could simply guarantee the continuation of present injustices. If peace is in the self-interest of the major powers, however, and if peace is only possible with justice, it is clearly in the self-interest of all parties to work toward ever-greater approximations of political and economic justice everywhere.

What conclusions can we draw from bringing together these theological and political representatives from three continents? Theology can be most useful to politicians and political analysts, it would seem, if the theological views spelled out here are allowed to supplement each other and are employed in combination. From the Niebuhrian approach come the necessary cautions and warnings that policies that do not recognize the persistent tendencies in human nature to seek security through power and control, control which by necessity must expand imperialistically, will be unrealistic. Thus the Christian doctrine of human sinfulness remains important not only to critique present injustices but to ensure that the new political structures which are built to serve the future include checks and balances that guard against the arbitrary use of power and protect the interests of the powerless.

From the political and liberationist theologies come appeals to recognize the claims to justice of all who are without voice in the dominant systems. Those in power and those representing power groups are usually successful in looking out for their self-interests, but their vision needs to be expanded to see how their own interests interpenetrate with the interests of those without representation—the poor, the disenfranchised, the exploited peoples and the exploited environment. That wider vision constitutes the "realistic" reading of political responsibility and likewise of U.S. interests in the world today.

As the mutuality of security and the convergence of self-interest are recognized, a hopeful prospect arises: new possibilities for the race are opened up without ignoring or glossing over the reality of self-interests. The politician is seldom able to win support for a policy based on theological motives or altruistic considerations alone, yet here Christian hope and Christian realism combine. And divine preserving grace puts even the sin of self-interest to good use to prod a reluctant and slow-to-learn humanity down the road toward peace.

Notes

1. Jürgen Moltmann, *Theology of Hope* (New York: Harper & Row, 1967), p. 25.

2. Jürgen Moltmann, *The Crucified God* (New York: Harper & Row, 1974), pp. 329–35.

3. Cf. José Míguez Bonino, *Toward a Christian Political Ethics* (Philadelphia: Fortress Press, 1983), p. 86.

4. Moltmann, *Theology of Hope*, p. 287.

5. Mikhail Gorbachev, "For the Sake of Preserving Human Civilization" (Moscow: Novosti Press Agency Publishing House, 1987), p. 9.

Theology, Politics, and Peace

Part One

From the Political Perspective

Chapter 1

Can Religious Faith Promote Peace?

JIMMY CARTER

The relation of religion and politics in the history of our nation has often been a problematic one. Hence it is with some trepidation that I enter these troubled waters. Nevertheless, I am convinced that religion has an essential contribution to make to politics—certainly that has been true in my own case—and therefore politicians and theologians owe it to each other to be in dialogue, as this conference seeks to demonstrate. Moreover, the avowed desire of both is to promote peace—not only individually and internally but internationally.

My own calling to become involved in politics was not unrelated to my religious background and values. We had a revival at the Plains Baptist Church in 1962, and the evangelist who came from Columbus, Georgia, to lead the week of morning and evening services was a distinguished preacher. He stayed with my mother during that week, and one evening after his evening service, he and my mother and I were sitting around the living room. I revealed to him my belief that I should run for public office, for the state senate. At that time, most political leaders in Georgia were determined to close the public schools if any black student were to sit in the same classroom with whites. It was in that political climate that I had decided to enter the state senate race. The preacher responded, "I hope that you will not do it. It's a terrible thing for a fine young Sunday school teacher and deacon like you to get involved in politics." I was taken aback. I answered, "Well, how would you like to be the pastor of a church with 75,000 members?" He said, "What do you mean?" I said, "The fourteenth senatorial district has 75,000 people in it, and I think that as a political leader I can serve them not incompatibly with the way you serve your own congregation in Columbus." That was probably a brash thing for a young man to say, but I never have come to the point in my life where I think I was wrong, because no matter what our chosen profession—farmer, medical doctor, college professor, minister of the Gospel, or leader in other religions—I think our own deep religious beliefs are imbedded and expressed in our daily actions as those actions relate to other people. But the relation between religion and politics in this country is a complex one.

Our nation was founded on the basic premise of separation of church and state. Until recent years, this has always been a firm belief of Baptists— and I happen to be a Baptist. But in the last decade there has been a countermove to break down this very careful separation, a move that in my judgment has been quite destructive. On the one hand, some Christian leaders, particularly among the television personalities and others of a more conservative bent, have tried to impose their definition of what is an acceptable American citizen. On the other hand, there have been efforts by politicians to define what constitutes Christianity and to determine what is a proper religion for our country. Some have even claimed that ours is a Christian nation, that those who do not believe in Christianity are not really equal or worthwhile citizens of our nation, and that they ought not serve in government posts. One of my own denominational leaders even asserted at one point that God does not hear the prayers of a Jew. These kinds of comments and these trends cause me great anguish and concern as a Christian. I hope that the recent developments in the television industry will cause these trends to be reexamined and perhaps even avoided.

At the time our country was founded, most of the nations of the world, then monarchies, had state religions that were almost totally dominant. In this country, with numerous religious sects, it was inevitable that religious beliefs would be highly fragmented. If this fragmentation were reflected in the political consciousness and political deliberations of the day and imbedded in political institutions and decisions, it would almost certainly be seriously and permanently divisive. Therefore, our nation implanted the principle of separation of church and state in the Constitution, and it has basically been observed.

I've had a chance, both as president and since my years in office, to travel extensively in foreign countries. One of the most intriguing things about these travels for me as a believer has been to observe different patterns of religion in different nations, and to observe with some degree of amusement and gratification the intense interest, even on the part of atheistic leaders in Communist nations, in my own faith. In some of the nations where the religion is adopted by the government and where the church functions are financed by taxes paid to the government—usually on a voluntary basis, and then allotted back to the churches—in my personal and admittedly biased assessment, the result is sterility in religion. There's a desiccation, a drying up of the dynamism, the fervor, the deep commitment, and the reaching out that ought to be characteristic of congregations. This is obviously the case in the Scandinavian countries. I've also seen the intense religious fervor that exists in nations where governments have been at least on occasion oppressive. I think the most dynamic growth within the

Christian church in recent years has probably been in nations like South Korea.

When I made my first trip to South Korea, I found the nation alive with religious fervor, with people seeking ways to understand more, including President Park, with whom I spent several hours privately. He confided to me that he had no religion, that he wanted to understand about my own faith, and that he wanted me as I left Korea to ask one of the religious leaders there to come and talk to him privately about his religious faith.

The first foreign country I visited after I became president was Poland, a Communist country, but with a great commitment among the people to Christianity. This was in 1977. First Secretary Edward Gierek seemed obsessed with my belief in Christianity. He wanted to know why his mother persistently urged him to return to the church. He was contemplating a visit to the Vatican, which he made soon after I left Poland. And he wanted to know how he as a Communist leader who professed to believe in atheism could deal with a Christian faith. When we normalized diplomatic relations with China and had the state banquet, after a few perfunctory but required remarks about politics, Deng Xiaoping turned the subject to Christianity and to religious faith in general. He had fervent believers in his country — a few Jews, a large number of Muslims and Christians of many denominations — and he wanted to know what could be done that would make his country's policies more acceptable to our country. I was not totally unprepared; I had three requests to make of him. I said, "First of all, you don't permit Bibles to be distributed in China. I wish you would eliminate this restraint. Secondly, you don't guarantee freedom of religion; there's some persecution of those who believe in religious faiths of different kinds. I wish that could be changed. Third, I wish you'd let Western missionaries come back into China." I told him that when I was a little child, I gave five cents a week to build hospitals and schools for Chinese children, and the most famous person in my life, the one whom I admired most of all, was not the president of the United States, not even an outstanding athlete, but it was Lottie Moon, a woman who went to China as a missionary. This was ingrained in my soul when I was four or five years old. And he said, "Well, I'll see what I can do about the first two requests, but we're not able to let Western missionaries come back." Subsequently, the constitution of China was changed to guarantee freedom of religion, and there has been burgeoning growth of the churches. Now the government has even established a factory for the production and printing of Bibles.

In Nicaragua, there is a dynamic, unshakable element of religious faith, primarily Catholic but also Protestant, that has kept this nation from moving toward Communism. You know of my work with Habitat for Humanity, which builds homes for poor people in this country and in some twenty-five nations abroad. We have ten different projects going on in Nicaragua. On my last visit there I spent a lot of time with the Sandinista leaders — President Daniel Ortega; Sergio Ramirez, the vice-president; Miguel d'Escoto, the foreign minister, who went with Rosalynn and me to do some manual labor in building homes for poor people in need of housing. When I went to the Baptist church in Managua there was a spirit of excitement and faith that was truly impressive. And even more impressive was the Catholic service in the church of Cardinal Obando y Bravo. I have never experienced more awareness of the hunger and commitment of people to their faith than I did during that exciting visit to Nicaragua. I think that the recent developments toward peace there have been heavily influenced by the unshakable commitment to the principles of faith in the churches that have thrived, even under an administration controlled by Marxists.

Our own cultural relativity can never be ignored in discussing justice or defining human rights. We cannot afford to be arrogant about our record on human rights. The United States didn't invent human rights; human rights invented our country. But when we define human rights we tend to do it in terms of our own tradition. Human rights are freedom of speech, of religion, of the press, and the right to be tried by a jury of our peers. These rights are imbedded in our Constitution. But when we talk with the Soviets about these matters, as I have with Dobrynin, or Gromyko, or Brezhnev, or more recently with Gorbachev, the Soviets' idea of the goal of human rights is the right to have a decent home, the right to have a job, the right of a family to have adequate medical care. We don't have those rights in our country in any way that would give us a basis for self-congratulation. We can all learn from each other, and not approach the questions of peace, human rights, prosperity and progress on the basis of a strictly American, or European, or Latin American definition.

In the United States there seems to be a growing split between two basic ways of understanding Christian faith. On the one hand, there is the belief found in those churches which look upon Christianity as a faith that rewards Americans. The material benefits we enjoy are viewed as an accolade by God. Such churches provide their adherents comfort, and there's an evangelistic zeal that is quite impressive. Moreover, these churches have become politically active and are a force to be reckoned with. On the other hand are those who interpret Christian faith as ministering to the poor, to the deprived, to the forgotten, to the ill, to the discarded, to the despised, to the homeless. The first group looks upon the second as less than Christian. The phrase "secular humanism" is used. I've been accused, as have other people who have worked to build homes for the homeless, of being communistic in my beliefs. A high official of the Southern Baptist Convention came into the Oval Office, and I had no sooner shaken hands with him and his wife than he said, "Why are you a secular humanist?" I didn't know what it meant then and I'm not sure what it means now. But I think it's obvious that there has to be some understanding of these differences that divide one group from another and which sap away a tremendous portion of our ability, our time, our efforts, our money, and our influence. As a result, our energies are not spent in the promulgation or the purposes of our religious belief, but are spent in internecine warfare, in arguments and debates that are not only divisive between people who believe almost exactly the same thing, but incapacitate them to work effectively, in the case of Christians, in the name of Christ.

I think it's obvious that the monotheistic religions, the great ones that came out of the Holy Land as we know it today, all profess to believe in justice, in human rights, and in peace. But this has not always been characteristic of the results of these religious beliefs. I have observed that the more narrow the difference is between two groups who believe something, the more likely they are to have combat, even bloodshed. The Persian Gulf War is between two groups in Islam whose differences are almost indiscernible to an outsider. But these narrow differences that divide them create hatred and mistrust and tension in one of the most bloody and long-lasting wars in the history of humankind. With amazement and concern we observe the terrorism on both sides in Northern Ireland between Protestants and Catholics, all of whom profess a faith in Jesus Christ. One of the reasons why Israel has not been able to make progress toward the hopes and dreams that permeated Zionism and the Jewish faith in 1948—hopes and dreams that are deteriorating under the more and more troubling circumstances in the West Bank and Gaza and within Israel itself—are sharp divisions among the more progressive, the orthodox, and the very conservative Jewish believers, some of whom deny that God wants there to be a Jewish state at all before the return of the Messiah. The conflicting attitudes of these groups toward one another and toward non-Jews have brought violations of human rights and a breakdown of progress toward peace. So, in many ways our religious faith and theological commitments carried into the political world have resulted not in peace but in war. We have a responsibility—those of us in the community of Islam or Judaism or Christianity who have devout beliefs—to see what's wrong and to work individually, and through prayer and supplication and the use of our influence among those who make decisions (most of whom share our faith, by the way, just as devoutly as do we), in order to bring about some resolution of these conflicts among us and to work toward peace.

When we first organized the Carter Center of Emory University, we assembled a group of people representing the university and members of my own White House staff and Cabinet, including the former Secretary of State, the Deputy Secretary, the National Security Advisor Zbigniew Brezenski, and others. We went around the room and asked them what they thought the major thrust of the Center should be, and Dr. Brezenski said, "I think that one of the first topics that the Carter Center should address is the relationship between religion and politics, because," as he pointed out, "this is a relationship that could be beneficial for the world, but quite often the results have been the opposite."

Examples of success are few and far between. But I don't believe we would have been successful in forging the Camp David accords, which led to a peace treaty six months later between Israel and Egypt, had not Anwar Sadat emphasized the common brotherhood that he shared with me and Menachem Begin in believing in the same God. He emphasized over and over that we were all sons of Abraham. I responded to this with enthusiasm—while Prime Minister Begin was always a little embarrassed and tried to change the subject. The first thing we did when we got to Camp David was to meet privately. I met with Sadat and then I met with Begin. It was obvious to me that the differences between these two men were almost irreconcilable. So, Rosalynn proposed that we issue a joint communique to the outside world asking all those who shared our faith in Allah, in the Hebrew God, and in Christ to join us in a prayer for success. I drafted the little communique and took it to Sadat and he approved it; I took it to Begin and, after a couple of hours of editing, he approved it as well. So we sent out a communique. While you may or may not remember that communique, it was the first thing on which we could agree. We met for three days together. The two leaders were almost totally incompatible, and for the last ten days at Camp David they never saw each other. Yet the success of that interrelationship between two courageous leaders, Begin and Sadat, was quite notable. And the margin for success was so narrow—we so easily could have failed—that I have no doubt that our shared religious faith was a crucial factor in success.

Those principles still prevail. I wrote a book a few years ago called *The Blood of Abraham*. The title has a double connotation: We are sons and daughters of Abraham; and the blood being shed today is shed in the former home of Abraham. The beginning of the book describes how the ancient evolution of Islam and Judaism and Christianity are interrelated. I think this common heritage holds obvious possibilities for the future.

Nowadays, the examples of unity to be derived from religious faith are rare. I would say that the Nicaraguan situation which I've already described, is one example. Much more common, unfortunately, are conflicts exacerbated by religious loyalties. The Carter Center sponsors a major project in the Sudan to try to teach small farmers how to grow more food grain. And we work with hundreds of them. But our project is endangered because the country is strictly divided along religious lines. The majority of the nation is under the control of Muslims, under Prime Minister Sadiq al-Mahdi, who I think is a very enlightened person; the so-called southern revolutionaries are under the leadership of Dr. John Garang (who received his Ph.D. in the United States, by the way), who resides most of the time in Addis Abbaba in Ethiopia. Here is a nation torn apart by differences in religious faith they can ill afford. We're making some faltering efforts working with others to try to heal this chasm. But to our distress the chasm is widening, because now marshaling behind Sadiq al-Mahdi and the Muslim majority is a growing number of Muslim countries that see this as a test case in the struggle between Islam and Christianity. And lining up behind John Garang are the leaders of nations that are predominately Christian. So in some ways these two men, who themselves have a desire for a resolution of the conflict, are constrained by others who have joined them because of religious faith or religious enmities.

I don't know the answers. There are problems within the world of Islam; there are problems within the world of Judaism; there are problems within the world of Christianity. For us to find, in this conference on Theology, Politics, and Peace, ways to realize the highest hopes and dreams and professions of peace on earth with justice is an elusive goal. In the last few years, I would say that we have been further from that goal than we were before. The divisions are becoming deeper, the suffering greater, and the deaths more manifold. Unfortunately, religious leaders have been either uninvolved or ineffectual. We discuss these matters, but there has been little effective way to marshal influence. My hope is that out of this conference might come new possibilities.

I would say that in the hoped-for increase of justice and peace through the political world, religion and religious believers have largely failed. But that failure need not be permanent, because all our religious faiths have within them a seed of hope. I think through prayer, shared hopes, and searching for common ground, ways can yet be found to promote peace and justice through religious faith.

Chapter 2

The Economics of Peace

KURT BIEDENKOPF

What are the essential factors to be taken into consideration in working politically for peace with justice? And, as a person actively engaged in politics, what assistance do I receive from theological principles, analyses, and values in approaching these issues?

My comments will focus on the subject matter of economics and peace. Given the vast amount of material, I will obviously have to be selective and have chosen three areas that I see as most relevant to the subject of economics and peace. In order to narrow down the subject, I have chosen, with primary emphasis on the responsibility of the developed countries, to raise first the question of our policies toward the poor, the needy, and unemployable among us. How do we arrive at peace in our societies in the light of these needs at our own doorstep? How can those who need our help, those who in many cases are in effect illiterate, be included in our society, not only as the recipients of welfare but as equal members of society? Second, what should be our relationship to the lesser-developed, especially the underdeveloped, countries? Third, what is our relationship and responsibility to future generations?

This relationship to future generations takes two forms. The first is the ecological aspect, the continued viability of this earth which we understand theologically as "creation." President Carter has made an important contribution to this in his "Global 2000" project, analyzing the effects on the planet if we continue to do what we are presently doing. The other form, the financial aspect, includes the long-range consequences of debt policies and the loads such policies create for future generations. Both of these are forms of drawing on the future to cope with the present. In the ecological as well as the financial areas, we are in effect using future resources, future opportunities, and future possibilities to ease the burden of solving present-day problems. These questions do not, of course, exhaust the subject. We have other questions relating to economics of peace. If peace, as Jürgen Moltmann says, is not the absence of force or violence but the presence of justice, innumerable other issues arise to which I will not be able to address myself: the problems of distribution; of the organization and institutional framework of social justice; the securing of equal opportunities in our highly developed societies, not to mention this in relationship to lesser-developed societies; the opening of chances for participation in the economic process at large; controls of government versus the development of personal freedom in the area of business, i.e., the right to freely associate in business versus the need to exercise control in the light of larger interests, and so on.

It is obviously not possible to plumb the depths of the three areas I have just outlined. Each is in itself very complex, full of problems and issues. I have chosen them because they have something in common. They are all influenced in their actual reality—the reality we have to shape politically— by a basic feature of our economic thinking rooted in our understanding of freedom, of self-fulfillment, of emancipation. This has developed as a result of the Enlightenment, of the secularization of our society, and as a result of our experience with the development of industrialization, especially with the expansion of technology and science. What I am referring to, and what will be the red thread running through my reflections, is the *expansionism* in our thinking. And I mean quantitative expansion. Our institutions, organizations, and more generally our patterns of economic and political behavior are all imprinted, formed, shaped, by the idea of quantitative expansion. I would like to put forward several theses on this subject and then explain them.

First, our concept that the expansion of material, measurable, quantitative wealth and growth is synonymous with progress. This assumption is rooted in our experience during the last couple of hundred years and was generally correct as long as material progress and the increase of the quality of human life were more or less synonymous. Today, however, this is no longer the case, at least not in our highly developed societies. By continuing practices from which in the past we could have expected more progress, we are increasingly producing side effects that are canceling out what could be defined as progress and increasingly creating costs beyond reasonable justification.

From the outset of the development of industrialization until the middle of this century it was assumed that material expansion and progress were synonymous. In industrialized societies this was the case. It was never correct to assume—and this is my second thesis—that the material expansion of our societies was synonymous with progress for the rest of the world. As long as we had colonialism, and indeed right down to the present, the rest of the world has been making contributions to our expansion of material resources, wealth, possibilities, and opportunities defined in material categories that have not been offset by similar improvements in those countries. In other words, if we look only at our own societies and their development and do not consider the costs that we create externally with our policy and philosophy, we can say that growth and progress are synonymous. If we look at the globe as a whole and apply the idea of justice to this equation, we cannot say that material expansion in modern Western industrial societies is equal to progress. We have not fulfilled this equation in those parts of the world on whose resources we have built our own growth. We have not fulfilled it in those parts of the world where our expansionism has intervened in cultural and structural processes of other people and has changed them without taking responsibility for the consequences of these changes. Much of the upheaval, unrest, injustice, and uncertainties in many parts of the world are the consequences of interventions that Western civilization and the Western way of life have made.

Not only can we no longer identify material expansion with progress, we find ourselves unable to strike a new balance among those three basic political priorities—freedom, communal solidarity, and justice—that could function to overcome our present plight. For my party, the Christian Democrats, this balance of priorities should be rooted in the Christian concept of humanity. Today we do not have this balance but have instead an imbalance, fueled by an expansionist drive and propelled by demands for more material expansion. Why? Because we assume we can solve our social and economic problems and bring about greater freedom, solidarity, and justice only if we continue to grow in a quantitative sense and produce greater resources to go around—or to trickle down, as the case may be. This philosophy of quantitative growth, as practiced in the industrial economies and considered indispensable for their governance, is in my view not qualified as a principle to be applied generally.

My third thesis is, therefore, that we cannot apply worldwide the principles we have developed for our economic order—they will not work! One of the conditions on which our present economies are based is that we can expand into more resources and exploit more markets outside our countries. If you apply such a principle generally, you will not get a peaceful order on the planet. So what I am saying is that the principles we presently apply in our traditional concepts of economic policy in the highly developed industrial democracies are not applicable worldwide if we seek worldwide justice.

This means that we have to overcome—and this is my fourth thesis—the principle of quantitative expansiveness. We must develop new forms for the evolution and development of our societies and institutions that permit such developments to fulfill our main political purposes, namely, a growth of the quality of our institutions and societies. When I speak of quality, I mean to develop institutions and organizations to better serve human rights and dignity. President Carter referred to the interpretation of human rights by Mr. Gorbachev. It may strike us as unusual to permit a Communist to define human rights, but it is a challenge. It is a challenge if someone like Gorbachev asks Western society whether it is capable of supplying everybody who wants to work with a job, a decent living and decent housing, and conditions, generally speaking, that permit that person to develop his or her dignity as defined by Christian principles.

I don't want to leave any doubt about what I am proposing. I am saying that we have to think in new ways. We have to overcome what we have traditionally learned as a way of life: that things have to grow quantitatively—a company has to make more sales, and have more profits, a labor union has to have increases in membership, everything has to expand in order to be successful. It is not possible to apply this kind of principle to a limited globe. Therefore we have to change not only our outward institutions but our thinking—in German *unser Bewusstsein*—nothing less than transformation of our mind-sets as well as of our institutions.

Now my fifth thesis: In order to accomplish this we have to rely on religion. I'm quite convinced that such a change in policy is impossible without the help of religion. If we want to overcome the dynamics of material expansion and define freedom in a way compatible with communal solidarity and justice, not as an abstract goal, but lived and experienced, if we want to arrive at a dynamic equilibrium between our priorities of freedom, solidarity, and justice without having to depend upon exponential material expansion, we will have to rely on the strength of religion. We have to have religion, not in the sense of aesthetics, but real religion—applied, serious, relevant religion—to make the kind of sacrifices and exercise the self-discipline that will be demanded. It is my conviction that nonreligious societies, societies that do not root in and draw strength from religion, will not be able to strike that kind of equilibrium. They will not be able to redefine the borders of freedom to limit the scope of freedom in order to give room for solidarity and justice.

As a sixth thesis, I would like to say that I do not think that secularized humanism can do the job. By secularized humanism, I mean humanism dissociated from its religious base. Such a humanism is not in my view a viable substitute for religion in facing the fundamental problems that confront us. Solidarity and justice administered by well-off majorities in highly industrialized nations can be promoted as a matter of self-interest. For example, if we don't handle the poor properly they may create trouble. Or, it is worth some sacrifice not to be burdened by uneasy consciences. These arguments may look rational on the surface; they may be cost-effective, rational evaluations of benefits that majorities may secure for themselves while exercising a form of solidarity and justice toward disadvantaged minorities, but such policies are not reliable. They can be revoked. And because they can be revoked by majorities they are not humane or humanistic in the sense that I comprehend solidarity. The covenant that is necessary to establish common bonds, and is stable enough to continue even in the face of substantial conflict, cannot be created on the basis of human rationality alone. This covenant requires God as the instituter, as the guarantor. That is why I am convinced that you cannot replace the indispensable help, assistance, and base provided by religion with a rationalized humanism.

My seventh point is that to define freedom in a way compatible with solidarity and justice as I have described them will mean restructuring not only our thinking but our social institutions. This is a very tough job. It will mean a new approach to our basic institutions and therefore a fundamental reorientation of our economic and social policies. If we do this, we will incur substantial political conflict. It would be a great mistake to believe that the application of religion to politics would mean harmony. The contrary is the truth. If we take seriously what we are discussing here and apply it in terms of political decision-making, there will be very substantial social and political conflict and strife. The vested interests in the traditional structures will not surrender without a fight. Since we all participate in these vested interests in one way or another, we will not be able to solve the problem by shifting the burden to our neighbor. We will have to share the burden. It will bring the kind of conflict that ensues if you move from abstract to concrete application of basic religious categories—if you really do what you say. It means to invite conflict where now there is relative harmony. But our task will be to ensure that solutions to such conflicts are found by orderly procedure compatible with human rights and dignity, which will be a major task of our Western democracies and a major challenge to their institutions.

Let me make this more concrete. At the economic summit in Bonn in 1978, in which President Carter participated as the president of the United States, the statesmen assembled discussed the economic developments of the highly industrialized nations and the economic developments of the world. One major issue of that economic summit was the question of economic growth, the growth of GNPs. Growth policy was held to be indispensable for highly developed societies for the following reasons: Without growth, they felt, you could not secure full employment, without material growth you could not ensure social justice, without growth you could not aid poor countries, and without growth you could not ensure governance. In the final communique, the seven chiefs of state agreed that without growth modern industrial democracies could not satisfy the expectations of their people and could not be governed. The fascinating thing was that in the years that followed, several of those modern industrialized democracies had no growth—and nothing happened. They were quite capable of solving the problems, at least initially. However, they used one way to avoid the real problems that would arise under such conditions; they went into debt. In other words, they created growth artificially by burdening future generations. Theologically speaking, referring to Professor Moltmann's formulation, they violated solidarity with the coming generations.

Growth and full employment are considered very closely intertwined. Increase in GNP in measurable categories was required and still is required today. However, in my country we are now beginning to have an intelligent debate on whether that assumption is correct. This debate I find of extreme importance because it may lead to a difference of economic policies between the United States, which has traditionally championed growth, and Europe, especially Germany. If such reassessment takes place, my country may very well say that to generate additional quantitative growth by going into debt is not the right answer to problems of instability and disequilibrium in international monetary situations. The latest platform discussed by my party included a change in formulation as to the importance of economic growth. While ten years ago we were saying that growth is indispensable, the platform proposal now says that growth is "helpful" in solving these problems. And helpful it obviously is, but we have abandoned the idea that it is indispensable. This is a major shift. We will need more such shifts.

Why do we believe in economic growth as we do? Why do we look at it as an indispensable feature of the economy? One of the reasons, as I have mentioned, is that we have experienced during the past 150 years that growth betters our way of living. We have therefore learned to understand it to be an expression of progress. This has been deeply ingrained in our political thinking and in our institutions. The consequence is that governments go into debt in order to stimulate growth or to substitute for it. The increase in deficits at the same time that the standard of living continuously rises is an unresolved paradox of Western industrial society. It makes no sense that in the long run, in spite of a continuous increase in material well-being, our societies have to go ever deeper into debt. Why is this so? There is considerable speculation that the structural composition of modern industrial society and democracy has its price and that the deficit is the price. Because majorities cannot be made to change their thinking and because vested interests cannot be overcome, we simply have to continue on this path. I am not as fatalistic as to believe that this is so, but I'm fully aware of the tremendous difficulty, being a member of parliament and being daily faced with the practical consequences of what I'm saying. Modern Western society in the past has accepted both forms of deficits that we incur — our national deficits and the increasing deficit that we ourselves help to create in the under- and less-developed countries. There is no question, if we are honest with one another, that we have been lending happily to these countries in order to enable them to buy our products and thus increase our own standard of living on money that we lent the buyer. Very often these were products that the developing countries could not put to use for increasing of their own welfare. Or at least, the net result of their buying these products was much less than it could have been had the money been used otherwise. So we now have a very substantial responsibility for that international deficit. And I think that we have to assume that responsibility and find ways to take our share of the burden. The reduction of these deficits is a matter of survival for the countries in question. Con-

ditions that we would think unbearable in our own societies would for many
of them be progress. Therefore it is unfair to ask them to make yet more
sacrifices. Our Christian heritage requires that we address the problem of
international debt and be prepared to share the cost.

At home, we continue to try to stimulate our economies by going into
debt with the idea that the stimulation will repay the debt. The problem
is, this method is no longer working. A favorite device that accompanies
this shot in the arm of greater deficits is lower taxes, with the result that
any increase of wealth due to the stimulation has been channeled to increase government spending. So we have a long record over the last twenty-
five years of disappointed assumptions as to our capability to repay debt
that we accrued to solve certain short-term problems.

We have not only gone into debt in order to support our philosophy of
quantitative growth, we have also exploited nature's resources in two ways.
With ever-increasing speed we are using up the world's energy capital. We
have not restricted ourselves to the energy income of the world. We began
about one hundred fifty years ago to draw upon the energy capital of the
planet. Just to give you an impression of the dimensions of this process,
this energy capital — coal, oil, gas — was built up on this planet in a period
of roughly 600 million years. If we continue to use up this capital at our
current rate, we will succeed in reducing this capital to nonusable quantities
at conceivably affordable prices within five hundred years. Now, if we com-
pare the time span in which this capital was created with the life of a human
being and set that at eighty years, the consumption of this capital will take
place in half an hour. This is the rapidity with which these resources are
being exhausted. If we talk about the world as God's creation, and about
our responsibility to future generations, this is an issue that must be faced.
Moreover, our use of our natural resources is burdening the ecology. Not
only the radioactive waste but our chemical products and the way we have
produced these products for the past hundred years has not taken into
account their consequences when they have to be absorbed within the ecological system. We assumed that the ecology could take care of things, and
for a time it seemed it could. Now we know it cannot. This calls for a basic
restructuring of our inventive and productive processes. I'm not suggesting
doing away with chemistry — that would be stupid. I'm saying, search for
ways to make chemical products compatible with nature, and of course
human inventiveness is capable of doing that. But it requires a rearranging
of our priorities and an application of the principle that we are trustees of
creation. We violate that trust if we do not include as an indispensable
criterion for scientific success the question of whether what we produce is
compatible with nature.

As I have suggested, in order to address these fundamental issues we
must change our way of thinking. We have to find new standards to measure
progress. We are presently working on the question of alternative standards
we can use in order to judge the performance of society. How can we make

sure that our social institutions do not privilege two-thirds of society and leave one-third of society out? How can we make sure that the way we spend money, both government money and private money, and the way we organize society in its various economic spheres, can lead to better results as far as our economy is concerned, both with regard to the poor today and future generations tomorrow? We have piled up huge deficits. Now we have to find ways to restrain that process. We can do this by redefining the concept of freedom in such a way as to include the *capability to share* as part of what we consider to be self-fulfillment and emancipation. We have to develop new forms and expressions of self-fulfillment that include restraints, and these restraints must be institutionalized. How this will be done will of course vary from nation to nation and society to society, but there will be many things in common. In my Bonn institute, where we work with these issues on a comparative basis, we find that in the various industrial societies—Great Britain, Switzerland, the United States, Sweden, Germany, Holland, Belgium—people are thinking along similar lines, and we have an increasing interchange of ideas and cross-fertilization. We have to reconstruct our social systems, our housing systems, our labor markets, and our whole approach to unemployment.

The big problem in democracies is that we can only do this with majorities. That means we have to convince a majority that is self-satisfied and pretty well off that it is necessary to change what it presently considers a highly desirable set of circumstances and lifestyle. We have to convince a majority to cooperate with the necessary restraints and sacrifices. Of course, I would not underestimate the importance of minority groups—church groups, civil rights groups, environmental groups, and others—who with the sometimes rather shrill voices necessary to be heard in our societies formulate and articulate the needs of society and bring pressure to bear. But finally you have to convince the majority. My conviction is that this is not possible without the assistance of religion. Without the values that are rooted in the religious heritage and the commitment that religion engenders it will not be possible to redefine our approach to basic economic questions in a way that is more compatible with our basic obligations in the area of human solidarity and justice. Religion is needed for the individual. I need it. Concretely, I need its assurance that it is justifiable and right to put society through the turmoil such a readjustment will bring. Many people will say, "You are creating social strife. Why aren't you satisfied with the situation as it is? Isn't it enough to do something for the poor here at home?" The answer is, we can never do something for *all* the poor if we apply principles that cannot be applied worldwide in our economic structure. I want to make it clear that I am not preaching the philosophy of non-growth; some people promote that philosophy, but I am not one of them. I am saying that something else has to grow: the intelligence of our societies, the quality of our institutions, the capability of institutions to conform to our basic principles better than the present institutions do. In other words, our energies should be directed to increasing the level of quality and intelligence and not the amount, the sheer quantity of what we have been doing in the past. We need a *qualitative* change in our development.

In the history of humankind, qualitative changes do occur from time to time — new outlooks on life, new ways of seeing things. But they occur when the situation demands a change. I think we are approaching a time when such change is necessary if we are to survive. If these changes do not come, we will not have an economy that creates peace. We will have an economy that increasingly foments unbearable strife, conflict, and terrorism and gives rise to a sheer unwillingness on the part of the majority on the planet to allow a minority to continue a privileged way of life to which the major portion of the human family will never have access or the opportunity to enjoy. To maintain a privilege requires a very solid justification. We have to think about that justification, because we are tremendously privileged. We assume our privileges are more or less brought about by nature or by our virtue, or by the fact that we have been selected specially by God. None of this is correct. If we are Christians, we cannot accept as God-given this kind of a privilege purchased at the price of inequality. There has to be a justification, and the only justification that I can think of is that we use the opportunities afforded us by our present privileges to cultivate on a broad base in our populations the kind of capability, knowledge, and intelligence necessary to understand and respond to the challenges we face. We who have created the present structures of the world economy have an obligation to develop a new economic order that is compatible with a limited globe and a growing population, and that in the long run — not from today till tomorrow, but in the long run — can guarantee justice and solidarity for all humankind, and not just for the privileged Western world.

Chapter 3

Political Realities
and the Witness of Religion

MANUEL ANTONIO GARRETÓN

As a social scientist as well as a politician, I will take a somewhat different approach from that which I anticipate the theologians will take. Mine will not be a normative approach which says how things *should be.* Instead, I will attempt to be descriptive and to understand how things *are.* I will devote the first part of the chapter to analyzing the characteristics of the specific problematic of politics in Latin America. Then I will move to some facts concerning religion in Latin America during the last two decades that seem to me important. Finally, I will present the challenges and problems in the relation between religion and politics.

Looking at the Latin American reality and the Latin American model of development first from the economic point of view, the important thing to remember is that its main characteristic is the phenomenon of *dependency.* Latin American development has not been autonomous, building from within with its own resources; it has always been heteronomous, controlled, dominated and exploited by outside interests.

The second feature from the economic point of view is that in the last decades there has been a consolidation of what has been called the "informal sector," the masses who are economically marginal. Even where the process of industrialization has taken place, this industrialization has been unable to incorporate these masses into organized labor. Thus there is a large sector of the population, the so-called marginal people, not incorporated into the welfare state or into the formal economic productive process. The third aspect to be noted is the role played by the state as the agent and engine of economic development. Finally, in the last decade the traditional economic dependence has been intensified and changed through the process of external debt. This has put severe limits on the process of economic growth. It is important to say that until the seventies, Latin America had significant rates of economic growth as compared with other zones of the world. But these rates of economic growth were not accompanied by a process of redistribution. As a result, inequalities have increased.

If we look now at the social and cultural aspects of this development, we see that the process has created a situation where there are in effect different civilizations co-existing in tension with one another. In Latin America we live in a premodern, a modern, and a post-modern world — all at the same time. This is clearly illustrated, for example, in the novels of Nobel laureate Garcia Marquez. Modernization imposed from without rather than built from within has left the lower and middle classes without an economic base or clear identity and completely dependent on the political system, either the party or the state, to accomplish anything. There has not been the classic capitalist type of development: class, party, state. Instead all these elements are fused. What is especially weak is what we call the "political regime," the institutional relation between the state and the people. Moreover, this ordering of society creates a great autonomy for ideological and cultural phenomena. There can be an important development of a socialist ideology, for example, without a working class that supports this ideology. The result is a disarticulation between economics, social actors, and ideologies as Alain Tourain has recently observed. This disarticulation can be unified through only one element, the state — and that means politics. Because the society is so fragmented, so heterogeneous, the unity of the nation is not to be found in the economy. It is not the rationality of capitalism that unifies the nation. Nor can unity be found in race or in institutions. And so unity must be found in the state. As many historians have observed, in Latin America the state precedes the nation, the state has created the nation. And if the state is so crucial, that means that politics — the relation between people and the state — is crucial. Politics penetrates the entire society; society and politics are absolutely intertwined; the culture is a political culture. All the aspects of society and culture depend on politics. In that sense, although it varies from country to country, it is civil society that is weak and politics, or the state, that is strong.

Politics in Latin America, according to Tourain, typically includes an appeal to masses, an appeal for modernization or development, and an anti-imperialist appeal to nationalist sentiment. Populism has been always the main way to do politics in Latin America because it combines these appeals. This populism is found in all countries and takes a variety of forms. But alternatives to populism have also emerged, such as the appeal to class struggle by the guerrilla movements in the sixties; the appeal to communitarian Christianity by the "base communities"; and the appeal to the order guaranteed by authoritarianism.

Because of the crucial role of politics, because politics penetrates all the society, there is a fusion of the dimensions that are in the developed countries usually separate, and politics is burdened with the weight of passions.

In that sense, the *symbolic-expressive* character of politics predominates over what can be called the *instrumental* character of politics.

In the international context, Latin America belongs to two worlds. It is part of Western civilization, but it belongs also to the Third World. It is torn between these identities, as is well revealed in Latin American novels. Integration into the world community has always been seen as a subordinate part of a major economy. In recent decades this has meant subordination to the economic and political interests of the United States. This is intensified by the fact that the hegemony of the United States over Latin America involves the evident incapacity of the United States, with rare exceptions, to understand the independence of Latin America. Instead, Latin America is viewed as part of the U.S. struggle against its own perceived enemy, the Soviet Union. As a result, the problems of Latin America are consistently seen not from the Latin American point of view, but from the point of view of the conflict between the United States and the Soviet Union. The most tragic example of this is the case of Central America, but it can be seen in other instances as well.

Some countries are still in the kind of struggle that was typical of the nineteenth century or the beginning of this century, the anti-oligarchy struggle and the struggle for national independence. This is especially characteristic of Central American countries. But in other countries, the oligarchic system collapsed with the economic crisis of 1929 to 1931. What emerged has been referred to as "the state of compromise," a kind of arrangement between the old oligarchical sector, a new bourgeoisie and middle class, and, in a subordinate way, organized labor. This unstable combination of interests created modernization and partial industrialization, accomplished at the cost of marginalizing two main sectors of the population—the peasantry and the urban poor. In the sixties, there were some attempts to integrate these two marginalized sectors through reforms such as agrarian reforms and benefits and participation extended to the urban poor. But dependency-style capitalism set very real limits on what could be done, and political factions were unable to find an agreement that genuinely and effectively incorporated the necessary structural changes. As a result, the earlier state of compromise began a process of deterioration. The deterioration gave rise to the guerrilla movement, on the one hand, and on the other, to a more class-oriented politics but under a democratic regime, as in the example of the Chilean *Unidad Popular* and the Allende government. These two approaches failed, but another way of transforming the state of compromise and overcoming populism has emerged, a new kind of authoritarianism. The military regimes that developed in Latin America in the sixties and seventies in the Southern Cone (Brazil, Argentina, Chile, Uruguay) have sought to eradicate and eliminate the trend toward redistribution and mass participation in government and to revive capitalism by reinserting their economies into the world capitalist system. The only actor capable of doing that was one that had the monopoly of force—and that was the military. So military regimes combined a typical military ideology, learned in the United States and based on the U.S. national security doctrine that led them to a very repressive system, with an attempt to restructure capitalism, setting aside previous attempts toward popular redistribution and participation. In some countries these regimes have lasted over twenty years. In others the experience has been briefer.

The evolution of the Latin American political *problematique* can be further seen in the main political debates. In the fifties the main themes were modernization and development. In the sixties, because of the influence of the Cuban revolution and because of the mood of the sixties everywhere, the main theme was revolution. The ideal was a socialist society. In the seventies and the eighties, the main theme is the concept of democracy. One hears less about development and even less about revolution and socialism, but everywhere the terms of democracy and democratization appear. In Latin America, however, democracy is an ambiguous concept. It has at least two meanings. One arises out of the opposition to authoritarianism, what everyone in Western society knows as political democracy. But in Latin America this concept of political democracy has had associated with it what Karl Mannheim called "fundamental democratization," the incorporation of all of the people into the benefits of modern life and a process of participation in the decisions that affect collective and individual life. In some countries there has been a process of democratization without political democracy. For example, under Peronism in Argentina, or in Bolivia where the working class experienced a process of democratization, but not in the framework of political democracy. What we have learned from experience, however, is that there is no way to have democratization without political democracy, and that there will not be a stable political democracy without a process of democratization. This means that it is one thing to eliminate authoritarianism and establish the institutions of political democracy, and another to create a political majority that will be able to combine political democracy with social change. The forces that would have to cooperate to do this have, until the seventies, been fighting one another. The problem today for Latin America is how to combine political democracy as a *conditio sine qua non* with increased and more profound democratization, while avoiding undermining the stability of political democracy. This situation of delicate balance is made even more difficult by the problem of the limits imposed by dependency resulting from overwhelming external debt.

If this analysis is accurate, the problems of peace and security in Latin America must be redefined. The central problem of national security is not the problem of the aggression of the Soviet Union, the communists, or Marxism. Understanding and accepting this crucial difference is for some North Americans puzzling, as caught up in East-West geopolitics as they are. For us the problem of national security is internal and political in the sense that millions and millions of people who have been shunted to one side by modern civilization must be incorporated into political and economic life. The problem of national security is political in the sense that a stable political democracy is a prerequisite. That means control over the military. The problem of national security is economic in the sense that with the kind of bondage to debt that plagues most Latin American countries, benefits from development cannot flow to the people. So the problems of security and peace in Latin America can be understood only by analyzing the challenge of democracy and democratization. Peace and national security are linked to the internal process of democratization and to the external process of the agreements necessary to solve the economic problems facing not only Latin America but the whole developing world, problems that have little to do with the struggle between the Soviet Union and the United States. Therefore, Latin America must be allowed to be a zone of peace and not embroiled in the fight between the U.S. and the Soviet Union. I would like to say that in recent years there has been only one administration in Washington in which the problems of Latin America were considered as problems of Latin America, in which the national security of these countries was defined as a problem of human rights and not as a problem of the interests of the U.S., and that was during some periods of the Carter administration.

Let us turn now to the problems and the relations between politics and religion. First, we must remind ourselves that Latin America is still a Catholic continent even if, because of the identity crisis of the Catholic church, Protestant religion, especially of a conservative variety, has made impressive gains at the popular level among the masses of the poor. Second, I would say that two tendencies have been present in the Catholic church since the sixties. On the one hand, the Catholic church and some of its hierarchy have assumed progressive positions in certain countries in the fight against dictatorships. The church has provided a space where social activists who were expelled or repressed could find a place to reconstruct themselves and rethink their mission. The church has been not only a space but an actor and has played an active role — as in my country — against the military state. We must not forget that the theme of human rights has been put on the agenda by the church. On the other hand, this sociopolitically progressive aspect of the Catholic church has tended to be counterbalanced in recent years by tendencies emanating from the Vatican that lead to an ecclesiology in which the nation and the religion are the same, where religion is the civil society and the church is seen as the institution that possesses the truth. This seems to me to be an ecclesiology that is counter to the Second Vatican Council and the Council's insight that the church can learn from human experience. Restructuring has been undertaken to develop especially the nonpolitical aspects of the church. In general, the new bishops appointed by the pope are what are called "pastoral" bishops, who do not understand politics and contemporary issues and try to confine the church to its old abstract mission to preach the faith but without the accompanying commitment to the redemption of society.

A third characteristic of religion in Latin America in the last two decades has been the vigorous development of Christian thought with a very important political content that emphasizes the prophetic dimension—commitment, faith and praxis—with the theme of liberation. This is in some ways summarized in the "preferential option for the poor." This intellectual position is paralleled by the massive participation of Christians in politics and the creation of popular organizations at the grassroots level with a commitment to social democracy, exemplified in the *communidades de base*, the base communities. But it can also be seen in the student movement, the workers' movement, and the shantytown movement—everywhere you find Christians at work. In any case, one can no longer say what was formerly said of the Christians, that they were unpractical and went into the battle "with a flower in their hand!" In this phenomenon of political participation, the role of the clergy and church workers, male and female, has been very important.

In the fourth place, there has also been a development in the religiosity of poor masses, the popular religiosity so inseparable from Latin American cultures. This phenomenon is ambiguous and complex in its meaning and implications. On the one side, it tends to be conservative and to invoke ritual and magic, isolating people from political life and its problems. On the other, this kind of religiosity has sown seeds of protest, of criticism. It sets the religious community against the world, and in that sense it has within it the germ of social change, even if this is obscured by ritual and magical beliefs.

Finally, the fusion of the different dimensions of social life in Latin America—politics, culture, economics—gives to religion a political function that goes beyond its cultural dimension. We can summarize this political function in the roles that religion fulfills. One is as the inspiration and motivation for political thought and action. Another, more complicated, is the role religion plays in the legitimation and delegitimation of political positions and political regimes. That is why the leaders of military coups will always try to have a bishop by their side to legitimate the new order. A third role of religion is that of active mediator of social conflicts. This means that there will not be significant changes in Latin America's future without the involvement of the church. But this also raises the problem of the difficult, but I believe necessary, future secularization of politics.

In conclusion, let me address briefly the three areas which seem to be problematic in the relation between religion and politics. One concerns the role of the church as such; the second, the role of Christians in politics; and the third, some issues of a more theological nature.

Concerning the role of the church, if this role is seen in the context of the democratization that I have described as a main challenge in Latin America, and if we say that the church will play a mediating role, we must recognize that this mediation will always be biased, just as the Spanish king who mediated the transition from the Franco regime to democracy was biased in favor of a democratic monarchy. In some countries, the bias of the church is still conservative. This is the case, for example, in the role of the church in Nicaragua. In the other countries, and this is true in Chile, the church mediates with a bias toward a progressive position and favors the process of democratization. However, even if the church plays a positive role in the process of transition to democracy by protesting military dictatorships and promoting political democracy, the question still remains, What will the role of the church be in the future process of modernization? It seems to me possible to hypothesize that the church will play a twofold role, progressive in some regards, conservative and even reactionary in others. When the church speaks of a "preferential option for the poor," it provides a kind of permanent pressure to avoid getting bogged down in the persistent institutional problems of democracy and move toward the goal of genuine democratization. When the church speaks about preferential option for the poor, it is saying it will always oppose all forms of domination and oppression. When politicians get too imbedded in the problems of constructing democracy and neglect necessary social changes toward a democracy more open to the people, the church will always remind them, "Listen, there are still some things to change because of the preferential option for the poor." However, in areas such as education, the role of women, interpersonal relations, and sexuality, the role of the church may be very conservative. Thus the influence of the church, because of the legitimacy the church has won in the fight against dictatorships, may in the end be a conservative influence that obstructs necessary moves toward modernization. We should not be surprised then if the church which has played a progressive role in fundamental questions of justice turns conservative when it comes to the modernization of cultural traditions.

The second *problematique* concerns the role of Christians. We will not discuss here the very positive role of Christians in organizing the working class and the poor or their commitment to the political process. But there is an absolutizing tendency in their commitment. They move too quickly from the prophetic dimension to political specifics without understanding that politics also means negotiation and compromise. There is a messianic tendency to turn politics into religion and to expect new political institutions to establish the perfect community, the final solution. Thus Christians may become more radicalized than the people to whom they appeal and whom they say they are representing.

Finally, I have difficulty with some typical Christian ways of thinking and therefore have a few bones to pick with the theologians. This is said against the background of profound appreciation, for in situations of social crisis, when aspirations are raised for justice and human rights but the daily reality in a military dictatorship is the ongoing drama of life and death, the language of the churches and Christian traditions become very important. They interpret the basic human situation, both its hopes and its tragedies. Religious language and interpretation will therefore play a crucial role in setting the norms for concrete historical changes and future political developments. And theological analyses will be an important part of this contribution. But the social analysis undertaken by liberation theologies has been heavily dependent upon socioeconomic theories and has not given sufficient attention to political processes. The utopian dimensions of Christianity could thus create problems in understanding the constraints and limits of politicians and politics.

Another issue has to do with the relation with Marxism. It is not so much a practical problem because on the practical level in Latin America Marxists and Christians collaborate in daily political life. But the church and some theologians still tend to treat Marxism as a monolithic system, a competing religion, as it were, and then they draw the conclusion that it is incompatible with Christianity. The fact is that Marxism has itself undergone a demythologizing and secularization process which makes it not so much a theory of salvation as a tool of analysis. As such, it remains most helpful when kept within sharply defined parameters. To continue to condemn Marxism as a monolithic system is to set up a straw man.

A third theme I would ask theologians to rethink is the subject of violence. Typically we hear the church say, "We condemn violence per se—all types of violence, regardless from whence it comes." This tends to be abstract and unproductive. No one is advocating violence as such. Belief in violence as such was a phenomenon of the sixties, when there was a blind faith in revolution. What is needed today is a strategy for necessary change. The abstract condemnation of violence per se, which one often hears in church circles, is not very helpful in situations where violence is already present and a way must be found to move beyond it.

Fourth is the theme of liberation. The concept of liberation has an incredible power for political action, but liberation is a prophetic and utopian principle. And so the concept needs to be accompanied by a theory of political means and mediations, the different measures and stages that can translate liberation into a democratic order. That is also the case with the concept of the "preferential option for the poor." What does this mean in political language? Are the poor a distinct class who should have their own political identity, party organization, and power? Or do we mean that we ought to pay more attention to the diversity of the poor as social actors, and to the problem of pluralistic political representation of the poor?

Finally, it seems to me that it would be helpful for the dialogue between theology and politics to clarify the distinctions as well as the points of intersection among the three types of utopian ideals. The Anglo-Saxon liberal utopia is freedom, not liberation but *liberty*, the unfettered independence of the individual, and is expressed in political democracy. The socialist utopia is *equality*, expressed in social and economic democracy. The Christian utopia is *solidarity*, love, genuine community. It seems to me that Christians need to ask what their utopia has to contribute to the other two, and to ask what the others contribute to the concrete realization of more perfect community. Only by the cooperation and integration of the three is a viable common life possible. But this presupposes more serious respect for one another and dialogue toward common goals than we have seen thus far. In the past, representatives of these three orientations have regarded their utopias as mutually exclusive and in competition.

In Latin America, you cannot think of politics without also thinking of religion, nor of religion without thinking of politics. But we need today a secularization of politics, an end of competing claims to be the only way to salvation. Politics is too subject to becoming "religious," to claiming an unwarranted comprehensiveness and finality for its institutions and solutions. The role of Christianity therefore should be prophetic, to point to the true utopia of absolute justice that serves to expose the inadequacies of every political solution along the way. But we must keep politics both realistic about its limitations and at the same time constantly pursuing its task of overcoming injustice and making relative justice possible. Thus religion and politics are interrelated but at the same time different in their roles, and therefore autonomous.

Christianity is prophetic: it fights against injustice in order to put an end to it. Politics is the art of the possible. It fights against injustice in order not to be destroyed by it. This is the drama that links, yet distinguishes, these key components of Latin American societies.

Part Two

From the Theological Perspective

Chapter 4

Political Theology and the Ethics of Peace

JÜRGEN MOLTMANN

As early as 1946, Albert Einstein wrote the prophetic words: "The unleashed power of the atom has changed everything except our ways of thinking. We shall require a substantially new manner of thinking, if mankind is to survive." Today, more than forty years later, the destructive power of atomic weapons has been raised to the immeasurable, but we are still looking for a "new manner of thinking," so we can escape this deadly threat to humankind. Since Hiroshima, "the bomb" has abruptly changed the world, but Christian theology has only slowly become aware of the new situation in which all its traditional concepts for dealing with power, with terror and with war have become antiquated.

In the first part, I would like to speak about the conditions of the world in a nuclear age and about the origin of a new "political theology" in Europe, which in both German states today is turning more and more into a "theology of peace." In the second part, I shall attempt to define anew what it means to be a Christian in the midst of these apocalyptic dangers. In the third part, I want to unfold the *ethics of peace* in a nuclear age in order to define finally the *categorical imperative* of every human ethic of life in this age.

The location for my perspectives on theology, politics, and peace is divided postwar Germany: Nowhere else in the world are per square kilometer so many nuclear weapons stored, so many missiles based and so many foreign armies stationed in addition to one's own as in West and East Germany. Moreover, we belong to the developed industrial nations in a global economic system that destabilizes the countries of the Third World and brings them into greater and greater debt slavery. Finally, because of the dense industrial development in our land the ecological crisis is ever-present in dying forests, poisoned waters and acid rain. I live in a center of these three crises, but I shall speak chiefly about the first.

I. The Nuclear Age and the New Political Theology

1. *The new sense of time.* Hiroshima in 1945 fundamentally changed the quality of human history: *Our time has become limited time.* The epoch in which we exist is the last epoch of humankind; for we live in the time in which the end of humankind can be brought to pass at any moment. The system of nuclear deterrence, which we have built up and continue to make more and more perfect, has made it possible to put an end to the life of most of humankind in a few hours. The nuclear winter that will follow a war with nuclear weapons leaves the survivors no chance. This time, in which the end of humankind is possible at any moment, is in a strictly secular sense and without any apocalyptic images truly the "endtime." For no one can expect that this nuclear age will be superseded by another age in which this deadly threat of humankind to itself no longer exists. The dream of "a world without nuclear weapons" is a pleasant dream, but only wishful thinking. No one seriously expects that humans shall one day again become incapable of doing that which they can do now. Whoever has learned the formula once can no longer forget about it. In Hiroshima in 1945 humankind lost its "atomic innocence," and it will never get it back.

If the nuclear age is the last age of humankind, then the struggle of humankind for survival means today the *struggle for time.* The struggle for life is the struggle against the nuclear end. We attempt to make our endtime as endless as possible by constantly granting the threatened life on this earth a new temporary reprieve. This struggle for the postponement of the end is a permanent struggle for survival. It is a struggle without victory, a struggle without end — at best without end. We can extend this nuclear endtime, but we and all succeeding generations must again and again negotiate a new reprieve for life in this endtime. The lifetime of humanity is no longer guaranteed by nature, as it has been up to now, but must be created by humans themselves through a deliberate politics of survival. Up to now nature has regenerated humanity after epidemics and world wars. Up to now nature has protected humanity from extermination by individuals. From this time on that is no longer the case. Since Hiroshima humanity as a whole has "become mortal," as Mikhail Gorbachev correctly observed. "Immortality," as he said (or more modestly, *survival*) has since Hiroshima inevitably become the *primary* task of human culture, and therefore also of political culture. It means that today all decisions must be considered in view of the life of the coming generations. This is a new, hitherto unknown responsibility of humans.[1]

2. *The nuclear age is the first common age of all nations and of all people.* Since Hiroshima the many, different histories of the nations on this earth have become the one common history of the one human race — but for the

time being only negatively, in mutual threat and common danger.

The nations today have entered into the first common age of humankind, because they have all become possible *common objects* of nuclear extermination. In this situation, survival of humankind is only conceivable when the nations organize themselves into the collective agent of survival. Since Hiroshima the *survival* of humans is inseparably bound up with the *unification* of the nations for the common defense against these deadly dangers. Only the unity of humankind guarantees survival, and the survival of every individual requires the unification of humankind. The lifesaving unification of humankind in the age of the nuclear threat demands the relativization of the individual interest of the nations, the subjecting of conflict-promoting ideologies to free, open and democratic critique, increased tolerance toward different religions, and the general subordination of all lesser interests under the common interest in life. The continuing rivalry of the superpowers and of the different social systems does not yet allow the necessary world organization. Nonetheless, a step-by-step building up of an international network of political responsibility for peace in regional security partnerships is possible, as for example between the two German states and the states of Western and Eastern Europe. Even in Moscow they speak of moving from confrontation with the West to an economic, ecological and scientific interdependence with the West.

3. *The military system of nuclear deterrence does not secure peace, but endangers it on a large scale.* It can only be a transition to another way of safeguarding the peace, namely a more political one. But it also endangers the peace in three other respects: First, the arms buildup of the northern hemisphere is a burden to the nations of the Third World, who are sinking deeper and deeper into poverty and debt. It has led moreover to the arming of the developing nations and the waging of numerous wars in these lands. Seventy-five percent of the weapons trade of the last two decades has been with the developing nations. Both crises are in various ways mutually dependent: without disarmament in the North, no justice in the South, and vice versa. Only through building up lasting development in the South can we come to disarmament and peace. A war with nuclear weapons is a potential danger for humankind. But the North-South economic conflict is a reality from which people are already dying today.

The second danger to peace comes from the fact that an atomic war would be the worst *ecological catastrophe* that could be wrought by humans, as the Brundland Report confims.[2] But the arms buildup in the First World is—together with other factors—already spreading ecological catastrophes in the Third World through the indebtedness of the Third World. Exploitation creates poverty; poverty leads to indebtedness; indebtedness forces them to sell and use up their natural resources, their own bases for life— to chop down rain forests, to overgraze the meadows, to drive out the rural population, etc.—which eventually can only deepen their poverty. It is a vicious circle: The arms race produces poverty and environmental destruction worldwide.

Finally, attention must be drawn to the *human problem in nuclear technology*: nuclear technology demands infallible human beings because it reacts in a quite unfriendly manner to human errors. Can this dangerous technology be controlled by fallible and corruptible human beings? The catastrophes from Windscale/Sallafield, Harrisburg, and Chernobyl as well as the diverse international corruption scandals in the nuclear industry all say no. The experimental, trial-and-error method has come to an end. We can no longer afford any error. This means we can gain no more experience. Humankind lives only once. And if we live only once we can experiment with nuclear war only once. But that means that either humans retire from risky nuclear technology and seek other energy sources which are ecologically more tolerable and friendly toward human beings, or they find a way to change human nature which up to this point has been described with the phrase "to err is human."

4. *New theological thinking in the nuclear age.* The new *political theology* arose in Germany after the end of the war under the dreadful shock of *Auschwitz*. For us young Germans who began the study of theology after the war, "Auschwitz" became a turning point in our thinking and acting. We became painfully aware that we must live, inescapably, in the shadow of the holocaust, which had been committed against the Jewish people in the name of our people. "After Auschwitz" became our concrete context for theology. With the name of the place of the crime we not only marked a political or moral crisis of our people, but also a theological and church crisis. For us, what was so incomprehensible about Auschwitz was not only the executioners and their assistants, not only the technical perfection of the mass extermination, and not only the experience of the hiddenness of God. For us, it was the silence of the men and women who had looked on, or looked away, or closed their eyes only to hand over the victims, so completely abandoned, to mass murder. For us Auschwitz did not turn into a question about the meaning of suffering, as it did for the Jews, but into a question about the strength to live with such a burden of guilt and shame and sorrow.

With this insight we began to examine the Christian and church traditions in Germany: Why did Christians and churches, aside from exceptions, for the most part remain silent? There was no lack of personal courage. But we discovered that the following cultural assumptions and prejudices prevailed. First, *"Faith is a private matter."* Faith is concerned with saving one's soul and the inner peace of one's heart, but not with politics. With the modern split of human existence into "public life" and "private life," governmental power politics without morality, on the one hand, and personal morality without power, on the other, arose. Many of the Christians who detested Hitler and deplored the fate of the Jews went into the so-called "inner emigration": They tried to save their souls by accommodating themselves to the political demands. They were not able to save their personal innocence. There is no chance for "moral man" in a really "immoral society."

Second, *the separation of religion and politics.* Since Reformation times, the Protestant "two kingdoms doctrine" has taught the distinction between the realms of church and state, religion and politics. From this distinction has followed the claim that the church must be unpolitical, and politics nonreligious. When Hitler came to power, the churches did not feel responsible for the human dignity and the civil rights of the Communists, Socialists, Democrats and Jews, who were the first to be persecuted. Only when Hitler wanted to subjugate the churches did the resistance movement of the churches emerge. Apart from individuals like Dietrich Bonhoeffer and Father Delp, there was no *political* resistance by Christians and churches. "The church must be the church," it was said, regardless of what happens in state and society. With this stance the churches were implicated in Auschwitz. Churches and theologies which declare themselves to be "unpolitical" always cooperate with the powers of the status quo. With their alleged political neutrality they pay the price for their privileges.

The new *political theology* does not want to "politicize" the churches, but it wants to make all aware of the political relationships of the churches and "christianize" the political existence of the churches. Christ's Church is "an institution of social-critical freedom" (Metz). For finally every church that bases itself on Christ must be reminded that Christ was not sacrificed between two candlesticks on an altar but was crucified on Golgotha, *outside* the city, between two Jewish freedom fighters, by the Roman occupation forces.

Third, we learned that the privatization of faith and the separation of the church from politics has resulted in a brand of politics called *Realpolitik,* with disastrous results for society and political life. In Germany politics became a matter of power politics without conscience and moral scruples. "With the Sermon on the Mount one cannot rule the state," said Bismarck, who in his private life was very pious. This German *Realpolitik* set off two world wars and destroyed our nation and people physically and spiritually in the long term, although it was rather successful for short periods of time. In comparison, it proves to be not only more responsible but also wiser to orient politics by standards of human rights and to regard national politics as a moral task in behalf of humankind. "After Auschwitz," morality and religion, conscience and responsibility will have to come back into politics, if we intend to save humankind from a nuclear holocaust.

The *Political Theology,* which we began in the 1960s in the awareness of the Jewish Holocaust, has since the mid-seventies turned more and more into a theology of peace in the face of the nuclear holocaust which threatens all humankind.

II. Being Christian in the Nuclear Age

When Christians think about the future of this society which lies under the threat of death, they begin with the experience that determines their existence as Christians. When the church intervenes in the conflicts of the society in which she lives, she does it for the sake of the God to whom she owes her existence. Christians respond to the challenges of their times with their own existence, their whole existence. For these are not only questions involving action, but also core questions of existence. Social involvement by Christians is the means of the witness of Christ; and the political responsibility of the church emerges from the innermost core of her divine mission. Otherwise the actions of both churches and individual Christians would be arbitrary and superficial. But what makes a Christian a Christian, and what makes the church the church of Christ?

First, at the heart of things is the justifying and peacemaking action of God through Christ toward an unjust and unpeaceful humanity. Christ "was put to death for our trespasses and raised for our *justification,*" says Paul (Romans 4:25). In the letter to the Colossians (1:19, 20) is a similar claim regarding peace: "For in [Christ] all the fulness of God was pleased to dwell, and through him to reconcile to himself all things . . . making *peace* by the blood of his cross." All that a Christian is, and all that the church is and can do, is derived from this justifying, reconciling and peacemaking action of God. The church of Christ cannot be anything other than a "peace church" and a "justice church."

From every *gift* (*Gabe*), however, arises a corresponding *task* (*Aufgabe*). If the Christians are the *handiwork* (*Werk*) of this justice-creating and peacemaking action of God, then they are also and with equal seriousness the *instrument* (*Werkzeug*) to express this divine action in this world. From the justification of the unjust humans follows their mission as peacemakers in the conflicts of this society. There can be no other response by Christians to their experience of God. The creative action of God and the answering action of humans certainly do not lie on the same level, because God is God and humans are humans. But no one should separate these two levels which God has put together. Just as humans owe their justification completely to God, so God is concerned with the just actions of humans. God puts the hunger and the thirst for justice in the hearts of those whom God justifies. Whoever rests content in the personal peace of God but does not become a peacemaker does not really know the dynamic of the Spirit of God. God gives us his peace in order to make us peacemakers.

The church exists in today's society as the product and instrument of God's justice. The economic, political, and social conflicts of society are also the church's own conflicts. All Christians experience them in their own lives. The stronger they believe the justice of God, the more painfully they suffer from the injustice they see. If there were no God, then perhaps one could come to terms with violence and injustice, because "that's just the way it is." But if God is, and if God is just, then one can no longer simply come to terms with it. Then one can never become accustomed to injustice, but will rather resist and oppose it with all one's strength. If there is a God, then there is a justice and a judgment—which no one can evade.

Second, if the Church of Christ is the handiwork and the instrument of God's justice in the world, then she is also the place where the signs of the coming creation of a new and just world begin: If the peace of God is experienced in the church, then the *hope* for "peace on earth" also originates here. If *faith* responds to the experienced justice of God with thoughts, words and works, *hope* anticipates a new just world. If *faith* embraces the peace of God, *hope* anticipates a new world of peace. If *faith* finds the comfort of God in all suffering, *hope* looks toward a new creation in which there will be no more suffering, pain or crying. To say it simply: those who believe in God have hope for this earth and do not despair.

Since the 1968 General Assembly of the World Council of Churches in Uppsala, this life in hope has been called in the ecumenical discussions, "life in anticipation": "Prepare the way of the Lord!" Even if the fears and apprehensions have become greater today, I consider the message from Uppsala to be as current and important now as it was then:

> The Lord says, "I make all things new." We ask you, trusting in God's renewing power, to join in these anticipations of God's Kingdom, showing now something of the newness Christ will complete. . . . Christ wants his church already to be a sign for, and an announcement of, a renewed human community.[3]

In fact, all humans live in anticipation: in fear and in hope we already dwell today in our destiny of tomorrow. By virtue of their hope Christians anticipate the future of the new creation, the kingdom of justice and freedom, not because they are optimists but because they trust the faithfulness of God. To be sure, we shall not fully realize the kingdom of justice in the world. But we cannot exempt ourselves from the task for God's sake.

III. The Ethics of Peace in the Nuclear Age

In this third part I want to develop five ethical principles of the politics of peace in Christian theological perspective which, in my opinion, follow directly from the experience of Christian existence in the nuclear age.

First, *Justice creates peace.* The biblical traditions and the Christian experience of faith say unambiguously that justice alone creates a lasting peace (*shalom*). All church pronouncements have correctly taken this view. But what is "justice"? Jews and Christians will start with their experience of God's justice when they want to bring justice into the world. God's justice is experienced by them as creative, justifying and justice-creating. God is just because God creates rights for those human beings who have no rights, and seeks to set right those human beings who are unrighteous. God's justice is not vindictive but saving justice. That is why we can pray with Psalm 31:1, "In thy righteousness deliver me!" God "executes justice for the oppressed," confesses Psalm 146:7. Through this justice God creates that kind of peace that endures: *shalom*. It follows from this that there is no peace where injustice and violence rule, even when "law and order" have been achieved by force. Peace does not bring justice, but justice brings peace. Injustice always creates inequalities and destroys balances. Unjust systems can only survive with violence. There is no peace where violence rules; for where violence rules, death reigns.

We relate this Jewish-Christian concept of justice to the concepts of justice in our legal culture:

An early concept of the European law defines justice as *justitia distributiva: suum cuique* — "To each his/her own." This ingenious formula combines equality in the eyes of the law ("each") with the real differences between human beings ("one's own"). It is reflected in the Hutterite Brethren's formulation: "Everyone gives what he can; everyone receives what for him is necessary." Or, as Marx restated it, "From each according to his ability, to each according to his need." This concept of justice is, however, mainly applied to goods and services: all humans have the human right to life, food, work and freedom.

The *personal concept of justice,* through which human community is established, goes beyond this goods and services concept, however. It consists in the mutual recognition of human dignity and mutual acceptance. This creates a humane and just community. And it corresponds to the Christian experience: "Accept one another, as Christ has accepted you, for the glory of God" (Romans 15:7). This personal concept of justice also underlies the modern concepts of democratic society like *covenant* and *constitution.*

But the highest form of justice is the *justice of mercy* through which those without rights receive justice. That is the justice of "the God of the widows and orphans." In this world of human injustice and human violence divine justice takes on the form of the *"preferential option for the poor,"* as the Latin American liberation theologians say. That does not mean that "mercy goes before justice," but that those deprived of their rights come to their rights, and the unjust are converted to justice. This divine justice does not stand outside of the human system of justice, rather it is the justice-creating source for that system which leads to lasting peace. Both the recognition of the human dignity of others and the creation and protection of the rights of the poor and the weak are at the foundation of every lasting human system of justice.

Second, *hope and the way of peace.* The biblical traditions and the Christian experience of faith speak of a *comprehensive* peace because they speak of *God's peace. Shalom* means the sanctification of all life which God has created, in all of its relationships. It is blessed life in communion with the life-giving God, with other humans and with all other creatures: peace with God, peace among humans, peace with nature. It is characteristic of *shalom* that it cannot be limited to a purely religious or individualistic interpretation. Because its source is in God, *shalom* is universal in intention. It follows from this that peace is not a state of affairs but a process, not a possession we have but a way in which we are. Peace is not the absence of violence, but the presence of justice.

In peace studies the distinction is made between a negative and a positive definition of peace. The *negative* definition says, peace is the absence of war, and thus the absence of the use of military force. This is the understanding of peace presupposed when it is said that the system of nuclear deterrence has "preserved the peace" for the last forty years. Apart from the fact that this is by no means the experience of all nations, peace in this definition is confused with "ceasefire," and the costs of the system of nuclear deterrence are concealed. A negative definition is more easily agreed upon, but it is insufficient.

The *positive* definition of peace defines peace as a state of social justice, with the democratic settlement of conflicts and conciliation in a lasting development of all. Some would consider this utopian, but without these positive elements the negative concept of peace does not function either.

The Christian concept of peace combines both definitions, but gives the positive definition of peace preference through the emphasis on justice. It follows from this that peace in history is a continuous process, a common way on which there are steps forward and steps back. On this way, the issue is the reduction of arms and violence and the building up of trust and community.

Lasting peace in history is peace viewed not just in terms of the present generation. Lasting peace arises out of the responsibility for justice between the generations. Humankind is created as a series of generations. That is why every generation is debtor to the past generations, and that is why every generation has responsibility for the life of the coming generations. Only an unwritten contract of justice between the generations promotes a lasting peace for humankind.

Third, *responsibility for the enemies.* "Love of the enemy" is, according to Christ's Sermon on the Mount, the perfect, God-like form of love and the way toward lasting peace on earth. Whoever gets involved in a disagreement and has a conflict comes under the law of retaliation, "an eye for an eye, a tooth for a tooth." Whoever accepts the law of retaliation in regard to the enemy falls into a vicious circle from which there is no escape: One is inevitably the enemy of one's enemy, and this hostility determines the nature of the relationship. If evil is repaid with evil, then the one evil always focusses on the other evil, because only in this way can it justify its hostility and right to retaliate. In the nuclear age the arms race, which works in a similar way, leads the world into the abyss of universal death. Liberation for life is possible only when the focus on the enemy ceases and deterrence by the threat of retaliation no longer reigns.

The attitude toward the enemy that Jesus puts in place of deterrence is "love of the enemy" (Matthew 5:43ff.). What is meant by that under the conditions of the nuclear age? Love of the enemy is not retaliation, but creative love. Whoever repays evil with good no longer retaliates but creates

something new. Love of the enemy requires great sovereignty with regard
to the enemy. The freer one becomes from fear of the enemy, the more
the love of the enemy will succeed. Love of the enemy can never mean
submission to the enemy and confirmation of his/her hostility. In love of
the enemy one does not wonder, "How can I protect myself against the
enemy and possible attack?" but instead, "How can I take away the enemy's
hostility?" Through love of the enemy we make the enemy part of our own
responsibility. We learn to look upon ourselves with the eyes of the other.
Love of the enemy is not the expression of abstract, good intentions ("ethics
of convictions"), but of concrete, realistic responsibility ("ethics of responsibility"). To be sure, the love of one's enemies is in private life and on the
interpersonal level extremely difficult. In a nuclear age, however, love of
the enemy is the only politically realistic alternative. We cannot secure
peace today by eliminating or threatening to eliminate all our possible
enemies, but alone by reducing hostilities and taking responsibility for our
common security and a lasting development. Politics in this first "common
age of humankind" requires that we think with and for each other. It
demands a large amount of empathy. The first question is not how can
Western Europe protect itself against the "Russian menace," but how can
we come to a common order of peace in Western and Eastern Europe?
We must demilitarize public consciousness and political thinking, and apply
how we deal with an opponent in a democracy to how we deal with so-
called "enemies" in international relations. "With the Sermon on the
Mount one cannot rule a state," said Bismarck. But I maintain that there
is no politics of survival in the nuclear age that does not learn from the
Sermon on the Mount.

Fourth, *nonviolent overcoming of violence.* Out of politics of love of the
enemy follows the politics of the nonviolent overcoming of tyranny. "Nonviolence" does not mean depoliticization or the renunciation of power. For
we have always distinguished between "power" and "violence." "Power"
refers to the just use of force, whereas "violence" refers to the unjust use
of force. The modern state has a "monopoly on force." And we speak of
"naked violence," "brutality," and "tyranny" where the state exercises its
force illegally, illegitimately, and in disregard of human rights. Christianity
has not been able to abolish the "culture of violence" in our societies. But
it has made it necessary to justify every use of force, especially the use of
force by the state. It has made no longer possible the "naiveté of power"
so admired by Nietzsche. The legal system also functions to set limits to
the state's monopoly of force, not only in domestic politics with regard to
its own citizens, but also in foreign politics with regard to other states and
humankind. Threatening humankind with a nuclear holocaust is an act of
violence which nothing can justify. The use, and the threatened use, of
nuclear weapons and other means of mass destruction exceeds the right
of every state: Is it not a crime against humanity?

The first way of overcoming violence is by binding every exercise of power to law. From this would follow the *duty of resistance* to every unjust exercise of power which is illegal, illegitimate or directed against human rights. The principle of "nonviolence" does not exclude the struggle for power when the issue in this struggle is the binding of power to law. Whoever joins the resistance in an obvious tyranny only does his or her duty as a citizen who has the obligation to stand for the restoration of law and the rights of the oppressed.

The power of people who suffer under tyranny is not terrorism but solidarity. Terror disqualifies the goals of liberation and only justifies the tyranny. Mass solidarity of the people, reinforced by the support of other peoples, deprives the tyranny of every right to exist and takes away the fear of its threats. Recently, we have had several examples in which peoples have overcome military dictatorship almost without bloodshed: Spain, Portugal, Greece, Argentina, the Philippines. Tyranny is built on sand. When it is rejected by the people and at the same time is isolated internationally, it is deprived of fear as well as trust.

Overcoming violence nonviolently is possible. But it can also require *martyrdom*. We think of Gandhi and Martin Luther King, Jr. We think above all of Christ himself. If we consider them, we discover that not only active action possesses liberating power and leads to "success," but that suffering also has liberating power and can work convincingly in the long term.

Fifth, *the categorical imperative of the ethics of life in the nuclear age.* The nuclear age is the first common age for all people and all nations. Through the nuclear threat all people have been condemned to death together. We need a convincing *ethics of common life.* Let me in closing name some conditions for it. (a) The current crises have arisen from competition and power struggles: The general assumption is that in the struggle for existence "the fittest survives." Success is therefore achieved at the cost of the other. Today this principle leads to the death of both the weak and the strong, and destroys the future of the earth. Today only peace can guarantee survival. The principle of life is: *respect for the interests of each is the condition for meeting the interest of all,* just as the only security that is secure is mutual security. National egoism, class rule and enriching oneself at the expense of others are reprehensible because they are deadly for all. Humankind and the earth can no longer afford this power struggle and rivalry. The first question in major political and economic decisions must be, therefore, *Does it, or does it not, serve the life of humankind?* (b) The current crises have further arisen from the egoism of humans in regard to nature. We have subjugated nature and exploited its resources. In the face of the ecological crises, this is no longer possible. Human egoism destroys the environment and finally even humankind itself. A primary question in major political and economic decisions must be, therefore, *Does it, or does it not, serve or destroy the integrity of creation?* (c) The current crises have arisen from neglecting the contract between the generations. The contract between the generations must therefore be publicly formulated and consciously kept, so that the current generation no longer lives at the expense of future generations. A primary question in political, economic and cultural decisions is, therefore, *Does it, or does it not, serve the life of the future generations?*

It follows from these three considerations that ethics has become a task oriented to humankind as a whole, and must therefore be freed from those particularistic national, economic and cultural interests by which it has been dominated thus far. The ethical values of the common life and survival of the earth have, in comparison with other more parochial values, become absolute.

It follows further that the separation of politics, economics, law, and the sciences from ethics can no longer be tolerated. The sad experience of the current crises is convincing proof that economics, politics, and the sciences become corrupted without ethical orientation.

Finally, it follows that the common formulation of an absolute ethical code for the community and for the life of humankind on this earth is necessary in order for the major problems of humankind today to be solved in a responsible way. Thus it is time for humans to remember the "eternal truths" which constitute the foundation of their humanity and order everything else with reference to these. The nuclear age has become the first common age of humanity. Let us then in all things think in the interest of our common humanity!

The categorical imperative of the life of the nations has become: Act as though the maxim of your action could become a universal law for all humanity.

Notes

1. Cf. Mikhail Gorbachev, "For the Sake of Preserving Human Civilization" (Moscow: Novosti Press Agency Publishing House, 1987), p. 8.

2. World Commission on Environment and Development, *Our Common Future* (New York: Oxford University Press, 1987).

3. *The Uppsala Report 1968: Official Report of the Fourth Assembly of the World Council of Churches* (Geneva: World Council of Churches, 1968), p. 5.

Chapter 5

Theology and Peace
in Latin America

JOSÉ MÍGUEZ BONINO

When we speak from a Latin American liberation theology perspective, we speak out of a commitment that is both a response to our situation and a point of departure for the analysis of that situation. The first word of theology of liberation is therefore a word of *commitment* in faith. Faith is, to be sure, a relation to God. In that sense it is an absolute relation to a transcendent reality and, in Christian terms, an absolute relation to God as manifested and enacted in Jesus Christ. But faith can only be lived in concrete historical conditions that shape the understanding and expression of the faith response. These conditions result from our heritage, experiences, relations, and social location. When faith begins to reflect on itself— i.e., to do theology—it makes explicit the rationality implicit in that response. Initially, the response of faith and its rationality are a sort of synthetic act which simply happens. Only afterwards do we think about what it means in rational terms. Theology attempts to develop critically the reasons implicit in that initial discernment of faith and commitment.

In Latin American liberation theology the initial discernment is what is called the "option for the poor." It is not first of all the result of an analysis of the situation; it is the concrete shape of an act of faith. The reason for solidarity with the poor in their life and death is, to use the words of Gustavo Gutierrez, rooted in "our faith in God, in the God of life."[1] For the believer, it is a theocentric option based upon God. The theocentric option is related to a situation; it is not a *discernment* produced in a vacuum. It is discernment of what faith is, and what the relation to God is, that emerges from a concrete situation. It is not a mere deduction from theological and biblical premises but a *discernment* in the light of the tradition we have received, a discernment of God's presence and calling in Latin

America today. As such, it is related to two facts that are signs of the times. The first fact is that the vast majority of our people are poor in the material, social, cultural, and even anthropological sense of the word—they are the great and growing masses of marginalized, oppressed and exploited, who on our continent and also worldwide have become increasingly visible. Whatever else faith in God may mean in Latin America today will have to be related to this reality. We have to respond to God in the context of the poor. Politically, this entails what economist Xavier Gorosteaga of Nicaragua has called the "logic of the majorities," which means not only that the point of view of the majority should be taken into account, but that political, social, and economic decisions have to be made with the condition of the poor majorities as the decisive criterion.

The other fact is the struggle of the poor. They are not only visible, but they have waged a many-sided, sometimes chaotic, but continuous struggle to change conditions. This struggle has had weak and strong moments; it has had small victories and serious defeats. But it is present in many forms and degrees throughout the continent. We can thus speak of the poor as a collective historical agent of social change. The option for the poor means at the political level, therefore, a commitment to social, structural change as required by the logic of the situation of the great majority and solidarity with the struggles of this majority to produce such change. Now, this option for the poor does not mean that one can neglect or reject other fundamental questions, such as peace. But it does mean that other important, burning, and urgent questions have to be related to the fundamental one of the worldwide plight of the poor.

With this in mind, let me merely enumerate some points with regard to peace. For Latin America, the central question in international relations is economic in nature and is most obvious in the foreign debt. Our countries are subject in international politics to the pressures of economic sanctions and rewards. As long as the present imbalance in terms of economic trade continues, we cannot really speak of our nations as independent and responsible partners in international relations. A new international economic order is the precondition for the possibility of genuine international cooperation. You cannot really cooperate if you are not to some extent free; otherwise it is not cooperation but simply co-option.

The violation of international law is another area in which reassessment is clearly called for in the quest for peace. The open defiance of the pronouncements of the international court at The Hague and of the recommendations of the U.N. Assembly, the refusal of the big powers to sign international conventions, for instance on torture, and the use of the veto power in the Security Council are some of the evidences that the international law and order are of no avail for international relations when the interests of the big powers are at stake and are in conflict with the rights of the small nations.

The third problem is the arms race and its consequences. It is not only that the resources needed for economic and social development are diverted, for they might be used in other ways were they to be saved through disarmament. It is not even that the arms race pressures Third-World countries to buy arms, frequently through earmarked loans which facilitate the disposal of obsolete weapons discarded in the constant updating of military systems by the major powers. The main consequence for Latin America of the two-bloc international policy, with its ideological support in the doctrine of security, is that it incorporates the Latin American nations into a security system in which the military become the protagonists and the privileged partners, with well-known consequences in the political and economic life of these countries.

Finally, in this two-bloc conflict the United States seems to operate on the theory of low-intensity and localized wars. The only trouble is that Third-World countries provide the battleground and the bodies for such political and military exercises. Even more seriously, these conflicts artificially dislocate the real problems of the societies involved and make it impossible to address them. And so, it is not that we Latin Americans are uninterested in the question of peace; we realize that it is a very basic question. However, we look at it not from the perspective of the major industrial powers but from the underside. And from that vantage point things often look different.

I now turn to the second question, theology and politics. I began by saying that it is our faith in God, lived out in the Latin American context, that leads inevitably to the option for the poor and, just as inevitably, into the area of politics. We could look at the question from another direction, however, from the specifics of political life in our part of the world. A look at the history of politics in Latin America will show the important role that religion and the churches, especially the Roman Catholic church, have played in our political life. To be sure, most of the time it has been as the legitimizer of the existing power structures. But religion has also played a role as protest, as a call for change, and even in some cases as inspiration for revolt. One may like or dislike this fact, but it is part of the picture. Such a role, far from declining, has become more and more visible and explicit in the present political crises and struggles going on in the region. The increase in the role of religion in politics is a fact not limited to Latin America. I have seen signs of it in this country as well. But for us there is no possibility of a neutral, uncommitted, or aseptic religious life and practice. The only question is how, from what perspective, in which direction, and on what basis will religion be present in political life? These are questions that require theological reflection. Thus we are led from the presence of religion in the political life to a theological concern.

If you ask how has religion been present in politics in Latin America, we could indicate at least three forms of this presence. In the first, which we could call the Christendom approach, the church is a formal part of the political order. This was the case of the Catholic Church in colonial society and in several countries after independence. As a state church, it functioned as a mechanism for the power of the state. Second, the church has functioned in a directive capacity, providing moral criteria for legislation in issues such as family, education, and penal law. Third, the church has been a leading factor in the creation and internalization of ideology—using the word *ideology* now in the more neutral sense of the sum total of social representations of reality dominant in a society or a social group. These three forms of presence are intimately related. But one can say that, although the first two—the church as part of the political society and the church as exercising a directive role—have lost some of their weight and influence, the third function has been and continues to be an important fact: religion as the instrument of the formulation and internalization of ideology. Moreover, if with Professor Garretón we distinguish the two dimensions of politics as *symbolic-expressive* and *instrumental*, it would seem that it is at the ideological level that religion plays a more significant role. This is so because, as state church or as moral director, the influence of religion is mediated through the power of nonreligious institutions, the church as an arm of the political order, or as the protagonist of moral legislation. In its third function, it works, so to say, directly; it doesn't work through political power, it doesn't work through a system of ethics. It works directly because the religious symbols themselves have political connotations implicit in them or are bearers of a political ideology which they have incorporated.

Both from a historical and from a systematic point of view, the reflection about theology and politics will not be relevant if it doesn't explore the relation between the symbolic function of religion and theology and the symbolic-expressive dimensions of politics. In this respect we can make a twofold criticism of much theological ethics of politics as it has developed, particularly in the northern world. On the one hand, it has not until very recently assessed critically the role of religion in the creation and internalization of ideology, both in terms of its alienating but also in terms of its conscienticizing potential. On the other hand, it has concentrated on deducing from theological premises a series of general principles and middle axioms which, because they are only indirectly related to the act of faith, do not carry the power of commitment. Now perhaps this procedure is more aseptic; perhaps it can be defended as guarding against fanaticism. My impression, however, is that the risk of fanaticism is not eliminated but rather it is masked. I think that experience in this country is that when the separation of religion and politics obscures the religious commitment inherent in politics, that political commitment implicit in religion at some point explodes, and it explodes as fanaticism. Fundamentalist fanaticism is the repressed power of the religious symbol which has now become explicit in its political meaning. A purely rational, instrumental understanding of politics fails to address the political reality adequately. The political reality is not merely the rational exercise of instrumental reason; it is the whole ensemble of representations, symbols, and utopias that are incorporated into political life. Other more moderate proofs of this observation would be the social gospel movement in this country, early in this century, black theology, and the recent impact of European political theology—theologies that not only can be debated and developed programmatically but also can be preached, prayed, and sung.

Now I want to explore a bit these symbolic motifs in Latin American religious life, two of which are very basic for the theology of liberation. The first one is the *epistemological* motif, theology derived from the suffering of the poor. In Latin America, two powerful symbols operate among Christians. One of them is christological, the other eschatological. Jesus Christ is the name of the symbol of God's identification with the suffering poor, the marginalized, the exploited, the repressed. This identification of Christ with the poor has a long history in Latin America. Already in the sixteenth century, at the time of the conquest, Bartolome de las Casas could write, "I see in the Indies [Latin America] Jesus Christ our Lord whipped and wounded, crucified, not once but a million times." And the mestizo artists of the school of Lima would carve the crucified, wounded, and bleeding Christ with the face not of a European but of an Indian. Recent liberation theology has developed this identification, both biblically and theologically in the doctrines of God and in Christology. The poor are the privileged locus, the place where God makes himself/herself present and invites all to follow. This relation—God, Christ, the poor—is not a deduction, it is immediate. The identification is theologically based because in the Christian mystery God and the poor are intimately united; there is a sort of kinship between them. The word in Spanish would be *parentesco*, a family relation between God, Christ, and the poor. This sort of blood relationship is rooted precisely in the mystery of the incarnation, the incarnation of the Word in the form of poverty. God is present as the powerless, as the abandoned, in the suffering of the poor. A Christian theology and ethics of politics begins at this point, not with the question of the powerful who ask, "How can I help the poor?" but by assuming the powerlessness of the poor and asking the questions that arise out of their suffering.

In political terms, this symbol expresses at least three things. First, it is from the experience of suffering that the gaps in existing reality can be perceived. In theological terms, the cross judges the present age. Ignoring this experience of suffering, the world can perhaps be justified or God can be viewed as the principle of a benign order. But the suffering of the poor is a critical principle that makes it impossible for a Christian to reconcile himself or herself with the status quo. Second, there is what has been called in Latin America "the epistemological privilege of the poor." This does not mean that the poor are more virtuous but that the perspective made available from their location on the seamy side of reality makes it possible for them to see things that other people cannot see. It is from this perspective that a political theology and ethics has to analyze reality and articulate such fundamental political categories as peace, justice, freedom, and democracy, and to assess the functioning of social institutions. This does not mean that the experience of the rest of society is not meaningful or valuable. It means that the experience of other sectors of society cannot be taken as autonomous data but must be considered in relation to the suffering of the poor. Third, since God has chosen in Christ to exercise God's power in the powerlessness of the crucified, a political theology and ethics will see the crucified of the world as the political agent, as the place from which power is built. Again, this does not mean a neglect or blindness to the existing power structures or to the other actors in the political arena. But it means relativizing these actors by introducing the suffering poor as a central actor in relation to which other agents have to be taken into account.

The other important symbol operative in the Christian consciousness of the poor in Latin America, especially in recent years, is the *eschatological*: the resurrection. As Guatemalan Julio Esquival has put it, we are "threatened with resurrection." The Brazilian song of the base communities says, "We are already risen, we are people on the march." Now, it is very interesting from a New Testament point of view to look at the relation in this song between being a resurrected people and being a people on the march. Look at the resurrection stories in the New Testament and you will discover how many are related to journeys, to migrations, or to hospitality to travelers. The resurrection does not cancel the cross, it does not explain or justify the cross, but it generates within suffering the promise of life and therefore the power for a praxis of hope. The affirmation of the resurrection is not merely the assertion of a fact. Even in the New Testament, when the resurrection is confessed, it is confessed in its meaning—all will rise, Christ is risen for our justification, we have risen with him, powers and dominions have been defeated, the risen one is the one who died, the Lord is *present*. Now, this is not merely a statement describing consequences deduced from the resurrection. It is that the words about the resurrection reflect God's present work; it is the presence of the resurrected, of life emerging from death, as the negation of the negative. This is the symbol that is sung, celebrated, and enacted in the political struggle of the poor. It is a promise that has no limits. Pablo Richard says this hope is without boundaries. It goes beyond all possible human limits, such as death, yet it is a hope lived within a concrete praxis of liberation.

This raises the thorny question of *utopia* that cannot be avoided in the comparison of liberation theologies with Niebuhrian realism. Utopian thinking is a strength, and perhaps also a weakness, of Christian political theology in Latin America. Most Latin American theologians have underlined, however, the distinction between eschatological hope and utopian thinking. The Kingdom of God cannot be identified with a social or political utopia, nor can a utopia be deduced from the Kingdom of God. Utopias are human creations, built by the exercise of creative reason, which extrapolates from and negates existing reality. Eschatological hope is not a utopia in that sense. Nevertheless, there is also a positive relation to this human utopian function, whether of a liberal capitalist or socialist variety. Theologically, by holding up transcendent hope, human reason is challenged to transcend the limits of existing reality. By holding up the testimony of the power of life transcending even death, it denies the fatalistic notion of a closed history. In Latin America, where religion has been the main instrument for injecting the poor with a fatalistic vision of the world and of their own lives, this power of hope to break the power of fatalism is indeed good news. Historically, biblical eschatological hope has been able to incorporate human utopias as bearers of transcendent hope, from the early Israelite dream of an egalitarian tribal society, as analyzed by Norman Gottwald, to the New Testament picture of the community of the New Age.[2] These utopias have created a powerful, expressive, symbolic language—shalom, justice, liberation, the rights of the poor, freedom—offering parallels to today's struggle. If it is true that such linkage of biblical precedents with human utopias may fall into the danger of sacralizing the human utopia, as Niebuhr maintains, it is also true that it opens any human utopia to the necessity for its own self-transcendence. This is what is happening in Latin America with regard to the socialist utopia. No doubt liberation theology has to some extent incorporated this socialist utopia in the thought and praxis of base Christian communities, but the relation of these groups to the socialist utopia and socialist parties is both a positive and a critical one.

Moreover, utopian thinking as a political factor has at least three significant effects, as demonstrated in Latin America. It unifies people by gathering them around symbols that carry and focus the memories of past struggles and by projecting them into future achievements. For a poor population that can easily be reduced to the anonymity of the masses and deprived of self-awareness and self-worth, to have this focus of hope is a fundamental asset. Utopian thinking also relates the small struggles and immediate goals to the larger issues of justice, freedom, and democracy. In situations where only minor, incomplete, and sometimes even ephemeral achievements are possible, the absence of a utopian horizon in terms of which these things have value results in a fragmentation of the people's struggle and even internal division and conflict. Moreover, utopia also has a power to anticipate a future that is already latent in the present but cannot be seen simply by exercising instrumental reason. It thus provides reason with the imaginative tools for designing a new scenario in relation to existing problems. For instance, the relation of the utopian vision of the land as being for all, found both in the biblical and in the Latin American indigenous traditions, has inspired peasant movements that have been one of the factors raising the issue of land use and planning agrarian reform. This links the utopian vision, the struggle, and the political rational attempt to alleviate the concrete problem.

To complete this comment on utopia, I want to address very briefly the current charges of lack of realism and of fanaticism. Perhaps it would be enough to quote the response of Rubem Alves to a journalist from the United States about our supposed utopianism. Alves commented, "Our utopianism is not the belief in the possibility of a perfect society, but rather the belief in the non-necessity of this imperfect order." Moreover, I want to question the claimed nonutopianism of so-called realism. We have a strong suspicion that behind the claims to realism — to rationality and pragmatism — there is in fact a sacralizing of the existing order that amounts to a negative utopia. Realists usually build their case on a pragmatic basis, which presupposes the ability of instrumental reason to discover the limits of the possible in a given situation. For example, Herbert Richardson refers to "that new knowledge whereby man exercises technical control, not only over nature, but also over all the specific institutions that make up society. Technical reason is able to control rationally the institutions of society just as it is able to control the forces of nature."[3] Now, this language betrays a religious faith in what Richardson calls a "social-technical intellectus." He speaks of the inevitability of this domination, this social-technical intellectus. Heiech speaks of "the necessary humility before the operations of this order." What we encounter here is a warmed-over version of Adam Smith's "invisible hand," the perfect equilibrium that is automatically, invisibly, and providentially achieved when there is free competition of all individual interests. If one dares to point out that this does not happen, at least has not happened so far, we are offered a theodicy: It doesn't happen because demonic forces, from the state for instance, transgress the law of free competition by interfering in the operation of the market. It is assumed that a transcendental order, the order of perfect free competition, underlies and supports the empirical existing order of the free world, which ought only to be changed in the direction of this transcendent horizon, the utopia of the perfect balance of interests.

The heresy of all genuine utopian thinking is that it challenges this social-technical intellectus and its myth of perfect balance. Genuine utopian thinking questions the present order and thus threatens to introduce disorder and chaos. So-called theological realism appropriates this balance theory in terms of an equilibrium of sin, in which each individual's or group's sinful nature would counterbalance and control the sinful nature of other individuals and groups. The optimism about technical reason, which to such a theology evidently appears less tainted than other forms of reason, and the pessimism concerning universal sin here join hands to outlaw all uses of creative reason to think the possibility of qualitative change. They claim, you can only think the possible; and the possible is only an extrapolation of the present.

The rejection of this sacralization of instrumental reason is the necessary presupposition for reintroducing instrumental reason in its *proper* place and for recognizing the relative autonomy of the political realm. The utopianism of a purely voluntaristic balance in society has led to disastrous consequences: to the isolation of the moral into absolute ideal principles which are irrelevant because they make no contact with social reality, or to the fanaticism of trying to introduce a utopia by force or by self-sacrifice with terrible human costs, or to the fanaticism that retains by force the conditions of the present order. There is an inescapable need for concrete measures that begin to actualize new possibilities and make the great utopian symbols operative in the life of existing societies for the purpose of justice, peace, and freedom.

What is the contribution of theological reflection to this question of the necessary means toward a better society? I think there are at least two important contributions. First, theology should make us aware that there are no *neutral* means and measures to work toward these goals. This might seem a superfluous point were it not for the fact that economists, political scientists, and sociologists usually begin by acknowledging in the prefaces of their books that there is no pure objectivity in social sciences and then proceed to develop their arguments as if in fact they could represent pure rationality. This is apparent to us in many of the North American social scientists, who tend to play down the fundamentally conflictive character of social reality. Conflict is understood simply as a passing phenomenon which can be managed within the presuppositions of the system by means of adjustments and compromises. It is not difficult to discover the social matrix in which this view originates. It is the perspective of those sectors of society that experience social reality as fundamentally friendly and favorable, and therefore think of change in terms that would not radically alter this order. But in our Latin American situation the unreality of this presupposition is glaring. So, I think that it is very important for the theological contribution to examine carefully the proposed means and methods of change, recognizing that there are no neutral means, no untainted methods. We are therefore concerned about the presuppositions implicit in the measures and methods for change that are proposed and articulated.

The second element theology can contribute is the discussion of the extension and intention of politics. When Aristotle defines politics as "the study of the forms of the political community that are best for a people to be able to pursue the most ideal forms of life," he is relating the *intention* of politics, the best of all forms, to the *extension* of politics, for a people to pursue the most ideal form of life. While theology should respect the autonomy of politics in the strict sense, its main concern will be to remind the political order that it exists for the sake of the life of the whole *polis*. This means that politics in the strict sense cannot be understood except in relation to sociological, cultural, and economic reality. While there is room for specific political analysis and theory—indeed, we need it—the main concern of theology is constantly to remind both governments and peoples of their obligation to the intention of the process and to critique the extension.

As we move toward the threshold of the twenty-first century, there are many places, particularly in the southern hemisphere, which are in transition to democracy. When we speak of a transition to democracy there are two things to keep in mind. On the one hand, this transition to democracy testifies to the strength of the struggles of the people, the constant protest, the extraordinary courage, persistence, and resourcefulness of their resistance. This is a political fact of major importance to be taken into account in political thinking and planning. On the other hand, the former, oppressive regimes have not simply left, nor have they been defeated—with the possible exception of Nicaragua. They have in many cases had to make compromises, but they intend to maintain control in the limited, restricted democracies that are emerging. They usually speak of a transition to democracy conditioned by a series of factors: the economic situation controlled by international obligations; the social conditions resulting from economic restrictions; the international security systems organized by the two blocs, which place Latin America in the security area of the United States; the militarization of society, an abiding consequence of the military regimes that permeates the whole life of society and does not simply disappear with a civilian government; and finally, the continued presence of a military force. The transition to democracy therefore needs to employ the very fruitful distinction between *democracy* and *democratization*. Democracy is a kind of political order in which there is division of powers and representation. The conviction growing in Latin America is that this political democracy is a fundamental presupposition for a process of democratization to occur, not only in the sense of participation of all in government but also for access of all to the basic necessities of life which the political order should make possible. Democratization is at the same time the ethical principle that is the presupposition or condition for the development of genuine political democracy. Political democracy as a space of freedom is necessary for the development of the poor as political participants. It is not only a means but the necessary climate for the social reality we seek, for that kind of socialism in which the popular majority not only receive benefits from the system but become active, participating agents in it.

Democratization is a process, and we are dealing with steps in the process. Traditional pictures of revolution convey the idea of abrupt, immediate overthrow of existing structures, the seizing of power, usually associated with armed struggle. While such an image does have a certain validity, and the possibility of such events cannot be ruled out, we must qualify it. A more careful study of the history of revolutions shows that they usually represent long processes. In retrospect, we can recognize different moments of repression which in the end have made change possible. Political thinking should not be so fascinated with the revolutionary moment that it becomes unable to understand the stages of the process. Moreover, under present conditions in which any change is immediately subject to being seen in the global context, we must reflect on forms of revolution that are viable in our time and circumstances.

Finally, a word about Central America, for a Latin American cannot speak about the relation of politics and religion without referring to this anguished and victimized part of our world. The Central American situation poses with particular urgency and sharpness the relation among social change, international relations, and peace. Nicaragua has become a test case for a number of things. In the first place, it has proved that under certain circumstances a broad alliance of popular forces with a project of building a pluralistic, political, and economic socialism, with widespread participation on the part of Christians, is possible. It has happened. Second, it demonstrates that the conception of security in the United States is hemispheric, and that the United States considers such changes as hostile and detrimental to its interests and will use all available means to reverse them. Third, it is a fact that in such hemispheric interventions there will be no regard for international law, institutions, or even constitutional or legal procedures. Fourth, these events have demonstrated the powerlessness of the international system—the United Nations, the Organization of American States—to prevent or counteract such acts of aggression, as well as the difficulty and precariousness of any multinational initiatives—the Contadora group, the Arias initiative—which the United States itself has not sponsored. The unavoidable conclusion is that processes of social change related to social conditions and political forces in any Third-World nation will be immediately distorted and relocated in international terms and taken out of local hands. Such situations, which will no doubt repeat themselves in many places, pose perhaps the greatest threat to world peace. As it has been frequently been noted, the Third World War, if it happens, will probably be an escalation of a Third-World local war. For Latin American countries, the awareness of this once far-distant tragic possibility has become a tangible, present reality which calls for our response.

Such a response must integrate several levels of reflection and action. At the symbolic-expressive level should be an emphasis on the biblical integration of peace and justice as inseparable in concept and reality. I am grateful to Jürgen Moltmann for what he and others have done in recent years to show that the Christian concept of peace is integrated with the concept of justice, which is basic to it. Then we need a more careful study by sociologists, economists, and political scientists of the question of world peace as it pertains to national economies and politics, to develop policies that will strengthen Latin American international coalitions to promote the cause of peace. We Latin Americans have been more or less reluctant to get into these things because we have had a different, more immediate agenda. We have to realize that this is *our* agenda, that we have to find our way into the agenda of peace. Third, we have to support attempts toward Latin American integration in order to obtain greater autonomy at the international level, as illustrated by recent discussions at the United Nations Human Rights Commission on the Arias plan for peace in Central America. The difficulties and frustrations of such plans and their execution should not lead to despair and indifference. Finally, there is a need for constant communication between popular liberation movements in the Third World and antiwar and antinuclear movements in Europe and in the United States. Such relations are not merely tactical alliances but a response that corresponds to the logic inherent in the theological/ethical understanding of the relation of peace and justice.

Notes

1. Cf. Gustavo Gutierrez, *A Theology of Liberation* (Maryknoll, NY: Orbis Books, 1973), pp. 301f.

2. Cf. Norman K. Gottwald, *The Tribes of Yahweh* (Maryknoll, NY: Orbis Books, 1979).

3. Cf. Herbert W. Richardson, *Toward an American Theology* (New York: Harper & Row, 1967), pp. 16ff.

Chapter 6

Christian Realism, Power, and Peace

THEODORE R. WEBER

Professors Moltmann and Míguez Bonino have addressed the issues of "Theology, Politics, and Peace" from their own theological perspectives, and I have been asked to do the same from the perspective of "Christian realism." It is appropriate that the Christian-realist orientation be included in this international and intertheological discussion. It was on the scene well before the appearance of European "political theology" and Latin American liberation theology, and through the influence of its founder and greatest exponent, Reinhold Niebuhr, helped shaped the attitudinal foundations of United States foreign policy in the years following World War II. Moreover, the central elements of Christian realism—its understanding of human nature and history and its attention to the realities of power— are elements of a perennial theology of politics. Whatever may be said of the historical relativity of Niebuhr's realism, it endures in the permanent political relevance of these theological and political interpretations of the human condition and its prospects. And however timely and prophetic the newer theological currents may be, their political proposals must stand the tests of this perennial theological-political wisdom. Therefore it is not only appropriate but also necessary that European political theology and Latin American liberation theology be drawn into conversation with the United States tradition of Christian realism over the issues of politics and peace.

However, my credentials as a representative of the Christian-realist tradition are not like those of Professors Moltmann and Míguez Bonino in relation to their own theological positions. Moltmann and Míguez are initiators and shapers of their theological movements. They are able to represent them with immediacy and authenticity, and to create the directions of the movements as they speak. I must speak as a "later generation" Christian realist, reflecting and improvising on what Niebuhr, Paul Ramsey, and others have said and done before me. My entry into this conversation is therefore on a different level of authority from that of my distinguished colleagues.[1]

Moreover, the label "Christian realist" does not describe the primary character of my own theological-ethical enterprise. My approach to political ethics, as to all questions of human responsibility, begins with Christology and the divine work of redemption. It places politics — and everything else — in the context of reconciliation, of God's work in Christ restoring and renewing the *kosmos* in its relationship to the divine selfhood and to its own created purpose.[2] The politics of peacemaking, in this view, is primarily and fundamentally a matter of finding a political place in God's efforts to bring wholeness and healing to a broken and suffering world. Its foundation is the human oneness established in the cross and resurrection of Jesus Christ, and it stretches toward that peace that is the fulfillment of divine promise. This theological orientation to politics is not so far removed from that of Reinhold Niebuhr, but it is sufficiently different in focus and emphasis to render the label "Christian realist" misleading as a matter of primary definition.[3]

Nevertheless, I accept — willingly and comfortably — the role of representing Niebuhrian realism in this conversation over politics and peace. I believe, as I have indicated, that its understandings of human nature and historical possibility are fundamentally correct as representations of political reality. Its perspectives on the political process, though subject to correction for historical distortion, serve as formidable monitors of any interpretations and proposals that take with insufficient seriousness the roles of power, national interest, and the state system in international relations. The influence of my somewhat different theological orientation will be seen primarily in the increased theoretical attention given to the process of *civilizing* power, a move that attempts to understand power as a dimension of community and not only as an instrument of particular institutions or societies.

But where should the conversation begin? It is characteristic of all three orientations that they reflect theologically and politically on particular situations of conflict. However, we did not decide in advance of the conference what the geographical reference of "peace" would be. We did not specify the Middle East, Central America, Northern Ireland, Ethiopia, Cambodia, Namibia, relations between NATO-Soviet Union, or even something as vaguely defined as "world peace." Therefore we are not committed to reflection on the same situation. Moreover, the speakers for the conference are drawn from three different continents, a factor that already promises differences in situational focus and angle of vision.

It appears that we must construct the basis of conversation inferentially by inquiring first into the geography of peace perspectives.

The Geography of Peace and the Issue of Power

Those of us who live on or near the Washington-Moscow axis always have in mind the relationship of the United States and the Soviet Union to each other when we think of the problem of peace. The most troubling aspect of that relationship is the capacity for worldwide devastation resident in the counterpoised nuclear weapons systems of these two superpowers. From this perspective, peace means primarily a stable political-technological condition in which war—specifically nuclear war between the superpowers—will not occur. What that stability entails and how the stable condition is to be reached are questions over which there is considerable disagreement, but there is no serious disagreement over the need to achieve that result and over the primacy of nuclear war avoidance in the concrete representations of peace. Even when the political-geographical focus is something other than the United States and the USSR, their relationships establish the primary context within which other conflicts are interpreted and assigned significance. Even when the nuclear threat seems fairly remote, and other values are more immediately dominant, the question of nuclear war avoidance is the ultimate criterion of risk assessment, policy planning, and policy execution.

The view from Latin America apparently is quite different—if one can take as representative José Míguez Bonino's *Toward a Christian Political Ethics.*[4] Professor Míguez has written an entire book on political ethics in today's world without dealing at all with nuclear weapons, their role in the conflict between the major powers, and their potential for massive destruction of life and property and for polluting the earth's life-space for centuries to come. Míguez writes of suffering and death as a *present* experience for millions of persons. Insofar as he concerns himself with suffering and death in the future, he perceives them as extrapolations of oppressive and death-dealing conditions already in place, not as the probable results of a possible nuclear war. The problem of peace therefore is not avoidance of conflict but the establishment of a just society through the elimination of the societal arrangements that produce suffering and death. Particular societies—and the world as a whole—must pass through conflict in order to realize that peaceful and just result.

Certainly Míguez is aware of and sensitive to the risks and probable consequences of nuclear war. A man who travels the world as he does, and who has served as a president of the World Council of Churches, could not be accused of a parochial or myopic view of global reality. The issue for him, as I understand it, is that the suffering of the oppressed has an immediacy for them which the prospects of nuclear war do not have. The structural violence of the systems under which they live constitutes a condition of real war in contrast to the hypothetical war of the superpowers. Their sense of time is defined primarily by the acuteness of their suffering, not by nuclear eschatology. The problem of peace, therefore, is the problem of moving from violent injustice to peaceful justice through the radical transformation of the national and international structures that are the source and occasion of their suffering. If the process of transformation runs risks of war at various levels, including the ultimate level of superpower conflict, those risks will be taken. The nuclear war risk, in any event, is more remote than the suffering and death they experience at the present time. Their historic situation with its attendant social pathology constitutes the locus from which they construct the world and define the problem of peace.

At first glance it seems unlikely that Christian realism can help very much to synthesize or otherwise resolve these variant perspectives. Historically, Christian realism is associated with the issues and struggles of World War II, the origins of the "Cold War," and the continuing contest between the United States and the Soviet Union for dominance in world politics. It is positioned fundamentally on the Washington-Moscow axis, to use the construction set forth above. Moreover, it arose on the Washington (or New York) end of the axis, and has served as a device for interpreting U.S. responsibilities in world affairs. In the eyes of its critics—especially its "Third World" critics and their sympathizers—it is therefore nothing other than a religious ideology that serves to justify U.S. power, or the power of establishments in other countries in league with the United States, and the "national security doctrine." The revival of Niebuhr in recent years to provide intellectual and religious support for President Reagan's Cold War and Central American policies does nothing to counter this accusation, however strained and distorted those uses of Niebuhr may be.

However, one can acknowledge the historical connectedness of Christian realism and its openness to misuse without conceding that it is either dated and irrelevant or simply an ideology of dominant power. Christian realism employs a method of analyzing power in relationship to values and goals that is necessary to any form and condition of political action and is movable from one geographical or political setting to another. It investigates the realities of power and human nature in relation to ideals pursued and objectives sought, calculates the probabilities of achievement, and helps to define and limit the appropriate means. It is a method characteristic of and essential to politics as such, and is not bound to any particular geographical area or time period.

If one makes political analyses and formulates foreign policy from the standpoint of the great powers and the aforementioned "axis," one must move sooner or later to a consideration of the realities and struggles of the so-called Third World. One must do this at minimum because these struggles are elements in the world political system and may become occasions if not settings for the conflict of the great powers.

To extend political analysis from the immediacies of great power conflict to include and connect with conflicts that are more remote and seemingly less significant from that viewpoint is a realistic maneuver. It is realistic also—one must emphasize—to give an honest and empathetic account of the nature of those "remote" struggles as defined in their own settings and by the immediate participants, and not impose ideological meanings on them or read them simply or primarily as projections or anticipations of great power interactions.

If one begins political analysis from the standpoint of societies of lesser international weight engaged in internal conflicts of social stasis and transformation, one already is calculating relationships with the weightier states, because the problems of the former are enmeshed with and to some extent generated by the interests and extensions of the latter. The method of realism therefore is present already in basic analysis. But one cannot stop there. One must analyze and calculate these relationships in terms of the state system as a perennial form and foundation of international order, and not as something reducible to the international economic system, or totally controlled by it. Moreover, as I argue below, one must assess the relevance of the threat of nuclear war to all risk-taking with regard to the transformation of systems of power. These considerations, also, are applications of the method of realism.

Having made these observations on realism as a political method of universal relevance and application, I must return to the differences of angle of vision and insist on recognition of the priority of the nuclear threat in the composition of the elements of world peace. That threat is an irreversible technological fact mixed into an unstable compound of volatile political compromises and countermeasures. There is no "realism," certainly, and no true political responsibility, in any inclination to ignore or denigrate the manner and degree to which nuclear weapons and their delivery systems have restructured the conditions of global politics. The prospect of windswept, cloud-carried radioactive dust poisoning the earth at random and depriving all animal and vegetable life of light and heat provides a unitive global perspective on the problems of peace that comprehends and qualifies all partial geographical perspectives.

Of course, it is the essence of realism to recognize that the nuclear risks are not the only ones, and to recognize also that not all dangerous political conditions are equally risky. If it is true that the United States and the Soviet Union are moving into a relationship of significant political accommodation, the likelihood of war, especially nuclear war, and even accidental war, decreases markedly. At the same time, however, it may increase in other relationships as more states enter the "nuclear club" and develop workable delivery systems. If the reports are true that Iraq has used poison gas in its war with Iran and in its attempted suppression of the Kurds, and that Libya has developed facilities for producing massive amounts of poison gas, obvious risks of another kind emerge. Moreover, we must heed José Míguez Bonino's argument concerning the relative immediacy or sense of immediacy of risks. If the prospective devastation of nuclear war rates highest in degree and extent of catastrophe, it nevertheless is less likely that children will die from that cause than from starvation and neglect in a system that deprives them of the necessities of life. Although the Israelis surely would want to avoid policies and actions that would draw the superpowers into direct conflict with each other, they nevertheless might take the risks of doing so if the failure to take such risks meant the loss of national existence. This point must be made over and over again to persons who assume that everyone wants freedom from the nuclear threat more than anything, and will sacrifice or put at fundamental risk every other value in order to achieve that freedom.

While allowing for these important qualifications, one must insist that the nuclear threat—especially as it involves the relationships of the two superpowers—establishes the ultimate framework within which other values and risks must be assessed and evaluated. Insurgency movements and smaller state conflicts do not always operate right up against the most sensitive nerves of great power relationships. There is a real if uncertain degree of distance within which they can range without activating the alarm systems, and this distance is established basically by the structure of the international power system itself. However, the alarm systems are in place, and the closer the insurgency and small state conflicts approach the neuralgic points, the more they will have to make the problems of great power relationships their problems, and the risks of nuclear war their risks. Moreover, the closer they approach those points the more they will be bound morally if not practically to give war avoidance priority over justice in the order of political values.

The notion of "nuclear free zones" is a case in point. Presumably the basic purpose of such zones is to remove the areas and their peoples from the threat and effects of nuclear war—an objective one can hardly fault. In some parts of the world an additional purpose may be to allow the conduct of other forms of war while keeping the nuclear powers at a distance—an objective that may be justifiable but probably not quite so meritorious. However, should any of the proponents suppose that a nuclear free zone can serve as *cordon sanitaire,* as a way of roping off and isolating the area from technological and political realities, they surely are working with an illusion, and a terribly dangerous and perhaps cynical illusion at that. The basic criterion of justification for a nuclear free zone is whether it makes the strategic balance of power more or less stable, that is, whether it makes a nuclear war more or less likely. The technologically governed geography of peace in a nuclear world will not allow anything less.

Peace as an Organization of Power

In all of these observations on the geography of peace, it has been necessary to refer to, or at least presuppose, power relationships. The next step in the conversation on peace therefore should be an inquiry into the relationship of peace to the organization of power.

Peace is an organization of power because its historical reality is that of a set of relationships moving on a continuum between unlimited force and unqualified consent. At one end of the continuum, force predominates in the organization of power. Its peacemaking in international politics is exemplified by the imposition of the will of a hegemonic state or group of states, terminating a brutal and devastating war, and thereby bringing order out of chaos and founding a new organization of power. At the other end of the continuum, consent predominates. Its peacemaking is exemplified by the enhancement of the authority of international organization and law and by the concluding of covenants and contracts centered on mutual recognition of interests and supported by a history of fidelity to agreements rather than by threatened sanctions for noncompliance.

The connection between peace and power is integral and definitive, not accidental or peripheral. Moreover, power, as the continuum notion suggests, is a variable combination of force and consent. It is not a synonym for force taken by itself, nor even for justifiable force, and certainly not for violence. Every peace is some particular combination of force and consent manifest in the relationships of an organization of power. The notion of peace therefore will have concrete reality at various points along the continuum, and not only at the consent end, and peacemaking will derive its orientation and programmatic substance not from abstractions or socially disconnected values but from the contours and dynamics of particular organizations (or disorganizations) of power.

If peace always is manifest concretely in the relationships of an organization of power, and if power is a variable combination of force and consent, then peacemaking is a process of transcending the arbitrariness of force by eliciting and institutionalizing the grace and rationality of consent. We may speak of this process of transcendence as one of "civilizing" or "politicizing" the organization of power, that is, of moving from anarchy to community, from war to diplomacy, from propaganda to respectful conversation, from security neuroses to confident vulnerability, from enmity to amity.[5] It is a process of bringing the qualities of *civitas* or *polis* increasingly to prevail over the egoism, alienation, and hostility of prepolitical, or only incipiently political, relationships in the organization of power.

Perhaps this is what Jürgen Moltmann has in mind in recommending the "democratization" of international politics (a concept taken over from the American Social Gospel theologian, Walter Rauschenbusch).[6] If so, one must expect Moltmann to look and account for the continuing role of force in the process. Democratization surely must mean something more than giving small states votes in an international assembly to outweigh the votes of large states, because as long as there are large and small states the large ones will find ways to use their power to support their own interests. If democratization requires the creation of a world public authority strong enough to dissolve the large states, or at least control them, that organization quite obviously would have to build in restraints on its own power sufficient to maintain its benign and democratic character.

Power will continue to be a variable combination of force and consent until the end of time. Organizations of power will continue to embody the varying combinations. Peacemaking must handle the historically related elements, and not assume that its vocation is to work the consent end only.

If what we have said about peace as an organization of power is analytically correct, what organization of power corresponds to the geography of world peace? The simplest answer to this question is a world government — presumably a representative, constitutional one, and not one established by the hegemony of one or more states. But the simplest answer is too simple, because it does not resolve or even confront the real problems of the transfer of power. If states were sufficiently secure to transfer their power and authority to a world government, there would be no adequate motivation for them to do so. If their insecurity were to be heightened enormously, the larger states surely would redouble their efforts to make themselves secure (thereby aggravating the situation), rather than trust their fate to a dominant power which they could not control.

The question of the international organization of power must be answered in two different but obviously related ways. First, what is the actual power combination at any point in history? That is, what elements predominate, and how are the other elements related to them? Second, beneath the shifting patterns of international relations is it possible to discern a perennial organizational principle that helps to interpret the elements in their relationships and to predict their behavior? Both questions must be raised and answered in the process of peacemaking. The second, however, is theologically more significant because it implies some fundamental and constant connection between human nature and politics.

For political realism, the second question is answered by acknowledging the state to be the principal actor in international relations, and pointing to the state system as the perennial form of the organization of power. The historic composition (i.e., the answer to the first question) of the state system changes. Early in this century, Britain, France, Germany, Holland, and Belgium were major shapers and occupiers of the world. Within a comparatively short time the pattern changed to reveal the predominance of the United States and the Soviet Union. What did not change was the primacy of states in international relations and the theoretical assumptions concerning their behavior in a world with no single governmental authority.

The main theoretical assumption is that states tend to maximize their power and will persist in doing so until effective constraints confine them to certain territorial and jurisdictional limits.[7] Constraints arise from various sources — from the nature of the internal system, the condition of land and people, the availability of resources, the authority of international law and organization, fidelity to treaties and other agreements, commonality of interest, "world public opinion," and so on. However, the principal constraint in international relations is set by the power of other states. It is the notorious "balance of power."

Balances appear — or ought to appear — at many points in the international system, but as a systemic principle the balance of power focuses on the relationships of the major states. Its main purpose is to prevent any one state or group of states from dominating the system as a whole. The organization of power therefore is centrally the relationships established through the balance of power. Peacemaking in international relations, we must conclude, is in large part an effort to enhance the efficacy of the constraints of state power, including especially that set of constraints known as the balance of power.

At least two major problems with this perspective on peace and power must be acknowledged. The first is whether we can continue to speak of the state as the principal actor in international relations and of the international organization of power as essentially a political organization, especially in view of the extraordinary expansion of capitalist economic power into a world system that seems to run on its own terms and to dictate policy to the states. For some Latin American liberation theologians, the contemporary international organization of power would appear to be the economic system of international capitalism, not the political system of states. The state—certainly in its mode of existence as "national security state"—is not the principal actor in international relations; it is a function of international capitalism and serves to execute its will.[8] Moreover, the international distribution of power among the states is defined in economic terms. In a pattern suggestive of older geopolitical models, the international system has a "center" and a "periphery."[9] But the center is an economic center, not a geographical one, and the states on the periphery are those that are dependent economically on the center, not those that simply are remote from the "heartland" of the "world island" (Eurasia).

If there have been attempts in Latin American liberation theology to analyze the state and the state system theoretically and in their own right, and not as functions of the economic system, I am not aware of them. However, the fact that part of the liberationist program is to gain control of the states for the purpose of countering if not destroying the power of international capitalism would seem to undermine the arguments for the primacy of economics over politics, at least with regard to the permanent and underlying character of the international system. Moreover, whatever the domestic patterns of economic organization may be, the control of military force—and therefore the disposition of nuclear, bacteriological, and chemical power—rests with the states as states. Accordingly, it appears that the realist argument concerning the political character of the international organization of power remains basically intact.

However, that conclusion can by no means be drawn as absolutely as classical political realism might have drawn it. The conspiratorial theories of Trilateral Commission control may be overdone, as may claims of world domination by computer-driven global stock and bond markets or by consortia of international banks, but the roles of commerce, finance, and industry in international relations are massive and at times overwhelming. If it cannot rightly be argued that the state system has been replaced by an economic system as the international organization of power, it can and should be argued that the international system is much more complex and extensive than the state system alone. Nevertheless, when we approach the task of peacemaking in international relations we must have in mind primarily the interactions within the system of armed states. The ending of capitalism would not dispel that condition simply by bringing to an end whatever contradictions inhere in the nongovernmental ownership of property. A socialist world would be a world of states, with differences of interest and power and problems of nationalism and leadership egoism. The organization of power in a socialist world therefore would be at minimum an organization of the state system, with attention to constraints on state power, and especially to balances of power.

The second problem with this perspective on peace and power concerns the systemically operative concept of the balance of power. The question is whether it is in fact perennial in political relationships, and therefore always central to the peacemaking process, or whether it was merely a condition of power relations in nineteenth-century Europe, now irrelevant and inapplicable to radically changed international conditions.

Several points seem to support this challenge to the balance of power. First, the present international system is much more fully a world system, and not essentially a European system. It is much more diverse and complex, and therefore less susceptible to governance by a balancing mechanism. Second, in nineteenth-century Europe, England played the role of balancer, working with different combinations of European states at different times to prevent the domination of the continent by any one state or combination. At the present time, however, there is no state with the magnitude of power sufficient to play the role of balancer between the United States and the Soviet Union. Third, whereas the earlier arrangement presupposed the use of war as a rational instrument for restoring a failed or failing balance, the present arrangement—however labeled—is a war-avoidance device, or at least a device for avoiding war between the two states most likely to devastate the world were they to fight each other.

These points must be acknowledged, but what one should conclude from them is that the historic configuration and modes of operation of balances of power in international politics have changed, not that the notion of balance itself has become obsolete. We speak today of a "strategic balance of power," meaning thereby the pattern of world organization constructed and focused by the contest for world predominance of the Soviet Union and the United States. It is a pattern of mutual restraint which involves the other states of the world system and influences their movements and aspirations. It has no "balancers" functioning clearly and effectively as such, because other significant states are not free to shift back and forth in their applications of balancing power. Nevertheless, each of the superpowers is wary of its allies or client states, and the movements of smaller states serve often to keep the giants alert and cautious. It is not a balance that could be maintained or restored by fighting a war, but it is nevertheless fundamentally, even if not exclusively, a set of military relationships, characterized as mutual deterrence.

What can and must be said is that a balance-of-power strategy is not sufficient as a peacemaking strategy. Other, nonlethal, forms of power must be brought into play or enhanced in their effectiveness as modes of constraint, and dependence on the deterrent effect of lethal forms of power must be reduced massively. The relationships of power must be progressively politicized, moving them from the force end of the continuum of power toward the consent end. But no changes, however politically intelligent or structurally efficacious, will eliminate the need to balance power in the relationships of states, and most certainly in the relationships of those states whose interactions give primary shape to the organization of power in international society. Peacemaking strategies and tactics therefore always must reckon with the influence they intend to have, or will have whether they intend it or not, on the various balances of power in international politics, and especially the strategic balance of power.

Reinhold Niebuhr understood full well both the need for and the inadequacy of a balance of power as an instrument of preservation and justice. During World War II, he assessed the promise of a balance of power for restoring the peace and maintaining it, and argued that such an equilibrium would serve to some extent to mitigate anarchy in international society. He observed, however, that "an equilibrium of power without the organizing and equilibrating force of government, is potential anarchy which becomes actual anarchy in the long run."[10] Yet he did not expect a world government to emerge with power and authority sufficient to coerce the major states and, furthermore, did not encourage such a notion. He proposed instead an accord of the great powers to manage the organization of peace in the postwar world, while anticipating that the tensions in their relationships would make such an accord unlikely. When the advent of the Cold War proved that expectation to be correct, he found himself essentially where we are today—acknowledging the perennial and functionally necessary character of the balance of power, and arguing for the development of more consensual forms of power to cope with its inadequacies. "If we escape disaster," he wrote in 1959, "it will only be by the slow growth of mutual trust and tissues of community over the awful chasm of the present international tension."[11]

Niebuhr's theological understanding of human nature also supports the broader perspective on the organization of power. The persistence of sin in the behavior even of the best persons and in the most just and well-disposed structures implies the persistence of the need for restraint and at times the use of force in human relations, and especially in political relations. The freedom and self-transcendence of human nature, and the capacity for mutual if not sacrificial love, open the imagination to possibilities of agreement and cooperation beyond the present situation, and empower the will to at least a partial achievement of what is imagined. That analysis of human nature in its ambiguity of possibility and limitations corresponds to what we have said about power being a variable combination of force and consent, spread on a continuum from the predominance of the former to the predominance of the latter, with the organization of the combination at any given point in time defining the context and something of the substance of peacemaking.

Peace as an Organization of Justice

But why not characterize peace as an organization of justice rather than of power? Surely one desires a just peace, and not simply an orderly one. The problem with the question, despite its correct intention, is its supposition that an organization of justice will be something other than an organization of power. It is true, of course, that justice is not simply reducible to prevailing power. Some organizations of power are manifestly unjust, and none is completely just or unjust. Therefore it clearly is possible to distinguish justice from power and to set the notion of justice in a relationship of transcendence to the patterns of power. But the notion of justice as a political concept always is an idea of how power should be disposed, delimited, and coordinated. Hence, the appeal or demand for justice is concretely a proposal for the organization or reorganization of power.

To establish the position more firmly, let us consider the following points. First, we must return to our characterization of power as a variable combination of force and consent. As we have seen, peacemaking is a process of politicizing or civilizing particular historic organizations of power (in some instances, tearing them down first). It is a matter of bringing into membership all persons and groups covered by the organization of power, inviting and empowering their full participation, and employing the power of the organization to meet their needs and promote their interests and values. It is a process of moving from the force end of the continuum toward the consent end, thereby giving the organization increasingly the character of a community and legitimating the authority of those who exercise the power. Normally, it is a process of embodying greater justice in the relationships of power, or at least of spreading and strengthening the consensus that the relationships and uses of power are just. Where this process of transcendence, of movement from force to consent in the concretion of power, is prevented, what passes for peace is fragile and tentative, is enforced arbitrarily, and is an invitation to disorder. The proper understanding of the nature of power therefore eliminates the simple distinction between peace as an organization of power or of justice, but does so without canceling the distinction between relatively just and relatively unjust organizations of power.

Second, and following on what has just been said, justice is in large part a matter of the equitable and balanced distribution of power. Reinhold

Niebuhr was convinced at a fairly early point in his career that an inequitable distribution of power was itself a condition of injustice, and inevitably would result in abuses of power. If that insight encouraged his support of the proletarian side of the class struggle of the 1930s, it also prompted him to speculate that the union of political and economic power in the hands of victorious proletarians—or their "vanguard"—would produce tyranny. Moreover, it underwrote the crucial role of the balance of power in his thought on both domestic and international politics, and prompted him to urge the empowerment of "out-groups" for their participation in the struggle for justice. Justice is contingent on an equitable and durable distribution of power, and an organization of power thus distributed and maintained is a condition of peace.

Third, the distinctions between justice and injustice in specific cases usually are not as clear-cut as the partisans think they are, and even if they are clear-cut to nonpartisan observers, the realization of justice depends on the availability of power to reorganize the relationships. In the terrible conflict between Israel and the Palestinian Arabs, for example, both sides are convinced of the justice of their respective causes. Declarations concerning the radical separation of justice and power in that setting are more understandable as partisan rhetoric than as statements of objective moral-political reality. A particular relationship of justice to power would be established if one side were able to impose its will totally on the other. The prevailing side then would proclaim the victory of justice, whereas the losing side would bewail the total separation of justice and power. Or a particular relationship of justice to power could be established if both sides shared available power sufficiently to protect their own interests by restraining the other, thereby creating the conditions of tentative peace as absence of war. This tentative peace-through-balanced-power would then provide the context for negotiation over a compromise settlement of differences that each side could regard as relatively just.

If it were necessary to explore the question in more theological depth, one could begin with the Augustinian claim that every political order—including the most unjust—contains some element of justice in the relationships of power to the different expressions of love that organize and sustain it. Without some factor of justice, however minimal, the order would cease to exist.The claim is true, but its political effect often is to shield tyrannical regimes and oppressive institutions from radical criticism. It will suffice for our purposes to restate the point that justice concretely always is a particular organization of power. As the realists insist, the work for justice as for peace is a problem of confirming and improving or radically reworking the organization of power in the pertinent geographical setting. One cannot assume, however, that those who consider themselves realists, and who have a firm grasp of the intellectual principle, necessarily have a correct understanding of the concrete realities of power.

Military Power and the Next Step

The position established in this paper regards force as an element in power and therefore as a factor in peacemaking. It stands in clear opposition to approaches to peacemaking that simply oppose all evidences and uses of military power, condemn all budgetary provisions for military preparedness, and protest the development of every new weapons system. At the same time, it stands in opposition to predominantly military approaches to peacemaking—simplistic "peace through strength" concepts, commitments to military superiority, confidence in the enduring efficacy of security through credible threats of nuclear retaliation. In general terms, this strategy of peacemaking is neither mere opposition to force in international relations, nor excessive reliance on force, but the civilizing or politicizing of force. It assumes that force, in the form of military power, will continue to play a role in international relations, but one that is less self-determining and more governed by international decisions designed to limit its significance and especially to restrain its unpredictability.

The position we have taken on the organization of power prompts us to consider military power in terms of its total organization as a system and not simply in terms of its instrumental character. Instrumentally, military power is one of several means states use to pursue their foreign policy objectives. In realist thought, military power is to be developed to the extent and in the kind necessary to serve the strategic and tactical needs of those objectives. It is a subordinate element of statecraft, in the dual sense that political ends determine military means and the civilian heads of government outrank and command the generals.

In practical terms of the organization of power, however, the world is not simply a collection of states pondering the instrumentality of armed force and deciding case by case whether and how to apply it. Rather, it is a sociotechnological system of weaponry of all degrees and kinds of sophistication, transcending even the largest and most powerful states and pressuring if not determining their military and political decisions. In this respect, military power is environment more than instrument. The system itself is a fundamental policy problem. The system as environment is the context within which all military decisions must be understood and taken— those pertaining to the organization of power itself and its tendencies, and those pertaining to more discrete and selective exercises of national power in pursuit of national interests.

Similarly, the system is the context for understanding the applications and limitations of the just war ethic. Christian realism rejects both pacifism and the crusade and takes its readings of the morality of military power from the just war criteria.[12] Applying these criteria to nuclear weapons with their awesome effects of blast, fire, and fallout, and doing so with respect to their systemic reality, it is difficult to avoid the conclusion that these weapons systems—even as deterrent systems—are morally indefensible. I drew that conclusion myself more than twenty years ago.[13] The problem with this conclusion, however, is that it does not suggest a self-evident and defensible policy. What is the next step, after moral approval has been withdrawn from nuclear deterrence? The weapons systems remain in place as the international organization of military power. The threat of war remains, and the moral condemnation pronounced on the weapons systems does not *ipso facto* make war less likely. Moral delegitimation alone obviously does not resolve the problem of war avoidance.

The logical next step from moral delegitimation is unilateral disarmament, with regard at least to nuclear weapons and delivery systems. But does that step serve the cause of war-avoidance, or simply introduce a different set of risks: that unilateral disarmament would raise the likelihood of war by destabilizing the international system; that the prospect of successful unilateralism would provoke unsympathetic right-wing groups and military establishments to seize power and control the weapons systems on their own terms? One does not know the answers to these questions. They are matters of speculation and of calculated risk-balancing, as is the question of continuing a policy of nuclear deterrence. What one should recognize, however, is that moral inquiry now begins with military power in its character as environmental system, not with military power in its instrumental character. Certainly the instrumental question is still of great moral significance, but its full and decisive significance must be determined with respect to political and military requirements for nuclear war-avoidance. What the next step may be is a matter not of idealistic dogmatics or of moral logic, but of realistic calculation. It must be disclosed from where we stand in the prevailing organization of power. The path it follows must be one that leads away from the brink of war and back to politics.

From this analysis it should be easy to understand why realists become impatient with persons who declare the immorality of nuclear deterrence and then advocate multilateral disarmament or an "ethics of reciprocity,"[14] as though they were simple alternatives to deterrence or military strategy. Multilateralism and reciprocity certainly are to be affirmed as essential to the peace process, but they become political possibilities in a hostile, adversary relationship principally because of the mutual fear that inspires the antagonists to cooperate and reciprocate in disarming. Military considerations and threats (implicit or explicit) are not excluded from the process of reciprocity in arms control or disarmament; they are part of the process itself. Apparently, therefore, the elements of deterrence retain some residual moral justification in the context of moving from war to politics as a means of resolving international differences, despite the judgments pronounced on the weapons systems and their war uses. How otherwise could it be morally right to retain morally disallowed weapons systems and rely on their intimidating effect to require the adversary to do jointly what one's own state is unwilling to do unilaterally?

It should be easy to understand also that persons who are serious about peacemaking should be prepared to recommend or support changes in weapons systems and military policies that make war less rather than more likely. The next step from war to politics may be, for example, the adopting of an effective, single warhead weapon in place of existing multiple warhead weapons, thereby making the total system of military power more stable. Or it may be the enhancement of conventional forces to fill the vacuum of power left by the dismantling of nuclear systems. But if it is easy to understand such readiness against the background of this analysis, it remains hard to do for persons convinced that to be for peace means to be against anything that has to do with war. The temptation is very great to escape into optimistic assumptions about the benign intentions of the opponents, or equally optimistic political or military calculations that dismiss the military proposals. However, if peacemaking has to do with civilizing the organization of power, one must test all peacemaking proposals in terms of the organization as it exists, and with reference to where one stands on the continuum from force to consent, and take one's next step from that point.

Questions in the Conversation

At this point in the conversation over theology, politics, and peace, I must press Professors Moltmann and Míguez Bonino to show how they would deal with the fundamental issues of the organization of power in the framework of their own theological approaches to peace. The question to Moltmann is this: Is there a distinctive political theory that derives from political theology? If so, what does it tell us about how the power of any society—in this case, international society—should be arranged so as to provide optimally for peace and justice? What are the relative roles of force and consent, and what is the role of military power in such arrangements? What theological understanding of human nature supports and comes to expression in this political theory?

The material and occasion for responding to these questions are present in some of Moltmann's essays on political issues, but he has not provided extended and systematic answers, so far as I am aware. He has stood for democratic socialism and the democratization of international politics, and has proposed that foreign policy should be the domestic policy of international society, but to my knowledge he has not confronted the structural difficulties of these proposals or made explicit their implicit anthropology. In his essay on "Political Theology," published in 1971, he acknowledged the need for representation in political society, but spoke of it primarily in terms of the risks of political idolatry and political alienation.[15] His contribution to political theory on this point seemed to be limited to a call for continuous democratization and political iconoclasm.

In *On Human Dignity*, Moltmann seemed to undercut the need for constructive political theory on Christian theological terms by arguing for "undivided discipleship of Christ *in* economic, social, cultural and political conditions" in place of "responsible support of the world orders *of* economics, society, culture, and politics."[16] He did in fact propose some specific next steps for moving the world away from the threat of war, but these recommendations then appeared to be compromised by a commitment to pacifism, which surrenders the power that states would need to carry them out. "Pacifism," he declared, "is the only *realism* of life left to us in this apocalyptic situation of threatened world annihilation. Pacifists are the realists of life, not merely voices of utopia."[17] Pacifism can be a hopeful stance for persons who trust God, and it may be, as Moltmann argues, the only stance Christians with an apocalyptic nuclear eschatology can assume, but it is not a state policy for changing the international organization of power. Moreover, that Moltmann commits to pacifism—at least partly on just war grounds—has something to do with where he is located in the geography of peace. He lives at an especially precarious point on the Moscow-Washington axis. The liberation theologians, located elsewhere in the world, do not readily commit to pacifism, and the Israelis clearly do not regard pacifism as realism.

A commitment to pacifism and a call for disarmament do not address fundamental problems of the organization of international systemic power to serve the ends of peace and justice. The question of "responsible support of the world orders" cannot be put aside, if one is to fulfill the expectations of Christian discipleship. What political theory, informed by what understanding of human nature, can political theology generate out of its own perspectives to assist these purposes? When a theology of hope reflects on the way states actually behave, what can it propose with regard to ways and means of organizing the future of international society?

The question to Míguez Bonino and through him to Latin American liberation theology is: What social science, backed by what theological understanding of power, human nature, and history, can account for the richness, diversity, and energy of international society, and thereby yield the understanding necessary to organize power for a just and confident peace? The Latin American theologians have found Marxist class analysis useful above other social sciences in disclosing their own reality to be a class struggle pointing to the necessity of revolutionary transformation. They have shown this reality to be part of a global process by linking the struggle in particular countries to the operations of international capitalism, to the problems of dependence and marginality, and to the role of the national security state. One should grant the importance of these methods and disclosures, especially for bringing criticism to bear on established and growing orders of power. But the question arises: Does the use of Marxist class analysis expose social reality in its fullness, or does it reduce this reality to structural economic factors, thereby obscuring other factors that bear powerfully on questions of the future distribution, limitation, and exercise of power? What are we to make of the fact that Mr. Gorbachev's *glasnost* has uncovered myriad national identities in the Soviet Union that are far stronger than class solidarity? What does it say about the sufficiency of class analysis that most Marxist states are incorporating some degree of market system into their economies, that Gorbachev has proposed joint ventures with "capitalist" countries and firms for doing business within the Soviet Union, and that Moscow soon may have a stock market? What is the international significance of the power of religion revealed by the resurgence of political Islam? Why do states with socialist regimes often have profound differences over foreign policy issues?

Obviously, class analysis does not explain all dimensions of corporate reality and conflict. Therefore it seems hardly likely that this social science employed by many Latin American liberation theologians can be the sole instructor in the future organization of power. That is clear in the case of domestic society, for which it does not provide in its own social theory for efficacious limitation of the power of the new ruling elite. It is even clearer in the case of international society. Once this social science gets beyond the critique of international capitalism, it cannot interpret and establish the conditions for the just and peaceful organization of international power. It cannot do so adequately without incorporating basic realist presuppositions concerning human nature, history, and power, and such a move would have the effect of changing its character as a social science.

The larger and more fundamental question, of course, is whether "liberation" is a symbol of sufficient comprehensiveness to fill out the dimensions of a political theology. That liberation is the necessary route for oppressed people is not to be denied, nor can one deny rightly that liberation is an essential element of authentically Christian theology. The problem is that the terms and conditions of the institutionalization of freedom are not contained in the notion of liberation itself. Liberation is potent as a critical concept, but not sufficient as a constructive concept. What is the nature and vision of the community within which the freedom of liberation is to be housed and exercised? How is its power to be organized to preserve and extend the achievements of liberation, and to restrain the liberated ones from becoming the new oppressors? What understanding of human nature supports and instructs the proposed power arrangements? These questions point to the fact that "liberation" does not define the scope and substance of a complete theology, and certainly not of a political theology. Therefore a liberation theology as such would appear to be too narrow to discern and describe the political conditions of peace.

Implicit in these questions to German political theology and Latin American liberation theology is the suggestion that they cannot complete their theological-political enterprises without accepting basic elements of the Christian realist position, specifically those having to do with human nature and its political implications. In Christian realism, human nature is understood to be an ambiguous combination of freedom and limitation, of aspirations to goodness and corruption of those aspirations by egoism. This ambiguity packages the capacity for justice with the inclination to injustice. It generates the possibilities for challenging and overcoming the limits of particular situations, but frustrates all prospects for transforming the earthly city into the city of God by political means. It acknowledges the sinfulness of structures but denies that radical transformation of structures will resolve the problem of sin and thereby allow the establishment of justice in pure and permanent form. With such ambiguities in mind it requires the organization of power in such manner as to restrain and control the centers and holders of power, while enabling the community as a whole—and the lesser members thereof—to pursue and enhance the possibilities of temporal justice.

Are these the anthropological assumptions with which Moltmann and Míguez Bonino analyze the issues of politics and peace, or do they hold others? I do not intend to attempt to answer for them, nor do I mean necessarily to imply that they disagree with this statement of the relationship of human nature to politics. Míguez's book on Christian political ethics reads to some extent like a treatise in the Christian-realist school, and Moltmann in some recent essays has written with recognition of the persistent realities of power. However, I do not yet see them employing their theological methods, with full awareness of these anthropological issues, to address the problems of the organization of power for the durable establishment of peace with justice. In my view they will have to occupy common ground with Christian realism in order to accomplish that task.

One must acknowledge the difference between the theoretical statement of a theological orientation to politics and its historical setting and appropriation. Niebuhr's emergent Christian realism of the thirties was focused heavily on prophetic critique of established and concentrated power. His more fully developed Christian realism of the forties and fifties was concerned with the responsible exercise of established and concentrated power, specifically that of the United States in world politics. Both elements—the prophetic and the responsiblist—were present in both historical settings and were related dialectically to each other. One element tended to predominate over the other, however, depending on where he stood in relation to established power and how he understood the relationship of power to justice. What has happened in the historical development of the second, i.e., responsiblist, case is that the exercise of dominant power has legitimated itself with the notion of responsibility while at the same time suppressing the prophetic-critical elements in the Niebuhrian realist dialectic. We do not hear much of Niebuhr's warnings concerning self-deception, the equation of national interest with international interest, or the messianism of American political consciousness. That may be why some present-day "Niebuhrians" could approve the Reagan Administration's unilateralism in foreign policy and its support for military dictatorships resisting liberation movements. It certainly explains why liberation theologians tend to be suspicious of if not hostile to the Christian-realist approach to peace and justice.

Given the relationship of theory to history indicated above, we can hypothesize that the liberationist critics of Christian realism are in the prophetic-critical stage of the historical development of political action. If so, they are making important contributions to Christian political consciousness as well as to the political struggle by emphasizing the side of the dialectic that cannot be sensed or understood as well by persons whose moral analysis of international politics is shaped by preoccupation with the responsibilities of dominant power. It is essential to the fullness of both consciousness and practice to hear voices from the "underside," from other parts of the globe, from different loci of historical awareness.

On the other hand, if these critics are in fact in the prophetic-critical stage, they are looking ahead to the stage of responsibility, that is, to a new organization of power in which they or persons with whom they sympathize will control, decide, and direct. What theological contribution can they make to the knowledge of how to design that organization, such that power will be exercised responsibly to pursue peace with justice, but without suppressing the critical perspectives and voices?

The Outlook

In a different sort of essay, I would have examined at some length the notion of the peace of Christ and would have stressed both the confidence the believer draws from that peace and the direction it gives for confronting the conflicts of the world. However, in a conference where differences over that notion are less likely to be as great as those generated by temporal agenda and points of view, I have chosen to examine theologically and politically some elements of that peace which the world is able to give. It is in this dimension especially that Christian realism makes significant contributions to the understanding of peacemaking.

Two types of "realities"—and their bearing on peacemaking—have received attention in the preceding pages. One is the objective historical fact of the creation of nuclear weapons and their development into an environmental system that exceeds all conceivable or allowable defensive purposes, and threatens the extinction of life on the planet. The other is the set of elements that perennially influence the recombinations of political society: the ambiguity of human nature, the character of peace and justice as political organization, the nature of power as a variable combination of force and consent. The latter "reality" defines the necessary theoretical framework of all peacemaking efforts in all times and places. The former identifies the practical limit of all conflict and struggle, however justified as to cause, wherever it takes place now and in the future.

Given this statement of realities, what is the hope for the future of peacemaking? In temporal terms, it is the hope for the continuing civilizing of power, of bringing consent into ascendancy over force, of strengthening the fabric of a community in which persons and groups will feel free to be vulnerable. Theologically understood, the process of civilizing power is a work of reconciliation, of creating a new and inclusive social reality which comprehends and redefines the parties that had stood in enmity to one another.

But realism requires honesty with regard to the limits of the process. It is a process of strategic and at times tactical military decisions, of redesigning of weapons systems, of dealing with opponents with threat and compromise, of renouncing comfortable ideological poses, of designing structures of balance and restraint that limit one's own material power. It is not one that allows the abandonment of such considerations if one's goal is temporal peace, especially peace with justice, or of fulfilling one's obligation through stirring calls to general disarmament or to personal renunciation of weapons.

Moreover, the process is limited in its possibilities of fulfillment. The scientific capability for nuclear weapons and delivery systems will not be unlearned, and the sophistication of military technology will increase. The ambiguity of human nature will continue to the end of time, and power always will have force as one of its components. The accomplished civilizing of power will remain tentative, never to be taken for granted, threatened from without by enemies who may appear in the course of time, and from within by the corruption of the ruling class, or the uprising of internal proletariats, or other centrifugal forces that never are far from the surface of any society. The hope for the coming Kingdom of God may inform the process, and it should, but the politics of peace will produce only better or worse versions of the earthly kingdom. As Reinhold Niebuhr wrote, "There is no escape from the paradoxical relation of history to the Kingdom of God. History moves towards the realization of the Kingdom but yet the judgment of God is upon every new realization."[18]

The process of promoting peace by civilizing power must be taken up daily. Peacemaking is a never-ending vocation, whose justification and promise are beyond the history of political systems. That is why the peacemaker must have the confidence and direction that come from the experience of the peace of Christ.

Notes

1. In his preface to *Christian Realism and Peacemaking* (Nashville: Abingdon Press, 1988), Ronald H. Stone writes of the "evolution" of Christian realism and the differences among its various later representatives. Regrettably, Stone's book was not available to me when I prepared this address.

2. I have developed the theme of politics in the context of divine reconciliation in several writings, including "Reconciliation as a Foreign Policy Method" in *Religion in Life* XXXVII (Spring 1969): 40–54, and "Security, International Respon-

sibility, and Reconciliation" in *Quarterly Review* (Summer 1986): 12–29.

3. In the question period following this address, Professor Alan Geyer of Wesley Theological Seminary pointed out these differences between my own line of thought and that of Christian realism. I am grateful for this clarification.

4. José Míguez Bonino, *Toward a Christian Political Ethics* (Philadelphia: Fortress Press, 1983).

5. See Arnold Wolfers, "Amity and Enmity Among Nations" in *Discord and Collaboration* (Baltimore: Johns Hopkins University Press, 1962), pp. 25–35.

6. See Moltmann's *Religion, Revolution, and the Future* (New York: Scribner's, 1969), pp. 39, 40. Moltmann quotes Rauschenbusch on pp. 34–35.

7. This claim is a point of contention among political realists, not all of whom see all states acting at all times to maximize power.

8. The most influential analysis of the national security state in Latin America is José Comblin's *The Church and the National Security State* (Maryknoll, NY: Orbis Books, 1979). Comblin regards the national security state as a United States export and instrument of U.S. imperialism. The interpretation of the national security states as a function of international capitalism is the one set forth by José Míguez Bonino, in *Toward a Christian Political Ethics*, chapter 5.

9. Enrique Dussel's adaptation of the center-periphery paradigm in *Ethics and Theology of Liberation* (Maryknoll, NY: Orbis Books, 1978), pp. 8–13, does not reduce the international order simply to economic relations, nor economic power to capitalist power alone. He considers the Soviet Union, for example, to be part of the center. However, the center is determined not by geography but by the locus of economic power sufficient to establish and control the relations of domination. The center shifts, depending on the locus of economic power.

10. Reinhold Niebuhr, *The Children of Light and the Children of Darkness* (New York: Scribner's, 1944), p. 174.

11. Ibid., p. x of the New Foreword.

12. In *Just War Tradition of the Restraint of War* (Princeton: Princeton University Press, 1981), pp. 330–38, James T. Johnson argues that Reinhold Niebuhr opened the way to recovery of the just war tradition in twentieth-century Protestant thought. However, the principal Protestant theorist of that tradition in this century was not Niebuhr, but Paul Ramsey.

13. Theodore R. Weber, *Modern War and the Pursuit of Peace* (New York: Council on Religion and International Affairs, 1968).

14. The proposal for an "ethics of reciprocity" was made by the United Methodist Bishops in their pastoral letter, *In Defense of Creation; The Nuclear Crisis and a Just Peace* (Nashville: Graded Press, 1986), pp. 15, 48. The bishops rejected unilateral disarmament, despite their denial of the moral justification of nuclear weapons and their war uses.

15. Jürgen Moltmann, "Political Theology," in *Theology Today* 28 (April 1971): 18–20.

16. Jürgen Moltmann, *On Human Dignity* (Philadelphia: Fortress Press, 1984), p. 113.

17. Ibid., p. 131.

18. Reinhold Niebuhr, *The Nature and Destiny of Man* (New York: Scribners, 1941), vol. 2, p. 286.

Part Three

Other Voices

Chapter 7

Martin Luther King as a Political Theologian

ANDREW YOUNG

If you were black, Christian, and a young ministerial candidate in the southern part of the United States in the 1950s and 1960s, you found attractive the Christian existentialism that characterized theology in this country just after the Second World War. That theology saw Western society in crisis and called for a personal and corporate response from Christians. It was no accident that Martin Luther King, Jr., gravitated toward the writings of Paul Tillich and Henry Nelson Wieman, and later Reinhold Niebuhr. He was very much a product of the theology of that period. But, more important, he was a product of a Baptist church in Atlanta, a Baptist church that had been pastored by his father and his grandfather, both of whom were in an Old Testament prophetic tradition, who Sunday after Sunday preached a powerful Gospel in which God was present with men and women. God was in the midst of us and doing something in our time to which we were required to respond.

There was almost no sense in which Martin Luther King thought of himself as a leader. He thought of himself as being pulled by forces beyond his control, forces which, as he reflected on it, were in some sense divine. It was very unreasonable for a young man with a Ph.D. degree to go to a little Baptist church in a southern town like Montgomery, Alabama. Martin chose to go to Montgomery because he didn't want to be involved in politics and didn't want to be pulled into a larger political environment, as he would have been had he accepted the position as assistant to his father at Ebenezer, or had he joined Benjamin Mays as vice-president of Morehouse College, or even had he gone to Dillard University as chaplain, which was also one of the considerations. Interestingly enough, the president of Dillard was rather glad, he said, that Martin decided not to come to Dillard because when he met him he decided that he wasn't a strong enough leader to lead students on a college campus. This was a genuinely shy man, a genuinely unassuming man, who found himself thrust into a leadership role by Rosa Parks sitting down toward the front of a bus. Now, I don't believe Martin knew Rosa Parks; certainly he did not know her well, though she was the youth director/advisor to the NAACP. Rosa Parks *always* got on the front door of the bus. In those days, however, black people were supposed to get on the front door of the bus, put their money in the till, then get off and go around and get on at the back of the bus. And most black people did that. Rosa Parks never did; she moved on down the aisle to the back. Most bus drivers tolerated that, but this particular bus driver always went past her when he saw her at the stop. This particular day, she came up after the bus stopped and she did as was her custom. Moreover, she didn't sit right in the front of the bus as a demonstration. Being "just plain tired," she slumped into the first seat available as she walked toward the back of the bus. The event of her being jailed for this simple act galvanized the community in such a way that Martin was thrust into a leadership position. This was only a few months after he had declined the presidency of the NAACP because he wanted to complete his Ph.D. dissertation. Rosa Parks sat down in the bus just two weeks after he mailed his dissertation back to Boston University and had it approved.

All of us, including Martin, always felt that he was put in this position by God, and his theology was a response to the leading of God in the midst of a dramatic social situation. When his home was bombed shortly after his first child was born and people came with guns to protect and avenge the bombing, that was the first occasion when he began to pull together the teachings of Mahatma Gandhi and the language of Jesus of Nazareth from the New Testament. He made an impassioned plea to those who came to defend him violently that "we must find 'a more excellent way.'" Out of his attempts to deal with a bus boycott, withdrawing the support of the black community from the buses, he began to forge a very powerful political theology and political methodology that had several characteristics. One was simply a quest for justice—it was not even a quest for integration at first. Martin and the committee only wanted black people to be treated courteously. There was no demand to desegregate the buses. They only asked that the Montgomery Bus Company apologize to Mrs. Parks and make it a policy to treat black people with some respect. They were refused. The refusal of that simple human courtesy involved denial of their fundamental human dignity and made it almost absolutely necessary for them to protest. But Montgomery was not a militant, protesting community. With its black bourgeoisie, it was a community as conservative and passive as any in the South. Yet they found themselves having to stay off the buses, first for a day, then for a week, finally for 381 days. In the midst of that long period of testing, Martin forged a concept of freedom and a concept of justice without violence that was different in the sense that he did not blame his oppressor for the condition. He adopted from Gandhi the notion that the oppressor was also a victim in the situation, for the whites who ran the bus company were born into an inherited tradition that they didn't fully understand either. He said, "We have allowed our white brothers to go on all these years and we have never questioned their dehumanizing us, and so we can't really blame them totally." He adopted what we might now call a no-fault concept of injustice. He didn't blame the injustice on anybody, black or white, but on an unjust situation. And he rallied people to deal not with each other but to deal with the situation which was as dehumanizing of whites in one way as it was of blacks in another. He was fond of quoting Frederick Douglass to the effect that the struggle for freedom is "a struggle to save black mens' bodies and white mens' souls." But it was always an attempt to establish justice in the midst of an unjust situation that we had all inherited.

There was also a strong note of New Testament reconciliation. He was very fond of the passages from Ephesians, and he used the image of "breaking down the dividing wall of hostility" that separated Jew from Greek in Ephesus but in the Southland separated blacks from whites. The legal system — the system of laws that segregated blacks from whites and whites from blacks — was the dividing wall that had to be torn down in order that we might be reconciled and truly become brothers and sisters. This was only possible by nonviolent means. He said, "We don't want to destroy the schools; we want to attend the schools. We don't want to destroy the factories; we want to be able to earn our living in those factories. We want to be a part of this society and we're convinced that as we become a full part of this society, it will become an even greater society."

His dream as expressed twenty-five years ago in the March on Washington was that America might begin to live out the true meaning of her creed. But there was also an underlying sense of the cross and resurrection, a notion that there is no remission of sin without the shedding of innocent blood. These were not statements that Martin learned in seminary particularly; this was black folklore. This was the kind of thing he heard in Ebenezer Church in prayer meetings. This was part of the conventional folk theology that was probably far more influential in Martin's ministry than this theological training. Even the sense of cross and resurrection came from his direct experience when, while signing copies of his newly published book, *Stride Toward Freedom,* he was stabbed by a demented black woman in Harlem. He always joked about that stabbing; he dealt with death with a sense of humor. But he was constantly reminding us, teaching us, joking with us, about the fact that what we were doing was very dangerous, that at any moment if we didn't really believe it, we shouldn't bother further with it because, as he said over and over again, "If you haven't found something that you're willing to die for, you're probably not fit to live anyway." You need to be prepared to die at any moment. And then he would launch into preaching our funerals. One of his great methods for relieving the tension and the anxiety of death was to decide who it was that was going to be killed in the next demonstration, and then he would preach the funeral, with all of the humiliating and embarrassing things that you'd never want said about you. It broke the tension while confronting us with the constant presence of death and with the constant realization that there could be no change without somebody willing to take on the role of suffering servant.

In his own ministry it was perhaps most dramatically expressed to us at the time of Birmingham. We went to Birmingham, Alabama, to end segregation. All of the brilliant young minds sat down around the table and drew up what we felt was a battle plan that would put an end to racial segregation in Birmingham. We decided where we were going to demonstrate, we decided how many people would go to jail this day and how many people would go to jail that day, and we decided which lawyers were going to appeal which cases—we had it all worked out. We went to Birmingham with the perfect plan, and we put it into practice. After about thirty-five to forty days, however, after we had done everything that was in our plan, after we were completely out of money, after we had about a thousand to fifteen hundred people in jail and after we had used up all of the bond money that we had raised and all of the property bonds we could get people to post, we had to face the possibility of failure. A group of black leaders and a group of white clergy had both made very strong appeals to Martin Luther King to get out of town. Interestingly enough, he was accused of being a Communist agitator. Sitting in his room in the Gadsden Motel, facing those black leaders who urged him to stop the demonstrations and gave all kinds of reasons why Birmingham was just too tough—it could not be changed; facing the fact that we had exhausted the human resources and the economic resources of that community; and though he was not sure what to do next, Martin was nevertheless convinced that what we were doing was right. He decided the best thing was for him to go to jail, to join the people who were already in jail and see what happened. We didn't realize it at the time, but the day that he decided to go to jail was Maundy Thursday. He went to jail and that weekend the white clergy of the community published an ad in the paper which was a condemnation of his whole effort.

Two things happened that Sunday. He was given a copy of the *New York Times* in jail which included an article on the white clergy ad. He was so furious at his brothers in the church for not understanding what he was doing and why he was doing it that he started writing a letter from the Birmingham jail. He didn't have any paper, so he wrote around the margins of the *New York Times* and, after going through all of the paper that he had, he wrote on toilet tissue. The letter that came out of the jail, piecemeal, was a brilliant description of the social dilemma of Christians in the South, and it had a liberating effect on the whole nation.

Also, the popularity of the Birmingham protest had been on the wane.

People were losing heart, people were beginning to be anxious. Only fifty-five people went to jail that day with Martin Luther King, and it was reported on page 36 of the Birmingham newspaper. Once the word went out that Martin Luther King was in jail on Easter Sunday, however, thousands of people turned up at church, ready to give themselves, ready to go to jail, ready to do whatever was necessary to bring about an end to racial segregation. Ironically, we marched to the jail simply to show Martin the numbers of people now supporting a movement that he thought was about to die. As we got several blocks from the jail, the notorious Bull Connor, the chief of police, was there with his army of police and with his fire trucks and police dogs. He formed a barrier of three obstacles: the dogs, the fire hoses, the policemen with guns. All we wanted to do was walk four blocks and pray and come back. I happened to be leading that line, and when we saw the police force, we didn't really know what to do. They were not the most rational people. People always say that nonviolence worked in the United States because of an enlightened police force, but it won't work anywhere else. At that time, those police had bombed and killed more than fifty black families in the year previous to our going there.

The kinds of things that you read about in Latin America or other oppressed societies such as South Africa were not unknown to us. We were expecting the worst. Because we didn't want people to panic, we asked everybody to get down on their knees. It was Easter Sunday, and people were all dressed up and they didn't want the police putting fire hoses on their pretty new clothes, but when they got down on their knees, they began to pray. And they began to pray in the old-fashioned traditional manner, not so much with words, but with moans and with sighs, with cries and with passion. I was trying to reason with the police chief, who was totally unreasonable, and I was getting nowhere. He was simply saying if we didn't move, he was going to turn on the hoses and turn loose the dogs, and the massacre would be our responsibility because we were disobeying his orders.

Just as I was about to give up, one of the good old sisters jumped up and got happy, and said, "The Lord is with this movement! We are going on to the jail!" Everybody just jumped up and started following this lady. Bull Connor began to give the orders to stop them. As I stood there, I saw this police force that had been hostile, that had been filled with hate, lose their anger. The dogs that were straining at the leash calmed down. They were no longer barking. The firemen who had fire hoses with the kind of water pressure that would have broken people's ribs if they had turned them on at that close range, were just standing there. And when Bull Connor jumped up and down and said "Stop them! Stop them!" I saw one of the firemen with tears in his eyes let the fire hose fall to the ground. As we marched through this red sea of fire trucks, the same old sister got on the other side and said, "Great God A'mighty done parted the Red Sea one more time!"

Later, as we reflected on it, we realized that on that Easter weekend what we had experienced in the course of a few days was in a very real social sense a crucifixion and a resurrection. We began to understand that this was the way the changes were going to occur. From that moment on, we didn't shy away from confrontations, we didn't shy away from dangers. Neither did we court them. For Martin Luther King never took on a new project without a great deal of difficulty and pondering the cost. He didn't want to oppose the war in Vietnam. He tried his best to get Coretta to be the spokesperson on the war issue. Coretta, who had been in her own right an active member of the women's peace movement, was very willing to take on that role. For a long time he operated on the basis that he would be the spokesperson for civil rights and would leave the question of war to others, until suddenly he decided this was segregating his conscience — that the bombs we dropped on Vietnam would explode at home in inflation and unemployment. Thus, it was after a long period of soul-searching that he finally began to raise questions about America's involvement in Vietnam.

His movement toward a poor people's campaign, which probably as much as anything led to his death, was out of a sense of near despair over the dislocation of poor people as a result of the mechanization of the rural South. With the automatic cotton-picker there was no need for the mass black labor that once had been so necessary. Not only was agriculture mechanized, but the federal government had a policy of paying landowners not to grow food or fiber. Yet no one was doing anything about the workers that were displaced. They were not just black; they were black and white, brown and red. He decided that we needed to get all of these forces together and go to Washington for one last appeal. Not that it would change our nation, for he had no illusions about being immediately successful, but he felt that it was important to raise the question of economic justice before the 1968 campaign. He thought that by raising the question in a dramatic way, with thousands of poor people of all colors coming to Washington, the next president, be he Democrat or Republican, would be forced to address the question of poverty and economic discrimination along with the problems of race. It was at that point that he was cut down by an assassin's bullet.

Even as he gave his life, some twenty years ago, a force was unleashed in this nation that was far more powerful than Martin Luther King, Jr., in his lifetime. We found the business community opening up its doors, suddenly realizing that they had to begin to hire and train black people not only as workers but as managers. We found the universities beginning to understand that there was an important academic role in providing opportunities for bringing along the least of these God's children — that university life was not a privilege for the upper classes, but an opportunity for all God's children. We found our nation's political process beginning to carry out governmentally and administratively many of those things that Martin only preached and dreamed about.

Martin Luther King lived the life that he preached and gave his life in service to the poorest of the poor. He didn't want to go to Memphis; Memphis was irrelevant to the plan that we had developed to change the nation through Washington. But here were garbage workers who were simply raising a cry for human dignity and the right to organize and bargain collectively and to elect their own representation. Martin said very simply, "Well, management has a board of directors and stockholders to make decisions; why shouldn't workers be allowed to organize and elect their leadership and participate in the decision making?" It was not in any sense a crusade, it was more a sense of compassion for a group of black men in Memphis that he saw being publicly humiliated. It was at the time of his identification with the least of these God's children that he was met with an assassin's bullet.

But that was not the end. It was only the beginning. We celebrate Martin Luther King's birthday as a national holiday now—although we're still not sure what we're celebrating. It appears to be something of a black holiday, something of a liberal holiday. In reality, it should be a holiday that celebrates the resolution of enormous tensions without resorting to means of violence. I always like to remind people in Atlanta that this city could very easily be Northern Ireland or Beirut, Lebanon; that everybody black and everybody white in the South after the Second World War had plenty of guns. My own family was a nonviolent household; we had only two or three guns. My wife's family had dozens! Had blacks and whites ever turned them on each other, we would be very much like Lebanon. And yet, in the midst of the tensions, Martin was a voice of reason, a voice of faith, a voice of compassion, willing to put himself forward and take the suffering of the evil world upon himself—not aggressively, not seeking martyrdom, but willing to respond with humanity to the needs of humanity. Who can say how far-reaching the effects of his life will be? Certainly his example helped to re-create the city of his birth, Atlanta. His example encouraged the Carter administration to rely on the methods of nonviolence in the independence of Zimbabwe and in the negotiations of the Panama Canal Treaty. Certainly this was a factor in the negotiations at Camp David. It was only in dealing with the Russians and the Strategic Arms Limitation Talks that we were less willing to trust nonviolent methods and became more "realistic" and "Niebuhrian." In other situations, we were far more willing, I think, to move ahead taking the risks involved in a creative, nonviolent approach— and made progress as a result. I still don't fully understand and appreciate all that happened to us during those days when we walked with Martin Luther King. For me, it was just a pleasure to have been able to walk along that way. And I am convinced that wherever there are men, women and children willing to walk that way, it remains the most viable means for effective and long-lasting change.

Chapter 8

Theological Resources
for the Political Task

GORDON HARLAND

A debate is raging in the churches. Sometimes it is fierce and frequently it is confused. This should occasion no surprise, for it is a complex debate concerning issues of great significance. It is an important debate. The subject shapes the way in which the churches view their responsibilities, conceive their agendas, and to some extent how they employ their resources. It also helps shape their thoughts and feelings about what it means to be Christian in the contemporary world and to participate in the Christian community. It is all this because the debate over the relationship between faith and society, between Christ and culture, is at bottom a debate concerning the nature of the Christian message itself. At the center of this debate are those biblical themes, images, and doctrines which inform Christian views of human nature, the meaning of God's work in Jesus Christ, the social significance of the paradigmatic event, and the consequent interpretation of history. The debate has brought to the front of the stage the grand old question: What *is* the relationship between our religious understanding and commitment and our pursuit of social and cultural values? What theological resources do we have that can significantly inform the political task?

The conviction informing what follows is that those central doctrines of faith — Incarnation, Atonement, Human Nature, and Justification by Grace — which are usually related only to our personal quests for forgiveness, meaning, and renewal, are also the basis for the most adequate political theology. For that reason I think that the center of the faith best provides us with a resource of insight and healing that can help us to keep the personal and social dimensions of life together and whole, and in so doing transcend the debilitating reduction and distortions represented by those wretched words *politicization* and *privatization.*

Theological Resources

Human Nature

Surely the realism of the Christian understanding of human nature can prove to be a significant resource for the political task. Anyone immersed in the Christian understanding of humankind ought never to be surprised by evil. The Christian understanding resists not only obvious evils, such as the grasping for tyrannical power and the exploitation of the weak, but it ought also to make us particularly alert to the way in which the good can become stale if it is not kept open to that divine judgment which is also the spring of renewal. The Christian understanding of human nature is the kind of resource that gives us a lively sense of what Reinhold Niebuhr called "ironic evil," by which he meant the tendency for our virtue to become vice, our strength to become weakness, and our wisdom to become folly, whenever pretension stretches them beyond their limits.

The Judeo-Christian understanding of human nature has a deep appreciation of the uniqueness and worth of the person. Of course, Christians have no corner on either the affirmation or the defense of the dignity of the person. The significance of the biblical view is that it locates our dignity in the position we hold before God. Our relationship to God, in this understanding, is not something added on to our being as an option or as an extra, but is constitutive of our being. Such a relationship, which is the very life of faith, can provide a significant leverage over the political order, and that is a matter of large significance in this technological age which facilitates such concentrations of power.

Christians, however, know not only the reality of sin but equally the reality of grace, and that means that we should always be alert to the possibility of the new in history. People informed by the Christian understanding are realists. Their understanding of sin makes them that. They agree with realists generally that self-interest is a fundamental datum of all collective life. However, they are not cynics. They do not believe that self-interest is the only thing operating in life. They know, value and nurture the human capacity to reach out in care and concern. Knowing both these things, they also know that the mark of leadership, or statesmanship, is the capacity to find the points of coincidence between the group or national interest and the needs and interests of the wider human community. Moreover, Christians live in the assurance that God ever goes before them, opening the doors to the new. In a word, the Christian understanding of human nature is a resource of insight for us because it provides such a balanced assessment of both the creative and disruptive effects of our freedom upon our communities.

Both aspects need to be emphasized. The creative goodness of the human spirit, the access to being that is gained through personal relationships and responsibilities, needs to be lifted up in this age when quantitative measures have gained such wide acceptance. But equally, any realistic analysis of the human condition must rigorously come to grips with the manner in which our existence is separated from what we essentially are or are meant to be, with that condition of the soul that we call sin, which is deeper than our conscious choices and intentions. It is recognized that we cannot be made whole again without some understanding of the broken situation in which we exist. There is a profundity in the Christian understanding of human nature that can be a much needed resource for us today. So it was not surprising to see the political philosopher, Kenneth Thompson, as he pondered the resources available for a wise foreign policy, remarking that "Christian realism by illuminating the misery and grandeur of man can be a textbook for the diplomatist. It can rid men of their illusions while preparing them for their 'finest hours.' "[1]

This heritage is not only a resource of insight but also a resource of *spirit*. By this is meant not only a general goodwill and kind feelings. Rather, religious faith nurtured by a biblical understanding of human nature ought to be productive of a peculiar quality of spirit that is a needed resource for the complexity of these days. What is the character of that spirit? It is a combination of *resolution* in the face of evil and a *humility* born of the knowledge that our cause, however right, however just, is not absolute. That is a tall order. Moral resolution and humility do not commonly travel together. This combination is especially difficult for participants in conflict. Yet one of the greatest examples in history was just such a central participant in a terrible conflict—Abraham Lincoln. He was a leader who, in the midst of the conflict of civil war, was richly informed by the biblical view of human nature and the spirit which flowed from it. *He was resolute.* He was much more resolute than his generals, as the Southern Confederacy, to its chagrin, was to learn. He was resolved (1) to preserve the union and (2) to abolish slavery. But his resolution was combined with the humility that came with the knowledge that although his case was relatively right, it was not absolute. It had been corrupted. It had been corrupted not only by Yankee self-interest but more importantly by the moral pretension that usually tempts the advocates of righteous causes.

This *combination* of resolution and humility was what was so important, and so rare. He did not allow his resolution, his moral commitment, to lead him into self-righteousness or moral rigidity. Nor, on the other hand, did he allow his great capacity for compassion to betray him into weakness or a sentimental analysis of the situation or the strategies necessary to deal with it. Reinhold Niebuhr's comment on Lincoln is pertinent to our discussion: "This combination of moral resoluteness about the immediate issues with a religious awareness of another dimension of meaning and judgment must be regarded as almost a perfect model of the difficult but not impossible task of remaining loyal and responsible toward the moral treasures of a free civilization on the one hand while yet having some religious vantage point over the struggle."[2] Lincoln remains not only a relevant example of wise political leadership in the midst of a terrible conflict but also an example of the perennial relevance of biblical insight into human nature. He gave expression to a perspective and a spirit peculiarly needed in our own time as we face so many tragic choices in our collective life.

It is, however, right here that the gravest deficiency of the American Religious Right is displayed. Instead of the tragic realities of human nature so profoundly articulated in the Bible and the Christian tradition, the Religious Right frequently presents us with a Manichaean view of human nature in which the world is divided into good guys and bad guys, the white hats and the black hats, which owes more to the legend of the American "Western" than it does to the Christian faith.

It is the role of biblical religion to provide a framework of understanding and value that will prompt a nation to seek to realize the greatest possible social values while at the same time keeping the nation keenly aware of the way in which those values and concerns are tainted by national self-interest. It was this understanding that Reinhold Niebuhr urged upon his fellow Americans over forty years ago when he wrote: "Thus a contrite recognition of our own sins destroys the illusion of eminence through virtue and lays the foundation of grace in the national life."[3] It is this sort of biblical understanding that is lacking in the new Religious Right where it would appear that an alien "secular," unself-critical, ideological approach has taken over.

The references to Lincoln lead us to consider the significance of the heart of the Christian faith for developing a political ethic able to face the tragic dimensions of our collective life. Specifically, I refer to the social relevance of an ethic shaped by the understanding of Justification by Grace.

Justification by Grace and a Political Ethic

We are a generation that lives with tragic choices. Every statesman, for example, is daily faced with trying to realize partially incompatible goals. To be responsible often means making the choice of suppressing one value in order to secure or preserve another. Moreover, the very struggle to secure justice itself involves the use of the instruments of power, and the instruments of power are always ambiguous. Nor can innocence be maintained or purity achieved by withdrawing from the struggle. The fact to be recognized is this: *There is no moral hiding place.* But it is precisely here that we see the genius of Christian faith. The central symbol of that faith is the cross of Christ. That cross discloses the tragic depths of life, the pervasiveness of human sin. It does this through the same reconciling act of God in Christ which provides resources to cope with those tragic realities.

The term Justification by Grace means the process by which we are made right with God, by which we are reconciled to God. Moreover, the heart of the Christian experience is that the grace we meet in Christ both illumines the depth of our need and is a power to reconcile us. Individual believers across the centuries have known what it means to experience the subtlety and depth of sin through an appropriation of the grace that brings both forgiveness and the energies of new life. Our contention is that this basic doctrine is also of social significance. To act socially in terms of Justification by Grace is to know three things: (1) that the Divine Love that has met us impels us to seek a greater justice in the community; (2) that the same Divine Love that impels us to justice also illumines the sin we will be involved in by our efforts; and (3) that this doctrine also assures us of a resource of mercy to cover the evil we do in order to be responsible. This is a perspective that saves us from both a paralysis of will *and* the pretension to which our righteous causes usually tempt us. It bids us to seek the combination embodied in Lincoln—a spirit of resolution against evil with an awareness of "the taint of sin in the cause of our devotion." Clearly, whenever the ambiguity of political decisions and the tragic dimensions of history are obscured, the full relevance of this Christian understanding will be lost.

This happened in the United States in the mid-nineteenth century. Indeed, to read much of the theology of that period, to say nothing of the literature of social and political conflict, is to be left wondering what happened to this cardinal Reformation doctrine. It was present of course, but one has the feeling that it was there only because it was supposed to be there. After all, the doctrine is an important part of the Christian heritage and theological discourse would be incomplete without it. It was, however, not informing religious thought and life in any vital way. Surely one of the reasons why it was not is that those who affirmed it failed to bring it into a living engagement with the great social issues of the day. That was a great pity, for if ever Christians needed the resources of insight and healing available in Christian faith to engage the ambiguous values and tragic choices of communal life, it was at that time and place.

Consider the debates that Christians had over the issue of slavery. As I read those debates, the thought would not die that a vital understanding of this evangelical doctrine of Justification by Grace could have been both illuminating and healing in that tragic situation. Why? Because the doctrine does two things simultaneously. It points to the riches of the Divine Love that throws a searchlight into the depths of the evil in which we are involved. At the same time, the doctrine points to the resources of grace enabling us to cope responsibly with a difficult situation. *It really is a doctrine that is indispensable for dealing with the tragic choices of life.* Therein lie both its truth and its relevance. It could have enabled those Christians to have said something like this: "We know that we are involved in an evil situation. We know also that there is now no easy solution. But we are serious about getting rid of this evil; we will set a realistic timetable to show our resolution, and we know that there are resources of grace to cover the evil we will be involved in, through our attempts to be responsible and just." But they did not say that sort of thing. The reason they did not do so would seem to be that moralism had become the content of their Christian understanding, obscuring the depths of both sin and grace. This ingrained moralism meant that they felt they must always be righteous, supporting righteous causes, instead of being forgiven sinners coping as best they could with an entrenched social evil in an ethically complex situation. This result was most instructive and we have seen similar results scores of times: *They deceived themselves, so that things could no longer be called by their proper names.* So slavery was no longer condemned as an evil, as it had been previously in the South; it was now even declared to be a "positive good." This failure was not simply a failure of courage. It was a theological failure. It meant that the depths of both sin and grace, and consequently the social meaning of the doctrine of Justification by Grace, were obscured by the all-pervading moralism. This means further that when the conflict was joined in bloody civil war, that this moralistic understanding, instead of illuminating the tragic dimensions of the conflict, served rather to intensify the crusading self-righteous moralism of both sides in the conflict.

The doctrine of Justification by Grace does not mean that we do not take sides in the struggle for social values. It does not say, "A plague on all your houses." It does not say that "since sin abounds, no significant distinctions are to be made." This is the fear expressed by Juan Luis Segundo. He fears that this "relativization of any and every political system" will end up "being a politically neutral theology" lacking the enthusiasm necessary for social change.[4] No! It is not an invitation to neutrality. It does mean, however, that the very faith that impels us to action also keeps us aware of the fact that our cause, though perhaps relatively righteous, is not absolute. This awareness will not get rid of conflict, but it will mitigate the ferocity of the struggle in which we are and must be engaged if treasured social values are to be secured and preserved. This emphasis upon the transcendent dimensions of divine grace is neither an excuse nor a summons to escape history. Quite the contrary. In the words of Reinhold Niebuhr, "It gives us a fulcrum from which we can operate in history. It gives us faith by which we can seek to fulfill our historic tasks without illusions and without despair."[5]

Certainly this doctrine of Justification has profound meaning for people in their individual pilgrimage. But just as the individual before God is kept from being sentimental by the reality of sin, and from despair by the largeness of God's mercy, so this center of the faith promises that combination of realism and hope that is at once the fruit of biblical faith and the perennial need of society.

It has been our contention that the central doctrines of Christian faith are significant not only for the personal religious quest but also because they provide the basis for the most adequate political theology. Development of the social significance of these themes could help Christianity make a contribution to a much-needed public philosophy and at the same time restore relevance and wholeness to the theological enterprise.

Notes

1. Kenneth Thompson, "Prophets and Politics" in *Christianity and Crisis*, May 16, 1966, p. 61.

2. Reinhold Niebuhr, *The Irony of American History* (New York: Charles Scribner's Sons, 1952), p. 172.

3. Reinhold Niebuhr, "Anglo-Saxon Destiny and Responsibility" in *Christianity and Crisis*, October 4, 1943.

4. Juan Luis Segundo, S.J., *The Liberation of Theology* (Maryknoll, N.Y.: Orbis Books, 1985), p. 145.

5. Reinhold Niebuhr, "Christian Otherworldliness" in *Christianity and Society* 9, vol. 1 (Winter 1943): 12.

Chapter 9

Theology, Politics, and Peace: A Jewish Perspective

MARC H. ELLIS

Some years ago, in an essay outlining Christian complicity in the Jewish Holocaust and the future of Christianity in light of that complicity, the German Catholic theologian Johann Baptist Metz wrote: "We Christians can never again go back behind Auschwitz: to go beyond Auschwitz, if we see clearly, is impossible for us by ourselves. It is possible only together with the victims of Auschwitz." When first read, this statement strikes one by its boldness, and later by its depth. For Metz, the Jewish victims of Christian triumphalism and power stand before the Christian community, challenging the past but also serving as the key to the future. Of course, Christian and Jew have traveled together on a tortuous and bloody road for almost two millennia before the Holocaust; however, the present calls for a radically new way of journeying together, one of trust and ultimately of embrace.[1]

With the eruption of widespread and violent demonstrations in the Israeli occupied West Bank and Gaza Strip, Metz's statement has assumed a new relevance in a different context. For, on the other side of power, the Jewish people have assumed a new and unaccustomed role in relation to the Palestinian people: that of the oppressors. As some Christians continue to have difficulty in admitting their complicity in the suffering of Jews, the Jewish people find it equally difficult to admit their own complicity in the suppression of the Palestinian people. Though Jewish empowerment, mandated by the suffering of the Holocaust, must be affirmed as a good, the present impasse in Israel and Palestine cannot be addressed outside the most obvious, and to some the most contradictory, of options: solidarity with the Palestinian people. To paraphrase Metz's statement, the challenge might be thus stated: "We Jews can never go back behind empowerment:

93

to go beyond empowerment, if we see clearly, is impossible for us by our-selves. It is possible only together with the victims of our empowerment."

Thus the question facing the Jewish people in Israel and the diaspora involves and yet moves beyond negotiation of borders, recognition of the PLO, the cessation of the expropriation of human land and water resources in the occupied territories, and even the public confession of Israeli torture and murder. For in the end the Israeli-Palestinian conflict involves the political, military, and economic spheres of Jewish life while at the same time addressing the deepest theological presuppositions of post-Holocaust Jewry. Without addressing the implicit and explicit theology of our com-munity, any adjustment of political, military and economic borders will represent superficial moments to be transgressed when the opportunity presents itself. Surely, political settlement of any significance in Israel and Palestine without a movement toward solidarity is, by the very nature of the conflict, impossible.

Unfortunately, the normative theology of the Jewish community today — Holocaust theology — is unable to articulate this path of solidarity. Nor can the most well-known of Jewish spokespersons, some of whom helped to create this theology and others who operate within it, speak clearly on this most important issue. There are many reasons for this inability to speak clearly on the subject of solidarity: Holocaust theology, emerging out of reflection on the death camps, represents the Jewish people as we were, helpless and suffering; it does not and cannot speak of the people we are today and who we are becoming, powerful and often oppressive. Holocaust theology argues correctly for the Jewish need to be empowered; it lacks the framework and the skills of analysis to investigate the cost of that empow-erment. Holocaust theology speaks eloquently about the struggle for human dignity in the death camps and radically about the question of God and Jewish survival but has virtually nothing to say about the ethics of a Jewish state possessing nuclear weapons, supplying military arms and assistance to authoritarian regimes, expropriating land and torturing children.

Though this information is readily available and accepted as documented by the world community, written about or even discovered by Jews in Israel and in the diaspora, Holocaust theologians often refuse to accept it, as if the suggestion that Jews could support such policies, rather than the poli-cies themselves, is treasonable and grounds for excommunication from the community. Because of the power of Holocaust theology in mainstream Jewish institutions, media and organized Jewish life, these "facts" are deemed outside of Jewish discourse *as if they are not happening because it is impossible that Jews would do such things.* Thus a community that prides itself on its intelligence and knowledge is on its most crucial issue — the future of our people — profoundly ignorant.[2]

That is why the dialectic of Holocaust and empowerment, surfaced in Holocaust theology, needs to be confronted by the dynamic and dangerous element of solidarity. Solidarity, often seen as a reaching out to other communities in a gesture of goodwill, at the same time necessitates a probing of one's own community. To come into solidarity, knowledge of the other is needed; but soon we understand a deeper knowledge of self is called for as well. If we recognize the national aspirations of the Palestinian people, that is only a step toward the more difficult and critical question of how Israeli policy has interacted with that aspiration. If we support the struggle of South African blacks, the relationship of Israel and the South African government needs a thorough investigation.[3]

Increasing numbers of Jews are beginning to understand that our historical situation has changed radically in the last two decades and that something terrible, almost tragic, is happening to us. With what words do we speak such anguished sentiments? Do we feel alone with these feelings so that they are better left unspoken? Do such words, once spoken, condemn us as traitors or with the epithet, self-hating Jew? Or does articulating the unspeakable challenge the community to break through the silence and paralysis that threaten to engulf us? And those of us who know and empathize with the Palestinians, can we speak without being accused of creating the context for another holocaust? Can we be seen as emissaries of an option to halt the cycle of destruction and death?

This is the challenge facing the Jewish people. And with it lies the task of creating a new Jewish theology consonant with the history we are creating and the history we want to bequeath to our children. It has to do with the way we exercise powers. Should we rest content with the proud claim that we are powerful where once we were weak, that we are invincible where once we were vulnerable? Or would we prefer to be able to say that the power we created, necessary and flawed, was simply a tool to move beyond empowerment to a liberation that encompassed all those struggling for justice, including those we once knew as enemies? And that our power used in solidarity with others brought forth a healing in the world which ultimately began to heal us of our wounds developed over the millennia?

Movements of renewal within the Jewish community point the way to this new theology. In Israel, Oz ve Shalom, Religious Zionists for Strength and Peace, argue for the end of the occupation on religious grounds and seek reconciliation with the Palestinian people. Even more to the point is The Committee to Confront the Iron Fist, made up of Israelis and Palestinians whose first publication carried the provocative title "We Will Be Free In Our Own Homeland!" Members of the antiwar movement Yesh Gvul, or There Is a Limit, made up of Israelis who refused to serve in the Lebanese War and today refuse to serve in the West Bank and Gaza, are courageous in their willingness to say no to the oppression of others.

North American Jews are increasingly vocal in relation to the pursuit of justice in the Middle East. New Jewish Agenda, a movement of secular and religious Jews, argues for Israeli security *and* the just demands of Palestinian nationhood. *Tikkun,* a progressive Jewish magazine, is in the forefront of vocal argument for a new understanding of the Israeli-Palestinian situation. And now with the recent crisis, mainstream Jewish intellectuals and institutionalists have voiced their horror at Israeli policies in the occupied territories.[4]

These movements represent a groping toward a theological framework that nurtures rather than hinders expressions of solidarity. It is almost as if a long-repressed unease is coming to the surface, breaking through the language and symbol once deemed appropriate. Of course the risk is that if the crisis passes without fundamental change the language of solidarity will recede and the more familiar patterns will reassert themselves. And, it is true to state that even the movements cited are often limited in their scope and vision, equivocating where necessary to retain some mainstream credibility.

Still the drift is unmistakable and the task clear. The theological framework we need to create is hardly a departure, but a renewal of the themes that lie at the heart of our tradition, the exodus and the prophetic, interpreted in the contemporary world. A Jewish theology of liberation is our oldest theology, our great gift to the world, which has atrophied time and again only to be rediscovered by our own community and other communities around the world. A Jewish theology of liberation confronts the Holocaust and empowerment with the dynamic of solidarity, providing a bridge to others as it critiques our own abuses of power. By linking us to all those who struggle for justice, a Jewish theology of liberation will, in the long run, decrease our sense of isolation and abandonment and thus begin the process of healing so necessary to the future of the Jewish community.[5]

Therefore, in this time of crisis we are encouraged to search for a Jewish theology of liberation requisite to our contemporary situation. The painful confrontation between Israelis and Palestinians on the West Bank and in Gaza is in reality a confrontation with the history we have created. It is a confrontation with who we have become and who we would like to be. If it is true that we cannot go back behind empowerment, we now know that we cannot go forward alone. The faces that confront us are those of the Palestinian people. Could it be that somehow in these faces lies the future of the Jewish people?

This is why a two-state solution is only the beginning of a long and involved process that demands political compromise and a theological transformation which is difficult to envision. For if our theology is not confronted and transformed, then the political solutions will be superficial and transitory. A political solution may give impetus to this theological task; a theological movement may nurture a political solution. However, a political solution without a theological transformation simply enshrines the tragedy to be repeated again.

Here we enter the most difficult of arenas: the presupposition that in the faces of the Palestinians lies the future of what it means to be Jewish, that at the center of the struggle to be faithful as a Jew today is the suffering and liberation of the Palestinian people. Such a thought *must be considered in Jewish theological circles.* At some point an essential integration of Jew and Palestinian in a larger arena of political, cultural, and religious life is integral to a Jewish future. But this assumes that a fundamental confession and repentance of past and present transgressions is possible and a critical understanding of our history can be uncovered.

Neoconservatism and Oppression

Every community has patterns of fidelity and betrayal, points of paralysis and breakthrough. For the Jewish community the issue of Israel and Palestine is central to these patterns and possibilities. Despite the fact that 75 percent of the Jewish people live outside of the state of Israel and that more leave Israel each year than emigrate to it, there is no question that psychologically and theologically Israel remains the center of Jewish life. Still, it is important to realize that Zionism has always been and remains today a minority movement within Judaism, no matter how Israel-oriented Jewish institutional life has become. Moreover, it is important to understand that this orientation toward, even preoccupation with, Israel was and continues to be a matter of disagreement and struggle within the Jewish community. That is, Holocaust theology was initially hardly welcomed by the Jewish establishment of synagogue, charities or other parts of Jewish institutional life. Holocaust theology threatened and ultimately deprived these traditional centers of their power within the community. Whatever one's perspective, all would agree that identification with Israel has profoundly changed the ethos of Jewish life throughout the world. At the same time it is profoundly altering our perspectives on justice and peace in the world.[6]

Nowhere is this shift more evident than in the progressive theologian and activist Irving Greenberg. In an important and radical analysis of the Holocaust and its implications written in 1974, Greenberg wrote that after the Holocaust "no statement theological or otherwise can be made that is not credible in the presence of the burning children," and that the victims of the Holocaust ask us above all else "not to allow the creation of another matrix of values that might sustain another attempt at genocide." Greenberg affirmed empowerment as an essential aspect of fidelity to the victims of the Holocaust, although he added the proviso that to remember suffering impels the Jewish community to refuse to create other victims.

> The Holocaust cannot be used for triumphalism. Its moral challenge must also be applied to Jews. Those Jews who feel no guilt for the Holocaust are also tempted to moral apathy. Religious Jews who use the Holocaust to morally impugn every other religious group but their own are the ones who are tempted thereby into indifference at the Holocaust of others (cf. the general policy of the American Orthodox rabbinate on United States Vietnam policy). Those Israelis who place

as much distance as possible between the weak, passive Diaspora victims and the "mighty Sabras" are tempted to use Israeli strength indiscriminately (i.e., beyond what is absolutely inescapable for self-defense and survival), which is to risk turning other people into victims of the Jews. Neither faith nor morality can function without serious twisting of perspective, even to the point of becoming demonic, unless they are illuminated by the fires of Auschwitz and Treblinka.[7]

By the 1980s Greenberg's understanding of the Holocaust as critique is overshadowed by the difficult task of empowerment. He comments favorably on the reemergence of American power, applauding Reagan's arms buildup, the stationing of medium-range missiles in Europe, the development of the Strategic Defense Initiative, supporting rebel forces in Angola, the withdrawal of the United Nations from UNESCO, and the continuing funding of the Contras in Nicaragua. Greenberg's emphasis on empowerment allows him to take the high road when analyzing Ronald Reagan's trip to Bitburg in May 1985.

Overall Ronald Reagan's record in commemorating the Holocaust has been very good. He serves as honorary chairman of the campaign to create a national memorial. He has held commemorations of the Holocaust in the White House and spoken passionately of the need to remember. His support for Israel—the single most powerful Jewish commitment that the Holocaust shall not recur, the haven where most of the survivors built their new lives—is exemplary. Our criticism of this particular callous misjudgment must not be allowed to falsify the total overall picture, which is a good one. And we shall have to work with him again.[8]

In a revealing theological and political transformation, the ultimate danger would seem to have become the prophetic critique of empowerment.

Greenberg is joined in these overall perspectives by the three best-known Holocaust theologians, Elie Wiesel, Richard Rubenstein, and Emil Fackenheim. And Greenberg's most recent statements concerning the uprising maintain his evolving position. Though Greenberg now publicly supports an eventual Palestinian state and is somewhat critical of certain Israel positions, his argument remains couched in *Realpolitik* with harsh words for moral argument and prophetic critique. That Israeli policies come into conflict with overall Jewish perspectives on justice and peace seems to elude Greenberg, as does the call for a radical evaluation of patterns that have evolved within Jewish life which make the brutality possible. Greenberg does present the crisis as an opportunity for peace in the Middle East. Beyond that there is silence, perhaps a theological inability to move to the heart of the problem.[9]

In a sense Greenberg illustrates the problem that faces the Jewish community at its most basic level. Unless Israel ceases to be a major isolated and hostile power in the Middle East it cannot but be dependent on American military and economic power. To maintain this role Israel must continue its unannounced policy of helping in the destabilization and underdevelopment of the Arab world, at the same time expanding its global military program of arms sales and technical training often to authoritarian regimes and right-wing rebel forces. Though surprisingly independent in many areas, Israel, in this scenario, maintains a surrogate role for the expression of Western power. Since Israel cannot through its own resources maintain a major power status or be received in the Middle East within this framework, and since no other Western power is capable of carrying this burden, America is crucial to the survival of Israel. It is therefore much easier to understand the responsibility felt by the Jewish community in the United States and the increasing impact of Israel on our worldview. When United States government aid to Israel surpasses four billion dollars a year and governmental foreign policy decisions and agency cooperation supply invaluable assistance, and tax-free contributions from Jews to Israel approach the billion-dollar mark, how can Jews in the United States be free to choose a different path? Is it surprising that Holocaust theologians, indeed the majority of the Jewish community, become increasingly neoconservative in their attitudes and policies?

As we become more and more powerful, the neoconservative trend is buttressed by fear, anger, and by a deepening sense of isolation. Anyone who works in the Jewish community recognizes immediately the almost uncontrollable emotional level that criticism of Israel engenders. To be accused of creating the context for another holocaust is almost commonplace, as are the charges of treason and self-hate. Yet on a deeper level one senses a community which, having emerged from the death camps, sees little option but to fight to the bitter end. It is as if the entire world is still against us, as if the next train departs from Eastern Europe, as if the death camps remain ready to receive us after an interval of almost half a century. This is why though the entire world understands Yasir Arafat to be a moderate there is no other name linked by the Jewish community so closely to Adolf Hitler. This is why Prime Minister Shamir spoke of the plans to launch a ship of Palestinian refugees to Palestine as an attempt to undermine the state of Israel, as an act of war. Years after the liberation of the camps, Elie Wiesel wrote, "Were hatred a solution, the survivors, when they came out of the camps, would have had to burn down the whole world." With the nuclear capacity of Israel, coupled with the sense of isolation and anger, Wiesel's cautioning words are unfortunately not irrelevant. Is it too much to say that any theology which does not understand the absolute difference between the Warsaw Ghetto and Tel Aviv, between Hitler and Arafat, is a theology which may legitimate that which Wiesel warned against?

The Occupation Is Over

Each morning over the last months we have awakened to reports of torture and death of Palestinian people, mostly children and young men in the occupied territories. But yesterday a strange and disturbing question came to me as I am sure it has to many of us: If Palestinians cease to die, will the uprising—at least for North American Jews and Christians—cease to matter? A horrible thought followed: For the Palestinian cause it is crucial that they continue to die in ever-increasing numbers if we in the West are to understand *that the occupation, as we have known it, is over.* Unable to accept this conclusion, I approached a Palestinian acquaintance and a Christian who had just returned from the West Bank: both had the same thoughts. It is true and the Palestinian leadership—as well as the Palestinian villagers—understand this tragic fact. The uprising is dependent on the continuing torture and death of children.

But can Jewish Israelis continue to torture and kill Palestinian children *ad infinitum*? Can North American Jews continue to support these acts? And can Western Christians, especially those who have chosen to repent the anti-Jewishness of the Christian past and who have accepted Israel as an integral part of the contemporary Jewish experience, remain silent on the uprising and Israeli brutality? Or, are we all hoping that somehow the situation will dissipate, go unreported, or better still, disappear? This much seems clear: The willingness of Palestinians to endure torture and death, and the willingness of Israel to inflict such acts of brutality, point to the most difficult of situations which many would choose to ignore, namely that some basic themes of post-Holocaust Jewish and Christian life are being exposed in a radical and unrelenting way.

If it is true that the occupation of the territories is in fact over, that it has moved beyond occupation to uprising and civil war, then the theological support for the occupation in Jewish and Christian theology must end as well. The focus of both theologies in their uncritical support of Israel has been shattered. The uprising, therefore, is a crisis on many fronts and is at its deepest level a theological crisis. Of course, like any crisis, the uprising presents us with both tragedy and possibility. By forcing the issue at the price of broken bones and lives, the children of Palestine force us to think again and to break through ignorance, half-truths and lies. But, will we have the tenacity and courage in safe and comfortable North America that the Palestinian children have on the streets of Gaza and the West Bank? Or will the inevitable allegations of Jewish self-hate and Christian anti-Jewishness deter us? Are we willing to reexamine our theological presuppositions as particular communities and in dialogue with each other, or will we attempt to pass over the question in silence?

It is not too much to say that the uprising poses the future of Judaism in stark and unremitting terms. The tragedy of the Holocaust is well documented and indelibly ingrained in our consciousness. Holocaust theology speaks eloquently for the victims of Treblinka and Auschwitz, yet ignores Sabra and Shatila. It pays tribute to the Warsaw Ghetto uprising, but has no place for the uprising of ghetto dwellers on the other side of Israeli power. It insists that the torture and murders of Jewish children be lamented and commemorated in Jewish ritual and belief, but has yet to imagine the possibility that Jews in turn tortured and murdered Palestinian children. Holocaust theology relates the story of the Jewish people in its beauty and suffering. Yet it fails to integrate the contemporary history of the Palestinian people as integral to our own. Thus, this theology articulates who we were but no longer helps us to understand who we have become.[10]

So Jews who are trying to understand the present become a contradiction to themselves, while others simply refuse to acknowledge the facts of contemporary Jewish life. A dilemma arises: Awareness of Jewish transgressions has no framework to be articulated and acted upon. Jews who become aware have few places to turn theologically.

Christians who have entered into a solidarity with the Jewish people are similarly in a dilemma. The road to solidarity has been paved both by Christian renewal, especially with regard to the Hebrew Scripture, and by Holocaust theology. But understanding the beauty and suffering of the Jewish people as a call to Christian repentance and transformation hardly prepares the community for a confrontation with Israeli power. How do Christians respond now when, over the years, the centrality of Israel has been stressed as necessary to Christian confession in the arena of dialogue, and no words of criticism against Israel are countenanced as anything but anti-Jewish? Too, Christian Zionism, fundamentalist and liberal, is ever present. What framework do Christians have within which to probe the present history of the state of Israel, to understand the uprising, to question the direction taken by Jewish empowerment? Can Christian theologians articulate a solidarity with the Jewish people which is a critical solidarity, one that recognizes the suffering *and* the power of the Jewish people? Can Christian theologies in the spirit of a critical solidarity open themselves to the suffering of the Palestinian people as a legitimate imperative of what it means to be Christian today?[11]

Clearly the Palestinian struggle for nationhood poses more than the prospect of political negotiation and compromise. For Jews and Christians it presents fundamental theological material which lends depth to the inevitable (though long-suffering) political solutions. Without this theological component a political solution may or may not appear. However, the lessons of the conflict would surely be lost and thus the political solution would tend toward superficiality and immediacy rather than depth and longevity. A political solution without a theological transformation would simply enshrine the tragedy to be repeated again. An important opportunity to move beyond our present theologies toward theologies of solidarity, which may usher in a new age of ecumenical cooperation, would be lost. Could it be that the struggle of the Palestinian people is a key to the Jewish and Christian struggle to be faithful in the contemporary world?

We are called to a theology that recognizes empowerment as necessary and dangerous in the journey toward liberation. It reminds us that power in and of itself, even for survival, ends in tragedy without the guidance of ethics and a strong sense of solidarity with all those who are struggling for justice. Today, the Palestinian people ask the fundamental question relating to Jewish empowerment: Can the Jewish people in Israel, indeed Jews around the world, be liberated without the liberation of the Palestinian people? Once having understood the question posed by the Palestinian people, the occupation can no longer continue. What remains is to build a theological framework that delegitimates the torture and the killing—a theology of liberation that sees solidarity as the essence of what it means to be Jewish or Christian.

A New Theological Framework

The development of a theological framework is crucial to delegitimate torture and murder—that is, to end theologies that rationalize occupations including, though not limited to, the Palestinian people. In this case we focus on the Israeli occupation as the breakthrough point for Jewish theology. The theological framework that legitimates occupation also, if we look closely, forces us to take positions on other issues that would be questioned, even abhorred, if the framework were different. If our theology did not support the occupation, its vision of justice and peace would be transformed. Thus we turn again to the prospect that the uprising represents a culmination and a possibility, if we only seize the moment.

An essential task of Jewish theology is to de-absolutize the state of Israel. To see Israel as an important Jewish community among other Jewish communities, with an historical founding and evolution, is to legitimate theologically what the Jewish people have acted out with their lives: the continuation of diverse Jewish communities outside the state. Thus the redemptive aspect of Jewish survival after the Holocaust is found in a much broader arena than the state of Israel and must be critically addressed rather than simply asserted in unquestioning allegiance to a state where most Jews do not live. De-absolutizing Israel hardly means its abandonment. Instead it calls forth a new, more mature relationship. Jews cannot bilocate forever and the strain of defending policies implemented by others, of criticizing without being able to influence directly, of supporting financially and being made to feel guilty for not living in Israel is impossible to continue over a long period of time. With this new understanding responsibilities between Jewish communities assume a mutuality that includes a critical awareness of the centrality of our ethical tradition as the future of our community. Therefore, the present crisis as well as any future crisis moves beyond the call for unquestioned allegiance or disassociation from

Israel to a critical solidarity with responsibilities and obligations on all sides.[12]

A second parallel task is to deal with the Holocaust in its historical context and to cease its application as a possible future outcome to issues of contemporary Jewish life. To continue to use the Holocaust with reference to Israel is to misjudge and therefore refuse to understand the totally different situation of pre- and post-Holocaust Jewry. Pre-Holocaust European Jewry had no state or military; it was truly defenseless before the Nazi onslaught. Israel is a state with superior military ability. Pre-Holocaust European Jewry lived among populations that varied in their attitudes toward Jews from tolerance to hatred. Post-Holocaust Jewry, with its population concentrations in France, England, Canada, and the United States, resides in countries where anti-Jewishness is sporadic and inconsequential. Pre-Holocaust Jewry lived among Christians who had as a group little reason to question Christian anti-Jewishness. Post-Holocaust Jewry lives among Christians who have made repeated public statements, writings, even ritual affirmations of the centrality of the Jewish people and Christian culpability for an anti-Jewish past. The differences between pre- and post-Holocaust Jewry can be listed on many other levels as well, which is not to deny that anti-Jewishness continues to exist. As many Jewish writers have pointed out, the paradox is that the most dangerous place for Jews to live today is in the state of Israel rather than centers of Europe and North America.

Even in relation to Israel the application of Holocaust language is clearly inappropriate. Israel has been involved in two wars since 1967 and can claim victory in neither; no civilian life was taken outside the battlefield. The great fear, repeated over and over again, is that one day Israel will lose a war and that the civilian population will be annihilated, i.e., another holocaust. Two points are important here. First, if the situation continues as it is today, it is inevitable that one day Israel will lose a war and face the possibility of annihilation. No nation is invincible forever, no empire exists that is not destined to disappear, no country that does not, at some point in its history, lose badly and suffer immensely. Can our present theology exempt Israel from the reality of shifting alliances, military strategies, and political life?

The only way to prevent military defeat is to make peace when you are powerful. Of course, even here there is never any absolute protection from military defeat, as there is never any absolute protection from persecution. But if military defeat does come and if the civilian population is attacked, the result, though tragic, will not be, by any meaningful definition, another Holocaust. And it would not, by any means, signal the end of the Jewish people, as many Holocaust theologians continue to speculate. It would be a terrible event, too horrible to mention, except for a clarification crucial to its prevention. And perhaps the differences between the Holocaust and any future military defeat of Israel are too obvious to explore, and would hardly need exploration if our present theology were not confused on this most important point.

To de-absolutize the state of Israel and distinguish the historical event of Holocaust from the situation of contemporary Jewish life is imperative to the third task of Jewish theology, the redefinition of Jewish identity. This is an incredibly difficult and complex task with parameters that can only be touched upon here. Yet it is the most crucial, raising the essential question that each generation faces: What does it mean to be Jewish in the contemporary world?[13]

There is little question that Holocaust theology is the normative theology of the Jewish community today and that at the center of this theology is the Holocaust and the state of Israel. Rabbinic theology, the normative Jewish theology for almost two millennia, initially sought to continue as if neither the Holocaust nor the state of Israel were central to the Jewish people. And Reform Judaism, the interesting, sometimes shallow nineteenth-century attempt to come to grips with modern life, also sought to bypass the formative events of our time. Yet to survive after the Holocaust and especially since the 1967 Six Day War, both theological structures have been transformed with an underlying Holocaust theology. Secular Jews, often affiliated with progressive politics and economics, have likewise experienced a shifting framework of interpretation. Though not explicitly religious, their aid has been solicited by Holocaust theologians to build the state of Israel as *the* essential aspect of belonging to the Jewish people. In sum, both those who believed in Jewish particularity and those who sought a more universal identification have increasingly derived their Jewish identity within the framework of Holocaust and Israel. And there is little reason to believe that any of these—Orthodox, Reform, or secular humanism— can ever again return to their pre-Holocaust, pre-Israel positions.

We can only move ahead by affirming the Holocaust and Israel as important parts of Jewish identity while insisting that they are not and cannot become the sum total of what it means to be Jewish. The point here is to take the dynamic of Holocaust and Israel and understand it in new ways. In both events there is, among other things, an underlying theme of solidarity which has been buried in our anger and isolation. This includes solidarity with our own people as well as others who have come into solidarity with us. As important, if we recover our own history, there is a theme of Jewish solidarity with others even in times of great danger. The latter includes some of the early settlers and intellectuals involved in the renewal of the Jewish community in Palestine, well-known figures like Martin Buber, Albert Einstein, Hannah Arendt, and many others.[14]

Even during the Holocaust there were voices, such as that of Etty Hillesum, which argued that their suffering should give birth to a world of mutuality and solidarity so that no people should ever suffer again. Hillesum, who voluntarily accompanied her people to Auschwitz, was hardly a person who went like a lamb to her slaughter. Rather she chose a destiny as an act of solidarity with her own people and the world. Is it possible that those who affirmed human dignity where it was most difficult and those who argued, and continue to argue today, for reconciliation with the Palestinian people even with the risks involved, represent a future worth inheriting and bequeathing to our children? By emphasizing our dignity and solidarity we appropriate the event of Holocaust and Israel as identity forming in a positive and critical way. They ask us to embrace the world with the hope that our survival is transformative for our own people and for the world.

The key to a new Jewish identity remains problematic unless we understand that de-absolutizing Israel, differentiating Holocaust and the contemporary Jewish situation, and recovering the history of solidarity within our tradition and with those outside it, leads us to a critical confrontation with our own empowerment. To celebrate our survival is important; to realize that our empowerment has come at a great cost is another thing altogether. Can we at the fortieth anniversary of the state of Israel realize that the present political and religious chauvinism can only lead to disaster? Can we argue openly that the issue of empowerment is much broader than an exclusive Jewish state and that other options, including autonomy with confederation, may be important to contemplate for the fiftieth anniversary of Israel? Can we openly articulate that as American Jews we can no longer ask American foreign policy to support policies that contradict the ethical heart of what it means to be Jewish? Can we say with Michael Lerner, editor of *Tikkun:*

> Stop the beatings, stop the breaking of bones, stop the late-night raids on people's homes, stop the use of food as a weapon of war, stop pretending that you can respond to an entire people's agony with guns and blows and power. Publicly acknowledge that the Palestinians have the same right to national self-determination that we Jews have and negotiate a solution with representatives of the Palestinians![15]

Notes

1. Johann Baptist Metz, *The Emergent Church: The Future of Christianity in a Postbourgeois World,* trans. Peter Mann (New York: Crossroad, 1981), p. 19. For a detailed discussion of this new way of journeying together see Marc H. Ellis, *Toward a Jewish Theology of Liberation: The Uprising and the Future* (Maryknoll, NY: Orbis Books, 1987), pp. 67–90.

2. For an extended discussion of Holocaust theology, see Ellis, *Jewish Theology,* pp. 8–24.

3. On the interaction of Israeli policy and the Palestinian people see Roberta Strauss Feuerlicht, *The Fate of the Jews: A People Torn Between Israeli Power and Jewish Ethics* (New York: Times Books, 1983), pp. 219–88. For the relationship of Israel and South Africa, see Jane Hunter, *Undercutting Sanctions: Israel, the U.S. and South Africa* (Washington, D.C.: Washington Middle East Associates, 1986).

4. Ezra Goldstein and Deena Hurwitz, "No Status Quo Ante," *Agenda* 24 (Spring 1988): 1, 3; Michael Lerner, "The Occupation: Immoral and Stupid," *Tikkun* 3 (March/April 1988): 7–12; Theodore R. Mann, "We Must," *Moment* 13 (March 1988): 18–22.

5. See Ellis, *Jewish Theology*, pp. 110–22.

6. For the shift of power within Jewish institutional life see Irving Greenberg, "The Third Great Cycle in Jewish History," *Perspectives* (New York: National Jewish Resource Center, 1981), pp. 32f. On the altering of perspectives in relation to this shift, see an analysis of Greenberg in Ellis, *Jewish Theology*, pp. 26–37.

7. Irving Greenberg, "Cloud of Smoke, Pillar of Fire: Judaism, Christianity and Modernity after the Holocaust" in *Auschwitz: Beginning of a New Era?* ed. Eva Fleischner (New York: KTAV, 1977), p. 22.

8. Irving Greenberg, "Some Lessons from Bitburg," *Perspectives* (May 1985): 4. For his political positions see Greenberg, "On the Third Era in Jewish History: Power and Politics," *Perspectives* (New York: National Jewish Resource Center, 1980), p. 6, and "Power and Peace," *Perspectives* 1 (December 1985): 3, 5.

9. Ibid., *The Ethics of Jewish Power* (New York: National Jewish Resource Center, 1988).

10. For an extended discussion of Holocaust theology, see Ellis, *Jewish Theology*, pp. 7–24.

11. An example of liberal Christian Zionism is found in the work of Paul M. van Buren. See *A Christian Theology of the People Israel*, vol. 2 (New York: Seabury Press, 1983). For my own discussion of developing a critical solidarity see Ellis, *Jewish Theology*, pp. 119f. This analysis points to a new ecumenical dialogue based on solidarity in the struggle for liberation rather than the status quo of Christian and Jewish institutional life.

12. The strains of this highly problematic and emotional relationship have increasingly come to the surface in recent years. Witness the upheavals in North American Jewish life relating to the Lebanese War, the massacres at Sabra and Shatila, the Pollard Spy Case, and now the Uprising. My point is simply that the relationship between Jews in Israel and Jews outside Israel cannot remain as it is without ultimately dividing the community at its very roots.

13. This ability to discuss the issue of Jewish self-identity assumes the possibility of moving beyond the typical epithet of being a self-hating Jew.

14. For Hannah Arendt's prophetic understanding of the choices facing the Jewish settlers in Palestine see a collection of her essays, *Hannah Arendt; The Jew as Pariah: Jewish Identity and Politics in the Modern Age*, ed. Ron H. Feldman (New York: Grove Press, 1978).

15. Lerner, "The Occupation," p. 7.

Chapter 10

Economics and Peace:
The Catholic Bishops' Approach

DENNIS P. McCANN

Recalling the American Catholic bishops' pastoral letter, "The Challenge of Peace: God's Promise and Our Response" (1983), may provoke questions as to its relevance today. After all, the INF Treaty negotiated in the meantime calls for more than the Nuclear Freeze, advocated by the bishops, itself dared hope for. The breathtaking vistas opened up by the Reagan-Gorbachev summits, the Soviet withdrawal from Afghanistan, and the significant tempering of anti-Soviet rhetoric in Washington, plus the growing recognition on all sides that the U.S. defense budget cannot be exempt from the retrenchment that must occur in order to shrink the federal deficit—these events, and many others, suggest that the "moment of supreme crisis" invoked by the American bishops' pastoral letter may have passed, at least for the time being. But does that make "The Challenge of Peace" as obsolete as a rerun of "The Day After"? I think not, and it is the burden of this chapter to show why not.

Much of the discussion of the peace pastoral focused on the American bishops' theological and ethical understanding of nuclear deterrence, and why, in their judgment, our current defense posture rates only a "strictly conditioned moral acceptance." The pastoral letter showed that Catholic social teaching's interpretation of the "just-war" tradition can continue to bring moral clarity to the so-called paradoxes of nuclear deterrence, and make important moral distinctions between some nuclear strategies and weapons systems and others, including the bishops' controversial moral advocacy of the doctrine of "no first use" of nuclear weapons. These and related issues, of course, were what made the pastoral letter so relevant when it first appeared. For such were the issues that dominated the discussion in that atmosphere of imminent nuclear crisis.

As the pastoral letter itself points out, a narrowly conceived focus on the morality of deterrence strategies hardly exhausts "The Challenge of Peace." The bishops' own refusal to accept the current nuclear stalemate as, morally speaking, the best that we can do is based not just on their analysis of the paradoxes of deterrence, but more so on their positive vision of what a peaceable community of nations might be. Fortified by a biblical perspective that emphasized the totality of factors—spiritual, cultural, and economic, as well as political and military—that make for peace, the pastoral letter recalled traditional Catholic teaching regarding "world order" and tried to rethink it in light of the growing trend toward "interdependence." This, I believe, is the point at which the American bishops' approach to the economics of peace begins to emerge. In what follows, I will outline this approach, tracing its theoretical development from "The Challenge of Peace" to the more recent pastoral letter, "Economic Justice for All: Catholic Social Teaching and the U.S. Economy" (1986). I will conclude by using various statements on the crisis in Central America issued in behalf of the bishops by the United States Catholic Conference (USCC), in order to illustrate the practical implications of this approach.

* * *

The strategy for peace advocated by the American Catholic bishops in their recent pastoral letters is nicely summarized by the bumper sticker: IF YOU WANT PEACE, WORK FOR JUSTICE. The force of this deceptively simple slogan would not be apparent if all we had to go on was "The Challenge of Peace." For although that letter does contain a section on "Shaping a Peaceful World" (par. 234–273), that section is easily overlooked as long as the focus of discussion remains fixed on questions of "just war" theory and its current applications. Only in the hindsight afforded by the bishops' more recent letter, "Economic Justice for All," does it become apparent that this section expresses the core of Catholic social teaching's vision of a political order alternative to the semblance of peace afforded by a protracted nuclear stalemate.

The roots of this vision, not surprisingly, are medieval. As "The Challenge of Peace" suggests, though they antedate the Peace of Westphalia (1648), they have been carefully preserved and nurtured by Catholic social teaching, particularly in the encyclical letter of Pope John XXIII, *Pacem in Terris* (1963). Viewed in the perspective afforded by this tradition, the nation-state sovereignty system, which tends to restrict conventional thinking about world order to the "balance of power" principle, is seen as merely "a step in the evolution of government" (par. 242). The next step beyond the nation-state sovereignty system would require the formation of a "properly constituted political authority," a kind of world government, for which the United Nations organization might serve as a prototype.

This proposal could easily be dismissed as a particularly devilish expression of that unique blend of romanticism and utopianism to which Roman Catholic social thought is all too often susceptible. The nation-state sovereignty system, among other things, is an expression of the political and military stalemate reached by the exhausted Catholic and Protestant powers after the Wars of Religion. The Catholic vision of world order, in short, is not entirely innocent of a romantic "Ultramontanism" that would foreclose the modern world's subsequent experiment in religious pluralism by reconstituting a papally-oriented Christendom. But the vision could be regarded as equally utopian insofar as it reflects the aspiration to escape from a situation seemingly designed to self-destruct at regular intervals.

It may be premature to dismiss the bishops' version of world order in this way, for such an interpretation flies in the face of their consistent attempt at Christian realism throughout the pastoral letter. Either the bishops' vision is radically incoherent, or we have missed something important in interpreting the vision. At several points in the letter the bishops refer to "The New Moment" in which they are assessing Catholic social teaching (cf. par. 126–138). The impression is created that the new moment is defined by the popular awakening to the actual consequences of nuclear warfare, instigated by, among others, the Physicians for Social Responsibility. But there are other ways to characterize the new moment scattered throughout the letter, the most important of which is the bishops' discussion of "interdependence." This term refers to one of those "signs of the times" by which Catholic theologians have been orienting their work since Vatican II. A theological interpretation of current social trends may yield some insight into the pattern of God's ongoing activity in history, in which case what to others may appear simply as a "fact," for Catholic social teaching becomes the basis for conscious "policy." Such is clearly the presupposition governing the pastoral letter's discussion of "Interdependence: From Fact to Policy" (par. 259–273).

What makes the American bishops' vision of world order as Christianly realistic as any other part of the pastoral letter is their reading of the trend toward global interdependence. Toward the end of World War II, Reinhold Niebuhr, the unsurpassed advocate of Christian realism in America, dismissed the possibility of "world government" because in his view the world was lacking the economic and cultural infrastructures necessary to give political form to that possibility. No less realistically than Niebuhr, the bishops describe a world in which these structures are emerging, though somewhat haphazardly. According to the pastoral letter, we've reached a point in addressing issues of global economic development where the problems being generated cannot be resolved apart from the creation of some "properly constituted political authority with the capacity to shape our material interdependence in the direction of moral interdependence" (par. 240). Specifically, "the need for social justice in terms of trade, aid and monetary issues . . . [should challenge the United States] . . . to rethink the meaning of national interest in an interdependent world" (par. 263–264).

However troubling this prospect may be, it is clear that the bishops expect only incremental advances in that direction. They recall "the spirit of generosity" that animated the Marshall Plan after World War II, and they call for U.S. leadership in effecting "significant reform and substantial change" in the United Nations organizations (par. 266–268).

* * *

The Catholic agenda for world order is not developed further in "The Challenge of Peace"; however, the American bishops do return to it in their next pastoral letter, "Economic Justice for All: Catholic Social Teaching and the U.S. Economy." Here, too, a superficial reading of the letter may dismiss the question of global interdependence as peripheral to the bishops' central focus on poverty and unemployment in the United States. But such is not the case: Not only are they aware of the trade-offs between resolving these problems in the domestic economy and our international economic policies, but they also devote a special section—which reads like a microcosm of the letter as a whole—to this topic of interdependence: "The U.S. Economy and the Developing Nations: Complexity, Challenge, and Choices" (par. 251–294).

Though there are other places in the pastoral letter on the economy that make explicit reference to "The Challenge of Peace"—for example, the discussion of unemployment notes the distorting and negative impact of the arms race on labor markets (par. 148)—this section takes up the question of world order once again, as part of the bishops' case for restructuring the international economic system. Though the pastoral letter is not specific about the political form this new international order might take, it does echo "The Challenge of Peace" in noting that "no political entity now exists with the responsibility and power to promote the global common good," and urges supportive reform of the United Nations (par. 261). "Economic Justice for All," however, does advance the discussion by giving a more detailed analysis of the "trade, aid, and monetary issues" merely alluded to in the previous pastoral letter.

What follows is a moral audit of sorts. The various elements of the emerging global infrastructure of economic interdependence, for example, the Bretton Woods institutions, the World Bank, the International Monetary Fund (IMF), the General Agreement on Tariffs and Trade (GATT), as well as the United Nations Conference on Trade and Development (UNCTAD), the Organization for Economic Cooperation and Development (OECD), multinational business corporations, and U.S. foreign aid policies are each examined in light of the bishops' overall moral agenda and the problems of global economic development. The moral principles that the bishops have clarified in relationship to the vicissitudes of the U.S. domestic economy, namely, the need to build a moral community based on "Christian love and human solidarity," a community in which "basic justice" means empowering people for full participation in the economy, in which "respect for human rights" is the hallmark of our public institutions, which finally recognizes "the special place of the poor," as priorities are set for social investment and the allocation of scarce resources (par. 258). These are used as a yardstick to measure the performance of institutions.

Commendably, the bishops have resisted the temptation merely to denounce them. Though many of these institutions are not coping very well with the problems of an emerging global market system—for example, the bishops' remarks on the so-called Third World Debt Crisis are particularly critical of the policies of the Bretton Woods institutions—they are regarded in general as acting in good faith and therefore as capable of significant improvement. Unlike those self-styled prophets whose response to the distorted patterns of international development is to blame "The System," the bishops seem to be saying that the real problem is the lack of an effective as well as equitable system. Rather than offer a blueprint for an alternative, they exhort the American people through its political and economic institutions to exercise responsible leadership:

> The United States represents the most powerful single factor in the international economic equation. But even as we speak of crisis, we see an opportunity for the United States to launch a worldwide campaign for justice and economic rights to match the still incomplete, but encouraging political democracy we have achieved in the United States with so much pain and sacrifice (par. 290).

The path toward realizing the Catholic vision of world order, in short, means an extension of the pastoral letter's "new American experiment" in democracy beyond the domestic political economy to the international arena as a whole.

* * *

Understanding the pastoral letter's new experiment in democracy, first of all, requires asking what the bishops think of the older experiment, that is, what their basic attitude is toward the experiment in self-government that issued forth from the American Revolution of 1776. Though that attitude is overwhelmingly positive, I must emphasize that it is not to be taken for granted. The separation of church and state that lies at the heart of the U.S. Constitution is not a Roman Catholic idea. The separation of powers and the theory of representative government articulated in *The Federalist Papers* did not correspond to the norms of Catholic social teaching at the time they were devised. Though Americanist Catholics a century ago struggled impressively and perhaps precociously to convince the Vatican of the merits of the American experiment in democracy, their efforts provoked from Pope Leo XIII a condemnation of heresy. Only during and after

Vatican Council II (1962-65) did American Catholics manage to secure the church's recognition of the unique fruits of their participation in the American experiment. I refer of course to Vatican II's epoch making *Declaration on Religious Freedom (Dignitatis humanae)*, whose principal author was the American Jesuit Fr. John Courtney Murray.

Seen in this context, the pastoral letter's appreciation for the genuine achievements of the original American experiment is itself revolutionary. "As *Americans,*" the bishops insist, "we are grateful for the gift of freedom and committed to the dream of 'liberty and justice for all.' . . . We are proud of the strength, productivity and creativity of our economy, but we also remember those who have been left behind in our progress. We believe that we honor our history best by working for the day when all our sisters and brothers share adequately in the American dream" (par. 9). In spelling out the rationale for the new experiment in democracy, the pastoral letter makes explicit its parallel with the original American experiment:

> In order to create a new form of political democracy they were compelled to develop ways of thinking and political institutions that had never existed before. Their efforts were arduous and their goals imperfectly realized, but they launched an experiment in the protection of civil and political rights that has prospered through the efforts of those who came after them. *We believe the time has come for a similar experiment in securing economic rights: the creation of an order that guarantees the minimum conditions of human dignity in the economic sphere for every person* (par. 95).

In contrast to Marxian-inspired ideologies which tend to play off economic rights against civil and political rights, the American bishops clearly envision the new experiment as an expansion of self-governing institutions, not their usurpation by the state. What the bishops have in mind is a social experiment that necessarily begins in the private sector of the economy and involves governmental intervention only as the scale and complexity of efforts at cooperation warrant it ("A New American Experiment: Partnership for the Public Good," par. 295–325). The policy recommendations outlined at the various levels of economic organization—partnerships (1) within firms and industries, (2) at the local and regional level of community, (3) at the national, and (4) international levels—represent a strategy for popular empowerment that cannot help but result in greater economic development, if the experiment is successful. What the bishops have discovered that many other observers have failed to grasp is that democratic institutions based on the principle of self-government are an important element in any strategy for sustaining economic development, not just politically but also and especially in the way in which business corporations, civic associations, and even schools and churches are internally organized. If social justice thus requires massive experiments in democracy, then by implication so does work for peace, as demonstrated in the grass-roots Nuclear Freeze movement.

The bishops' argument for a firmer government role in the economy is premised on Catholic social teaching's "principle of subsidiarity," which in application "calls for government to intervene in the economy when basic justice requires greater social coordination and regulation of economic actors and institutions" (par. 232, cf. par. 314). Their analysis suggests that equitable strategies for international economic development cannot be implemented effectively unless the United States takes a leadership role in creating such a regulatory framework. As in the previous pastoral letter, they offer no blueprint but instead express the hope that an evolutionary process based on the achievements of currently existing bodies, such as the Bretton Woods institutions, would be the most fruitful area of experiment.

The proposals offered in "Economic Justice for All" are based on a realistic assessment of the emerging global economy, measured in light of the bishops' moral principles—particularly the preferential option for the poor. The need for "greater social coordination and regulation" is expressed primarily in terms of what the lack of such an institutional system seems to be doing to the quality of life of the poor, considering their vulnerability to the economic gyrations of unregulated markets. Their analysis of the debt crisis in the so-called Third World, for example, offers a realistic description of the economic causes of the crisis and the impact of IMF efforts to relieve it; but the bishops' perspective remains unabashedly moral:

> The crisis, however, goes beyond the system; it affects people. It afflicts and oppresses large numbers of people who are already severely disadvantaged. That is a scandal: it is the poorest people who suffer most from the austerity measures required when a country seeks the IMF "seal of approval" which establishes its credit-worthiness for a commercial loan (or perhaps an external aid program). It is these same people who suffer most when commodity prices fall, when food cannot be imported or they cannot buy it, and when natural disasters occur. Our commitment to the preferential option for the poor does not permit us to remain silent in these circumstances (par. 274).

Yet when the bishops recommend policies for alleviating this distress, they presuppose the cooperation of the IMF and other institutions in a long-term process of internal reform, stimulated by the economic leadership of the United States. Finally, they suggest that such a process "is not only morally right, but is in the economic interest of the United States" (par. 277). They are referring, of course, to the destabilization of the international banking system that could occur because of mismanagement of the debt crisis.

It may be easier to make this argument from national interest today, in the wake of the October 1987 stock market collapse, than at the time the pastoral letter appeared. For beyond all the concern over the impact of computer technology on market trading, there is the intractable fact that Wall Street was merely reacting to the inability of the major economic powers to do anything more than pay lip service to the international financial system's need for "social coordination and regulation." The reality of economic "interdependence," even for middle-class Americans, ought to have become perfectly obvious as, in the days following that collapse, the stock market reacted to whatever the markets had done in the previous hours in London and Tokyo. The emerging vulnerability of the domestic economy of the United States to the patterns of "distorted development" that heretofore were characteristic of Third World dependency should now be apparent to the most casual of observers. Seen in this context, the requirements of national interest may indeed point in the direction that the American bishops advise. What might otherwise seem an unwarranted subversion of national sovereignty may, under present and foreseeable circumstances, be the only effective way to preserve and sustain the U.S. economy. What once may have been dismissed as utopianism may actually be the height of economic and political realism.

My reading of the American bishops' pastoral letters thus seeks to define the economic dimension of a strategy for waging peace, a strategy that at one and the same time will recognize, as the bishops clearly do, both the legitimate security interests of the United States and our moral responsibilities as a "Superpower" in a world of increasing "interdependence"— economic, as well as political and cultural. Informed by the traditions of Catholic social teaching, some of which antedate the advent of the nation-state sovereignty system, the bishops understand the problems in this economic dimension as symptomatic of the inevitable "defect" in world order implicit in that system. Their argument for establishing a significantly greater degree of political and institutional coordination at the international level is economic: the distorted patterns of global economic development cannot be overcome on any other basis. And those patterns, the bishops insist, represent a serious moral challenge, not just for Catholics but for all Americans.

* * *

Let me conclude this discussion by turning now from the two pastoral letters to the U.S. bishops' recent statements on Central America. My purpose in doing so is to test whether the bishops' foreign policy recommendations in that area are consistent with their overall strategy for waging peace, as outlined in the letters. For purposes of this inquiry I have restricted my focus to the bishops' statements over the past four years on Central America in general and Nicaragua in particular, that are available in *Origins: The NC Documentary Service*. A "Joint Communique" from a meeting of U.S.

and Central American bishops, July 21-23, 1987, in San Jose, Costa Rica, provides a fitting summary of the NCCB's basic perspective on that region.

Over the years, various U.S. bishops, as well as representatives from the United States Catholic Conference (USCC), have testified before Congress in opposition to military aid to the Contras. This much is generally known. Usually not understood are their reasons for doing so, and what policies they might propose as an alternative. Their opposition to military aid is not based on sympathy with the Sandinista government; on the contrary, they have consistently protested its pattern of human rights violations and repressive policies toward the Catholic church in Nicaragua. The bishops are not ignorant about the Marxist-Leninist scenario apparently unfolding in that country. They object to military aid because their perspective remains firmly attached to the concerns of the poor who inevitably suffer most during a civil war, and because they doubt whether a military solution to the Nicaraguan conflict is possible without direct and massive U.S. military intervention.

Alternatively, they recommend "diplomatic initiatives," ranging from the Contadora process to the Central American peace proposal developed by President Arias of Costa Rica. Within this context they typically insist upon what amounts to a demilitarization of Central America. Their purpose is emphatically not to disarm the Contras so that the Sandinistas will have the field to themselves. They recommend new experiments in multilateral assistance for economic development, some of them involving nongovernmental organizations, like the churches, in creative efforts to make sure that foreign assistance actually reaches those most in need of it. Above all, they insist that Nicaragua's problems cannot be solved apart from a new national "dialogue" within the country itself, involving the local churches and the full range of political and other civic organizations. Presumably, they would acknowledge the right of representatives of the Contras to participate in any such dialogue. Finally, they urge the U.S. government to explore ways to use the possibilities of nonmilitary aid to modify the Sandinista government's human rights practices. In short, their approach emphasizes the procedural: Though they apparently share with Contra sympathizers their opposition to Marxism-Leninism, they urge a package of nonviolent, nonmilitary strategies for transforming the situation in Nicaragua. Their remarks on social conditions in the other Central American nations follow a similar pattern: a generalized advocacy of human rights, equitable economic development, and nonviolently democratic means for achieving them.

The bishops' approach to waging peace in Central America thus is impressive for its consistency with their overall perspective on Catholic social teaching; for it is as if the answer to Central America's problems lies in having Central Americans conduct a "new experiment in democracy" of their own. Like the pastoral letters on the economy, this approach is to be commended for recognizing the realities of social conflict without losing faith in the prospects for a peaceful, political solution to such conflict. Like the pastoral letters, this approach envisions a role for the local churches, a kind of moral leadership in facilitating the public "dialogue" that will not be without political and economic consequences. IF YOU WANT PEACE, WORK FOR JUSTICE, the bumper sticker reminds us. In their approach to peace in Central America, the bishops recognize that problems of basic social justice cannot be solved through military force, but only repressed and postponed. It is far more promising to transform the existing institutional context or create a new one, if necessary, to coordinate the energies of the region's people in the direction of equitable economic development. That is the lesson of the pastoral letters.

Chapter 11

Political Fundamentalism: Distinctions and Directions

GABRIEL FACKRE

The influence of the Religious Right on the 1980 elections, its success in subsequent single-issue campaigns, the high visibility of television evangelists, and the media attention to all these things pointed to a new phenomenon in contemporary culture. But was it not, finally, one more transient American fancy? The Bakker and Swaggart scandals, the "invisible army" of Robertson that never materialized, Falwell's announcement that he was "backing off of politics" — are these not indicators of the end of a short-lived era?

To write the obituary of political fundamentalism now is a measure of the naiveté of any popular commentary. The invisible army that managed to propel a candidate into the presidential arena is still there, far more dispersed than was thought to be the case by the sages of "Nightline" and "Frontline." It lives still in the political arena. And it dwells as well in the church and as part of a wider evangelical constituency. Indeed, we cannot understand its political presence and future unless we grasp this latter ecclesial meaning. To that end we engage here in some necessary theological analysis. Such inquiry requires attention to basic definitions with special reference to key distinctions within and beyond the movement in question. With those in hand we will be in a position to discern potential directions.

Evangelicalism

The first set of confusions that must be addressed has to do with the words *evangelical* and *evangelicalism* and their relation to fundamentalism. "Evangelical," as a description of a theological point of view, came into usage in the sixteenth century to identify Protestants who believed that "the evangel," the good news, centered in justification by grace through faith, as that was attested to by the authority of Scripture. This double affirmation was sometimes called the material (justification) and formal (Scripture) principles of the Reformation.

Today evangelicalism refers to these same two accents as they have been radicalized and interiorized by the historic movements of pietism, Wesleyanism, Puritanism, the Great Awakenings, and modern revivalism. Evangelicals have an intense personal experience of justification (and thus are "born-again" Christians) and make rigorous use of Scripture, a piety that issues in evangelistic zeal and strong moral codes.

While these characteristics locate modern evangelicals within the current theological spectrum, they do not get us very far into the subject at hand. The reason is there are at least six major divisions within contemporary evangelicalism. I would identify them as "fundamentalist" (our topic at hand); "old evangelical" (Billy Graham and those who stress personal conversion and mass evangelism); "new evangelical" (a 1950s phenomenon associated in this country with the periodical *Christianity Today*, one which finds a place for apologetics and moderate social witness); "justice and peace evangelical" (with its representative journal, *Sojourners*, espousing a radical political agenda in the Anabaptist tradition); "charismatic evangelical" (practicing "speaking in tongues," spiritual healing and exuberant worship); and the growing presence of the "ecumenical evangelical" (with strong ecumenical affinities and associations). "Political fundamentalism" is a subset of our first type. We turn to the investigation of it.[1]

Fundamentalism

Political fundamentalism is both a version of evangelical faith and an expression of a more universal human phenomenon. In the latter respect, it shares with other religious and political movements a *mind-set*, as in Islamic fundamentalism, Roman Catholic fundamentalism, Jewish fundamentalism, Marxist fundamentalism, etc. (The literature of the organization Fundamentalists Anonymous—made up largely of Protestant ex-fundamentalists—is a storehouse of information on the mind-set.)[2] Associated therewith are the familiar words "absolutist," "dogmatic," and "polemical." These attitudes, however, are grounded in a deeper set of the mind, a worldview. In it, reality is viewed as at war with itself. History, indeed the cosmos, is sharply divided between the legions of light and the armies of night (coming to metaphysical expression in the dualism of specific religious traditions such as Manichaeism and Zoroastrianism). Thus a decisive line is drawn between "us" and "them," and the true believer guards it with the weaponry of inner conformity and outer assault. The "righteous empire" must by rigid discipline be kept unsullied, and the "evil empire" must be subjected to unremitting attack by means appropriate to dealing with satanic forces. Hence the campaigns mounted to purge its institutions (as in the 1980s efforts of fundamentalists in the Southern Baptist Convention), or to separate itself from the infidel parent organizations (the "independent Baptist" movement with which Falwellian fundamentalism is associated). When this mind-set is combined with an apocalyptic reading of current history—an imminent End—all these features are intensified.

Apocalypticism points toward an important theological aspect of fundamentalism. But before attending to these key eschatological themes we must understand fundamentalist hermeneutics, the interpretation of the Bible that warrants the end-time scenario of much political fundamentalism.

Fundamentalist Hermeneutics

Fundamentalist biblical interpretation is based on the principle of "inerrancy." The errorlessness of the Scripture was one of five planks in the early twentieth-century fundamentalist movement as it attacked "modernism." Fundamentalism today, however, fixes upon scriptural interpretation as the key issue, with ultra-inerrancy as the test of orthodoxy.

Inerrancy is the view that the original writings of Scripture—the "autographs"—are without error in all about which they speak, including science and history as well as faith and morals. Inerrancy, however, is not direct communication from the mind and mouth of God to amanuenses. This is the "dictation theory" that fundamentalists strenuously deny, one which applies to Islamic and Mormon hermeneutics, not Protestant inerrantists. In an inerrantist hermeneutic the words of the Bible are conceived to be those of human authors with their different environments and vocabulary pools, protected, however, from any error by the "plenary inspiration" of the Holy Spirit.

Yet even inerrantists disagree among themselves, a fact to keep in mind when attempting to understand major denominational disputes as well as the political landscape (as for example, the moderate inerrantists who teach in Southern Baptist seminaries and the fundamentalist inerrantists who want to remove them). Fundamentalists are ultra-inerrantists or "transmissive" inerrantists.[3] The transmission from God to authors takes place with minimal human contribution, and from authors to us with no human distortion, by virtue of a "grace of preservation." The intellectual expression of this view appears in the zeal to harmonize apparent conflicting historical narratives, and to treat biblical cosmology and nature marvels as scientific reportage.

Fundamentalism is a version of transmissive hermeneutics which uses this as the criterion of orthodoxy, with special attention to the accounts of beginnings (Genesis) and endings (Revelation), thus the "creationist" effort to rewrite public school textbooks, on the one hand, and the high profile of apocalyptic eschatology among many (not all) fundamentalists, on the other.

Apocalyptic Fundamentalism

Distinctive as it is from other kinds of evangelicalism, fundamentalism itself is not an undivided empire. Intense struggles go on within its own ranks, indeed, exacerbated by the "us and them" mentality that tends to make even small deviance cause for major splits. Touching the immediate issues of politics and apocalyptic, for example, four camps can be discerned: political and apolitical, apocalyptic and non-apocalyptic fundamentalism. The phenomenon we are examining is largely a case of political apocalyptic fundamentalism.

Apocalyptic fundamentalism refers to ultra-inerrantists who anticipate the imminent closure of human and cosmic history, discernible by secret knowledge of cataclysmic events either presently taking place or immediately forthcoming.[4] The form apocalypticism often takes in political fundamentalism is that of "pretribulational premillennialism" with its roots in the dispensationalist thought of John Darby and the Scofield Bible.[5] As *pre*millennialists, they believe that Christ will come from heaven with his church to establish a thousand-year reign of peace and plenty on the earth, a view to be contrasted with that of erring *post*millennialists who hold that Christ will come *after* a thousand-year period of peace, missionary success and plenty. As *pre*tribulationists, they hold that a "rapture" will take place in which Christ will "come for" his church (Christ descending halfway to earth to gather the living saints and the resurrected dead saints into the heavenly regions), thereby protecting believers from seven horrifying years of "tribulation" that will be then unleashed upon the earth before Christ comes to establish the millennium. This comforting thought of "pretrib premils" (as they are identified by the cognoscenti) contrasts with the discomforting thought of "posttrib premils" and "midtrib premils" who anticipate that the saints will have to endure all or some of the tribulation. Pretrib, posttrib, and midtrib premils watch carefully the signs of the times through the lens of the apocalyptic passages of Scripture (found especially in Daniel, Revelation, 2 Thessalonians, Matthew 24, and Mark 13), often interpreting the establishment of the state of Israel in 1948, the formation of ten nations into the European common market, and events in the Middle East as portentous of Things to Come. Posttribs and midtribs can identify tribulation figures of the anti-Christ, the "abomination of desolation," and so on, in the present, a practice denied to pretribs for whom these events can take place only after the rapture.

All premillennialists continue and conclude their apocalypse with a final uprising of Satan and his legions after the millennium, put down then by Christ who dispatches the enemy to a lake of fire and passes final judgment on the reprobate, sending them to eternal damnation and establishing a new heaven and a new earth where the saints dwell in glory.

Political Apocalyptic Fundamentalism

Apocalyptic premillennialism has in earlier eras tended to be apolitical: the End is coming, "rescue the perishing," gather the church apart from a world on the way to destruction. The groups under examination are, therefore, "neofundamentalists" in that they combine intense this-worldly political commitments with their apocalypticism. Neo-fundamentalists draw a straight line from the apocalyptic preview of coming attractions to specific programs, parties and candidates. The believers "prepare the way for the coming of the Lord" by service to causes that are commensurate with the standards of the arriving Kingdom. Loyalty to them pits the legions of the coming King against the satanic forces that now, as in the future, contest Christ's rule. The political *cum* evangelistic zeal and attendant organizational energy that arises from this kind of "theology of hope" is something to behold, as in the Robertson "crusade" and the vigor of neo-fundamentalist single-issue campaigns.

It should be noted in passing that the neo-fundamentalists who comprise much of the current Religious Right are different from the religious expressions of the "radical right" in this country. In earlier decades of this century, and still today, there are fundamentalists with pronounced political agendas of a hypernationalist and in some cases of an avowedly racist sort. Thus Carl McIntire is a "soft radical" of super-patriotic bent. And groups that range from the Klan and neo-Nazis to the newer survivalist movements who link Christian symbols and fundamentalist hermeneutics to nativist and racist programs with violent overtones are "hard radicals."[6] Neo-fundamentalists are distinguished from the radical Christian right not only in their rejection of avowedly super-patriotic and racist views but also their mainstreaming political intentions. They do not attack "the establishment" from outside in ad hoc raids and political hyperbole as is the case with radical rightists, but seek to change what they also believe to be a Satan-captive terrain from within by accepted processes of political and social action. Using many of the tactics employed by other movements of social protest — electioneering, petitioning for redress of grievances, letter writing, rallying, demonstrating, boycotting, and in some cases civil disobedience — they seek to change laws, lawmakers, and the social, economic, and educational institutions of society.

By mapping the territory within a section of today's "evangelical empire," I have tried to identify the features of one aggressive religio-political movement in our midst that will have significant impact on the future of this country, *including its quest for peace.* Understanding its politics requires this kind of theological investigation with all its distinctions, indeed tedious and fine distinctions. In sum, we are dealing with a *neo-fundamentalism* within evangelicalism, largely wedded to a *pretribulational premillennialism* with imminent *apocalyptic* expectations, drawing *political conclusions* and tapping *political energies.* With this understanding we are in a position to anticipate more clearly the directions this movement may take.

Before we turn to that, however, passing reference must be made to one version of political fundamentalism that is *postmillennialist* rather than premillennialist, one that has a growing following in the United States. This is the "reconstructionist" movement mentored by R. J. Rushdoony and given visibility in a recent Bill Moyers documentary. Reconstructionism is an intellectually complex ideology in the Reformed tradition that seeks to order society on the basis of very strict Old Testament legal as well as moral codes in the expectation that the biblicizing of society is promised as a millennial hope *before* the return of Christ.[7]

Directions

Political fundamentalism is a volatile movement, active in a volatile society going through volatile times. All this makes prognostication about directions hazardous. For example, while writing in 1982 about the Religious Right, I commented on its susceptibility to the seductions of power because of naiveté about its presumed righteousness. However, I was myself naive about the vulnerability of its leaders to more prurient temptations. Projections, while risky, are nevertheless possible, especially so when grounded in an understanding of the theological assumptions of the movement.

The apocalyptic premillennialism of neo-fundamentalism will fuel its own political fires for the foreseeable future. The invisible army will continue to march because (as Jürgen Moltmann has argued and history has demonstrated) ardent hope mobilizes for action. Certainly nontheological factors will play their part in its momentum, including the cultural and economic disenfranchisement felt by many of its participants. Indeed, the tumults and historical peril of our times are social facts that feed apocalypticism, for theological visions are inextricable from their socioeconomic habitat. There are enough analysts around to remind us of this earthy underside, but they regularly fall prey in their analyses to a reductionism that fails to assess the influence of belief systems in social change. This latter "sociologism," in combination with uncritical assumptions about an omnipresent and irreversible secularization process, makes it difficult for most popular and much academic commentary on political fundamentalism to grasp its factuality and durability. Neo-fundamentalism is here in force, and is here to stay.

Our mapping shows the diversity within a wider evangelicalism and in fundamentalism itself. That should tell us something about the ways it will influence the political process. Even secular commentators can see by now that evangelicalism is no bloc vote. The following Jesse Jackson has among black evangelicals who make up a large part of black church life should put to rest all early media stereotypes about the monolithic nature of "the evangelical vote." And the poor showing of Robertson forces, the fundamentalist leaders prominent in the Bush and Kemp campaigns, etc., should underscore the diversity in fundamentalist party politics. However, signs of fundamentalist political unity can be seen on single issues, both those which directly connect with its hermeneutics, such as public school textbooks and prayer in public schools, and those in which its agenda converges with the secular New Right on issues that run from personal morality to foreign policy.

The continuing presence and influence of political fundamentalism could be weakened or slowed down by two factors, one obvious and the other less so. The first is public exposure of the moral flaws of some of its leaders. Fundamentalists are supposed to practice what they preach, especially so when the lines are so sharply drawn between the forces of good and the cadres of evil. This sense of betrayal has already taken its toll on the income and thus the institutions of prominent media figures, including those not exposed for hypocrisy (the cutback on the television programming of Falwell and the unsuccessful effort of Robertson to distance himself from the scandals). Further, neo-fundamentalists are children of their times, whether they admit it or not, and thus are embarrassed by "bad PR," a fact that could account for such things as the final decision of the Assemblies of God not to exempt Swaggart from its rules for rehabilitation after a period of equivocation, and also the apparent slowing in 1988 of the campaign of Southern Baptist fundamentalists to take over Southern Baptist educational institutions.

The second factor that could significantly retard neo-fundamentalist political momentum has to do with a two-fold theological contradiction. First, in spite of its professed loyalty to biblical authority, including its rigorously literalist hermeneutic, the radical understanding of the fall found in Scripture is not espoused by neo-fundamentalism. Sin does not stubbornly persist in the life of the redeemed but has been evacuated to the exclusive region of Satan outside the precincts of the saints, creating the "us and them" mentality earlier discussed. Because the saints are so preserved in their saintliness and thus enjoined to carry on "holy wars" against the sinners, there is no place for a piety of self-criticism and no system of checks and balances or sober procedures of monitoring within its institutions that might anticipate the corruptibility to which all persons and institutions in a fallen world are susceptible. In the absence of both the spirituality (for example, no regular corporate confession of sin within its liturgies, and no modes of self-examination in personal piety and institutional self-scrutiny, as in financial accountability to its constituency or to the wider public), persons at the top of pyramidal organizations have fallen prey to the predictably attendant temptations. Indeed, "money, sex, and power," three seductions to which neo-fundamentalists have succumbed, are directly related to this naiveté about the invulnerability of saints, aggravated further by the "us and them" apocalyptic of neo-fundamentalism. An older tradition that demanded of its "saints" (the monks) the taking of vows of "poverty, chastity, and obedience" knew about the corruptibility of the pious, even though its ascetic alternative is inadequate. Given the universality of sin manifest in the temptations that grow with the accumulation of power, including spiritual power, both a sober piety and an institutional self-monitoring are necessary. Their absence in political fundamentalism could prove its undoing. Time will tell.

The second contradiction emerges when one asks the question: Can apocalyptic theology sustain over time its political rationale? If the End is coming soon, one in which believers will be raptured and a time of devastating tribulation expected, then why should they want to change political institutions? Apocalypse forecasts their imminent dissolution with the attendant removal to Heaven of believers. Why should a neo-fundamentalist want to build a university that will compete with Notre Dame (Falwell) or a Christian Broadcasting Network (Robertson) or Christian theme parks (Bakker) or publishing houses (Swaggart) or hospitals (Roberts) or run for president (Robertson)? It would seem that more hope and a longer future for human history are assumed by both the political and institutional programs launched than is allowed for by premillennialist horizons. This seeming theological incoherence has been noticed by the sociologist Jeffrey Hadden, who wonders if a postmillennialist turn is in the offing for the televangelists.[8] Indeed, the growth of the postmillennialist reconstructionist movement may be a straw in the wind. Then one must ask if the abandonment of apocalyptic that goes with such a move would, in turn, affect the degree of political energy generated by it. This second theological caveat may argue for a potential change in the political trajectory of the phenomenon.

While we cannot know the ultimate direction of political fundamentalism, any more than we can penetrate the eschatological future God has in store for us (seen as it is "through a glass darkly," and not through the transparencies of apocalyptic), we can make an educated guess about its penultimate future. Barring the pitfalls identified, this army will continue to be about its holy wars. And you and I will have to ask ourselves whether we have clarity about our own eschatological vision and an equivalent political will to pursue it.

Notes

1. These categories appear in the writer's entry, "Evangelical, Evangelicalism" in *The Westminster Dictionary of Christian Theology* (Philadelphia: Westminster Press, 1983), pp. 191f.

2. See *The FA Networker*, especially Vol. 3, No. 1 (Spring 1987), published by Fundamentalists Anonymous, P.O. Box 20324, Greeley Square Station, New York, NY 10001.

3. The transmissive view and other forms of inerrancy (and "infallibility") teaching are discussed in Gabriel Fackre, *Authority: Scripture in the Church for the World*,

vol. 2 of *The Christian Story* (Grand Rapids: Wm. B. Eerdmans Publishing Co., 1987), pp. 62–75.

4. Graphically portrayed in color, for example, by Charles R. Taylor, "The Destiny Chart" (Cypress, CA: Today in Bible Prophecy, 1978).

5. Described in such works as George Ladd, *The Blessed Hope* (Grand Rapids: Wm. B. Eerdmans Publishing Co., 1956); Ernest Sandeen, *The Roots of Fundamentalism* (Chicago: University of Chicago Press, 1970); Robert Gundry, *The Church and the Tribulation* (Grand Rapids: Zondervan Publishing Co., 1973); and Dave MacPherson, *The Great Rapture Hoax* (Fletcher, NC: New Puritan Library, Inc., 1983).

6. For an investigation of these distinctions, see Fackre, *The Religious Right and Christian Faith* (Grand Rapids: Wm. B. Eerdmans Publishing Co., 1982), pp. 1–5.

7. See Rousas J. Rushdoony, *The Institutes of Biblical Law* (Phillipsburg, NJ: Presbyterian & Reformed Publishing Co., 1973).

8. Jeffrey Hadden, "Religious Broadcasting and the Mobilization of the New Christian Right" in *The Journal for the Scientific Study of Religion*, Vol. 26, No. 1 (March 1987): 23, 24.

Chapter 12

War, Poverty, and Patriotism: The Theological and Moral Quandary of Black Americans

RIGGINS R. EARL, JR.

And you will hear of wars and rumors of wars; see that you are not alarmed; for this must take place, but the end is not yet. For nation will rise against nation, and kingdom against kingdom, and there will be famines and earthquakes in various places: all this is but the beginning of the birth pangs (Matthew 24:6–8).

The Bible has often been used by the poor of America to undergird their uncritical tolerance toward the notion of the inevitability of war. Many have believed that war is ordained of God. America's economic elites have known full well that there is a direct correlation between small-scale wars in distant lands and the nation's economic well-being; they are necessary for the growth of the military industrial complex. The ruling class understands that small-scale wars are initiated and controlled by the collective wills of superpowers. This difference in perception can, in part, be attributed to the way the two different groups view the Bible. The poor try to make sense out of the modern world by seeing it uncritically through the lenses of scripture; the ruling class is more inclined to use the critical literary tools of modernity to critique the world that produced the scriptural texts.

The passage of Scripture cited above portrays Jesus' disciples privately asking from him about the sign of his coming and the close of the ages. This account of Matthew credits Jesus with responding with two doctrinal positions about the phenomenal signs that will occur in both the natural order and the social order. Both orders must experience inevitable birth pangs before the dawn of the eschatological age. The famine-earthquake warning characterizes one doctrinal position; the wars-and-rumors-of-wars warning characterizes the other.

The poor are subject to seeing these teachings as being consistent with the notions of God and war that are evidenced in such Old Testament passages as Isaiah 13:17 and Genesis 25:22, 23. War and poverty might very well be perceived by them as the fulfillment of biblical prophecies. Theologically, they presuppose that God uses famines and earthquakes to humble those who ignore the need to confess total dependency on God; God uses war and violence to humble and punish haughty rulers of the kingdoms of this world. Those who read the text solely in this way will miss the connective links between peace, poverty, and war. They will not see that the ruling class needs small-scale wars in order to maintain poverty and manipulate peace. The makers and shakers of world powers, in the name of creating peace, initiate wars for the purpose of controlling and exploiting the natural resources of the world. They have at their disposal chemical defoliants, incendiary bombs, napalm, and even biological weapons for doing so.[1]

Black Americans have been among the primary victims of uncritical theological and moral presuppositions about the peace-poverty-war riddle in the modern world. Morally, they have subscribed to the unproven notion that unhyphenated loyalty to the nation's war causes would convince white Americans that black Americans are of equal human worth. Consequently, national and international theaters of battle have always been potential proving grounds for black males. They have enthusiastically volunteered for every war believing that they could earn the right to be respected as American citizens. Black Americans have been so seduced by this notion that many prominent civil rights leaders (e.g., Roy Wilkens and Whitney Young) could not comprehend Martin Luther King's prophetic critique of the Vietnam War. These leaders, perhaps unconsciously, presupposed that black Americans' human worth is tied to America's hierarchical scale of values. King, on the contrary, presupposed a value system, grounded in a radical vision of Christian humanism that critiqued America's system of values predicated on materialism, racism, and militarism.

It is my thesis that black Americans have failed to examine critically their theological and moral presuppositions about war and their involvement in it. I will illustrate my claim by descriptively examining the attitudes of blacks toward four major wars: (1) the Civil War, (2) World War I, (3) World War II, and (4) the Vietnam War. In each war blacks fought primarily to prove their humanity to their own nation. They fought for a moral victory. But no feats of military heroism have enabled them to answer this question: Why does our nation deny us the dignity of personhood which we have proven on the field of battle that we deserve? Theologically, black Americans have gone into each battle with the presupposition that God was on the side of their government; however, the government has failed to respond to them in a moral way for their sacrificial loyalty. I will show that blacks fought in the Civil War first to win their right to be free men and second to save the Union; in World War I they fought to save the world for democracy so they could be its recipients; in World War II they fought to globalize the world of democracy so they would have a place to be heard and recognized; and in the Vietnam War they fought to overcome the economic deprivation of American ghettos.

The conclusion of the essay will show that black Americans need to reassess their theological and moral presuppositions in the light of their nation's philosophy of militarism. It will make the case that blacks need to redefine critically their vision of patriotism. This can be done by seeing how Martin Luther King, Jr., critically assessed the correlations between peace, poverty, and war in a militaristic society.

1. The Civil War: From Slaves to Liberators

Slaves saw the Civil War as God's war to set them free; they had seen in the Union Army "the coming of the glory of the Lord . . . trampling out the vintage where the grapes of wrath are stored." They heard God call them by the trumpet to leave the plantations and join God's mighty marching army. Many did this only to learn that they were merely pawns in the struggle. Others saw the opportunity to join the armies of the North or the South as an opportunity publicly to affirm their loyalty. An anonymous New Orleans black accurately summarized the ethical dilemma black soldiers faced, whether they joined the men in blue or gray:

> It is retten that a man can not Serve two master. But it seems that the Collored population two a rebel master and a union master the both want our Servicss one wants us to make Cotton and Sugar And the Sell it and keep the money the union master wants us to fight the battles under white officers and the injoy both money and the union black Soldiers And white officers will not play togeathe much longer.[2]

The fact is that black soldiers fought a different war, although they wore the same uniform as white soldiers, observed the same system of military justice, and confronted the same enemy. Why? Because they struggled to end inequality as well as to save the Union. Blacks knew that a union without freedom for all would not be genuinely free; they made clear that freedom was the paramount principle for which they fought. One black writer of the period voiced the sentiments of millions of slaves when he wrote:

> Let the white fight for what the want and we negroes fight for what we want there are three things to fight for and two races of people

divided into three Classes one want negro Slaves the other the union the other Liberty. So liberty must take the day nothing Shorter.[3]

Slaves were undoubtedly convinced that God was the champion of liberty, the author and sustainer of those desiring freedom. Subsequently, they saw volunteering their services in the Civil War as being the equivalent of serving in the army of the Lord. Their belief was sustained by 200,000 enlisting in the Union Army and 30,000 in the Union Navy during the Civil War. Another quarter of a million black men and women labored for that Army and Navy as teamsters, nurses, cooks, river pilots, fortification-builders, and pioneers, while many more served as guides, spies, and scouts. Through this direct participation black people contributed, directly and decisively, toward the maintenance of the American Republic and won their liberation from chattel slavery. Blacks en masse believed God was working through President Lincoln and the Union Army for their liberation. Such sentiment is graphically portrayed in the description of a black soldier who fought with the 29th Regiment of the Connecticut Colored Troops. This anonymous freedom fighter documented via letter his observations of blacks' response to Lincoln's visit to Richmond following the fall of the Confederate capital:

All could see the President, he was so tall. One woman standing in a doorway as he passed along shouted, 'Thank you, dear Jesus, for this sight of the great conqueror.' Another one standing by her side clasped her hands and shouted, 'Bless the Lamb—Bless the Lamb.' Another one threw her bonnet in the air, screaming with all her might, 'Thank you, Master Lincoln.'[4]

The soldier-observer interpreted these unrestrained words of praise he heard from the women as being directed to God for using Lincoln as an instrument in the cause of their liberation: "They were earnest and heartfelt expressions to Almighty God, and thousands of Colored men in Richmond would have laid down their lives for President Lincoln."[5]

Such theological presuppositions about the Civil War were not restricted to untutored slaves. Literate blacks such as David Walker strongly believed God would rectify the injustice of slavery with violence. He had prophesied more than a generation earlier that God, because of God's just nature, would cause the violence endemic to institutional slavery to divide and destroy the household of the nation. W.E.B. DuBois later summarized the collective disposition of the victimized toward God during the period when he wrote approximately two generations after the war:

But to most of the four million black folk emancipated by the Civil War, God was real. They knew Him. They had met Him personally in many a wild orgy of religious frenzy, or in the black stillness of the

night. His plan for them was clear; they were to suffer and be de-
graded, and afterwards by Divine edict raised to manhood and power;
and so on January 1, 1863, He made them free.[6]

DuBois perceived that God, out of the carnage of the war, had exalted
an insignificant people to a position of triumph. Like deutero-Isaiah, he
used the poetic idiom to describe the glorious exaltation of a once down-
trodden people:

> To these black folk it was the Apocalypse. The magnificent trumpet
> tones of Hebrew Scriptures, transmuted and oddly changed, became
> a strange new gospel. All that was Beauty, all that was Love, all that
> was Truth, stood on the top of these mad mornings and sang with the
> stars. The great human sob shrieked in the wind and tossed its tears
> upon the sea—free, free, free.[7]

These reflective insights about the Civil War show the complex understanding blacks had regarding both God's and their own involvement in the
theater of violence. On the one hand they understood that God was fighting
the war for them; on the other hand they were fighting the war in partnership with God. It was their courage to be co-partners with God which
enabled them to conclude that it was a rite of passage to full rights as
American citizens. Sacrificial involvement in this war gave black Americans
an official place in the Americanization process. It provided the opportunity
for them voluntarily to become full members of the violent nature of America's national character. It was the official ritual for primordially binding
black warriors and their descendants to the land of the free and the home
of the brave; it gave them a deeper ontological sense of belonging to America. It created within them a notion of kinship to America as their place
that was stronger than death itself.

2. World War I: Saviors of the World for Democracy

Black soldiers fought valiantly in World War I under the slogan, "saving
the world for democracy," although for them there was precious little democracy to be experienced in either the civilian or military sector. America's
German opponents quickly exploited the racist treatment of black soldiers
during the war period. A classical example of this can be seen in an incident
where German soldiers, in the fray of battle, circulated circulars among
black soldiers that asked:

> What is Democracy? Personal freedom, all citizens enjoying the same
> rights socially and before the law. Do you enjoy the same rights as
> the white people do in America, the land of Freedom and Democracy,
> or are you not treated over there as second-class citizens? Can you

get a seat in a theater where white people sit? ... Is lynching and the most horrible crimes connected therewith a lawful proceeding in a democratic country? ...

Why, then, fight the Germans only for the benefit of the Wall Street Robbers and to protect the millions they have loaned to the British, French and Italians?[8]

Such frank inquiries by the Germans forced black soldiers, even while fighting, to face consciously the contradiction in their efforts to save the world for a democracy that their nation denied them. They were forced to examine the correlation between war and the economic deprivation of which they and their people were the victims back in America; they were introduced to a new way of explaining the phenomenon of poverty in the world. The modern paradox, however, is that the radical questions of the Germans to the black soldiers in the trenches did not undermine their commitment to "save the world for democracy." To the contrary, blacks clamored to serve in the military. More than 2,500,000 registered for the draft and about 31 percent were accepted for service, compared with 26 percent of the registered whites. More than 140,000 black soldiers were sent to France, but the vast majority were confined to menial duties and only 40,000 got to fight. For the most part, the combat soldiers were in units assigned to the French command.

A minority of black leaders did protest blacks' fighting abroad for ideals they did not enjoy at home. Some were even persecuted and jailed by the American government as being suspected friends of the Kaiser (e.g., A. Phillip Randolph and Chandler Owens). White newspapers deemed any anti-war comments by black protest leaders unfit to print. Government opposition, however, could not undo what blacks knew experientially about the nation. This was best articulated by the president of the Liberty League of Negro Americans:

They are saying a great deal about democracy in Washington now, but while they are talking about fighting for freedom and the Stars and Stripes, here at home the whites apply the torch to the black man's home, and bullets, clubs and stones to their bodies.[9]

Even in the face of such outrages the black apostles of American patriotism won the ear of the black masses. They championed the notion that it was incumbent upon the black Americans to see Kaiserism, portrayed as inimical to all forms of democratic government in the world, as *the* threatening issue of the day. Even the social prophet, W.E.B. DuBois, summoned hyphenated Americans to "close ranks" and defend the national space first; they could defend their ethnic interest following victory. DuBois said: "I believe that this is our war and not President Wilson's war, and that no matter how many blunders the administration makes, or how many obstacles it puts in our way, we must work the harder to win the war." He reasoned that blacks, even if denied a chance to fight, would benefit from the labor shortage caused by the war:

> Will we be ousted when the white soldiers come back?
> They won't come back.
> So there you are, gentlemen, and take your choice—we'll fight or work.
> We'll fight and work.[10]

DuBois reasoned that the war, whether blacks fought abroad or worked at home, would give them a chance to develop those sophisticated skills they needed for defending themselves and competing in the modern world.

> If we fight we'll learn the fighting game and cease to be so 'aisely lynched.'
> If we don't fight we'll learn the more lucrative trades and cease to be so easily robbed and exploited.
> Take your choice, gentlemen. 'We should worry.'[11]

Blacks followed the behest of DuBois and chose to serve enthusiastically on every front where the country would allow them. They served so willingly until some racist whites exploited their good intentions: "The Negro likes to go to church because God gives him equality. He likes to be in the army because there he approaches nearest to that equality with the whites which he enjoys in theory but never knows in practice. And in the army he wears good clothes, eats three meals daily, sleeps in a bed at night, and at the end of the month, has a little money in his pocket."[12]

The high note of patriotism was sounded throughout the black community by black leaders of every walk of life. A majority of the black editors rallied to the nation's call and wrote in a martial spirit; the black clergy put on the whole armor of patriotism and awakened the Negro laity to a sense of its duty, opportunity, and responsibility; black educators in all sections taught loyalty as a cardinal virtue and representative black public speakers sought diligently to maintain a healthy morale among the rank and file of black Americans.[13] Dr. Emmett Scott, private secretary to the late Booker T. Washington, was appointed special assistant to the Secretary of War to "look after" the darker tenth of the population. Scott, from behind his Washington desk, cautioned that the saving of America for democracy took priority over saving democracy for black Americans: "This is not the time to discuss our race problems. Our first duty is to fight, and to continue to fight until the war is won. Then we can adjust the problems that remain in the life of the Colored man."[14]

Instead of crowning the heads of her black soldiers for their unhyphenated loyalty in the war, the nation unleashed a campaign of violence against them. This could not abort, however, the fact that the experience of war itself had created a new black American who had lost his innocence and his illusions about the promises of the American government. This new black child of war substituted for faith in the white man faith in himself only; war had taught him self-reliance and peace taught him that self-reliance was all that could be believed in. The rest was pie in the sky. President Wilson complimented a group of blacks on the remarkable loyalty and patriotism of black Americans, despite the unjust and illegal treatment they had suffered in the past. Out of the war, he said, would come all the rights of citizenship. He warned, however, against impatience, saying that "great principles of righteousness are won by hard fighting and they are attained by slow degrees." The President quickly discovered that he was speaking to a new group of black warriors. Their new consciousness was typified by a member of the group who responded: "I fear, Mr. President, before the Negroes of this country again will submit to many of the injustices which we have suffered in this country, the white man will have to kill more of them than the combined number of soldiers that were slain in the great war."[15]

At the peak of the domestic violence against black Americans, DuBois in August 1919 put the same declaration of a war for equal rights in his ringing prose, a trumpet call welcome to the ears of the former black soldiers:

Behold the day, O fellow black Men! They cheat us and mock us; they kill us and slay us; they deride our misery. When we plead for the naked protection of the law, there where a million of our fellows dwell, they tell us to 'Go to Hell!'

'To Your Tents, O Israel!' And Fight, Fight, Fight for Freedom.[16]

3. World War II: Internationalizing Black Manhood

Approximately two decades later, America would ask her ebony sons for a demonstrated encore of valor in a second World War. More than 1,500,000 entered the armed forces during World War II. They volunteered as enthusiastically as had their predecessors in World War I. Again it was to prove their worth in the eyes of America and the world. This war, more than the preceding one, would allow them to exhibit their valor before the makers and shapers of world opinion. Three score and ten years after the Civil War, black Americans still had not convinced white Americans that they deserved to be recognized as full citizens. Black Americans were clearly the victims of America's institutionalized racist policies. W.E.B. DuBois, reflecting on the Civil War during the mid-thirties, characterized the totally racist nature of the nation's policy:

Everything black was hideous. Everything Negroes did was wrong. If they fought for freedom, they were beasts; if they did not fight, they were born slaves. If they cowered on the plantations, they loved slavery; if they ran away, they were lazy loafers. If they sang, they were silly; if they scowled they were impudent.

The bites and blows of a nation fell on them. All hatred that the whites after the Civil War had for each other gradually concentrated itself on them. They caused the war—they, its victims. They were guilty of all the thefts of those who stole. They were the cause of the wasted property and small crops. They had impoverished the South and plunged the North in endless debt. And they were funny, funny ridiculous baboons, aping man.[17]

In America, blacks were guilty just by virtue of being who they were. This might explain also why they welcomed enthusiastically the opportunity to be and do in a war context on another continent.

World War II, as did the war before, impacted the socioeconomic fabric of American society. Increased demands for factory workers, caused by male employees who volunteered for the armed service, called blacks from the rural South to the industrialized areas of the North; increased need for combat soldiers called black young men from the farms to the battlefield trenches in Europe and the Pacific. Blacks supplied the demands on all fronts—at home and abroad.

At the close of World War II, blacks would see themselves as members of a nation that quickly was recognized as the leading international power and shaper of world opinions. The world influence of America, needless to say, internationalized in a qualitatively new way the situation of American blacks. Out of the war would emerge the United Nations, and that international organization would provide a forum from which American racism could be indicted. The experience of fascism had convincingly demonstrated that there was not an absolute line between a nation's foreign policy and its own domestic society, and many would believe there was something profoundly wrong with a leader of world democracy that tolerated brutal treatment of minority people. Blacks were not naive. Though they were asked to support the war against Hitler, people in the South lived under a racist system more appropriate to a Fascist state than to a democracy. Even black servicemen were not safe in many southern communities:

They encountered resentment and reprisals from white citizens, officials and soldiers. It was common for a black soldier to experience verbal abuse and physical abuse, which sometimes resulted in death. Afro-American servicemen had undergone similar treatment in the Great War, but twenty-five years later the race was less tolerant and the times less receptive to such injustices.[18]

Such abuse only encouraged the new spirit of internationalism among blacks which the war had awakened. They were forced to break out of the mind-set of caste and to identify with the darker races of the world. The sociologist Horace Cayton observed in 1943 that "blacks no longer confined their demands to their own rights but championed the democratic rights for all people throughout the world."[19] Blacks had shifted from a position of some indifference to the war effort to one of demand for participation in every aspect of the war so as to be in a position to help shape the peace. They moved from a posture of seeking concessions to one of demands for full equality. A black woman in Cincinnati expressed her hope not only that the United States would win the war, but that "colored people get a fair chance to make a living and equal rights as the white man." She favored equal rights legislation, not only for Cincinnati "but all over the U.S.—even down to the deep south where they're treated like dogs."[20]

Interestingly, black Americans accepted the same theological and moral presuppositions about war as did their white counterparts: God was on the side of right, and America and her allies were right. This explains, undoubtedly, why many black American leaders, even clergy, had serious difficulty with King's opposition to the Vietnam War. It would be safe to say that the oppressed of America came to see war at best as an immoral means to a moral end.

4. The Vietnam War: A Loss of Innocence and Cause

The nation called another generation of black warriors; and they answered the clarion call. Poor black American males went to Southeast Asia, as did many poor whites, totally ignorant of what they were going there to defend. Class was a clear factor operative in selecting those who would go to Vietnam because of the draft deferment policy which favored the middle class. It allowed students who maintained a certain grade-point average special draft-exempt status. Those of a middle-class background undoubtedly were in a better position to meet this academic challenge. In addition to this, the poor often had to choose the military because they lacked economic resources needed to get into college or stay there. A new generation of primarily ghetto dwellers were sent to defend Southeast Asians against the invasion of communism. These young men came primarily from that segment of the society, as did their poor white counterparts, where they were taught that obedience is better than resistance when it comes to Uncle Sam. The following reflection from a young black soldier from Baltimore probably typified the uncritical mind-set of lower-class whites and blacks: "I didn't ask no questions about the war. I thought communism was spreading, and as an American citizen, it was my part to do as much as I could to defeat the Communist from coming here. Whatever America states is correct was the tradition that I was brought up in."[21] In addition, the veteran remembers seeing the military as being his corporate saviour from the economic deprivation of the ghetto: "And I, through the only way I could possibly make it out of the ghetto, was to be the best soldier I possibly could be."[22]

As had been the case in the three other wars, the battlefield was still a place where black Americans believed they could prove that they were as deserving as whites of full citizenship rights. Since it was not possible to prove this working the fields or bumming around the streets of Chicago or New York, relatives encouraged their sons, who were turning eighteen years old, to join the armed forces. One youngster remembered it as an opportunity to show his "devoted duty, to God, state and country." Black soldiers in Vietnam, as well as the preceding wars, had to prove that they merited an opportunity to fight even against the nation's common enemy. It has been the lesson that black mothers and fathers have handed down to their children. Another veteran of Vietnam remembered being told by his mother: "You're not white so you are not as good as they are, but you got to work hard to strive to be as good as they are."[23] His mother's instructions became an incentive for him to strive for excellence as a soldier.

Black veterans returned from Vietnam acutely aware of being unsaved, lost warriors. They had fought the nation's war but the nation ignored their plight. The following statement of a veteran reflects the tragic consequences of many poor victims:

> But they turn their backs on a lot of us Vietnam vet'rans. They say the only way to success is through education. I wanna go back to school and get my B.A., but I can't afford to. I gotta get out there and get a job. Ain't no jobs out there. So what I'm gon' do now? Only thing else I know how to do is pick up a gun.[24]

The unsaved black veterans, as had the black warriors of both World Wars, saw the nation promote the welfare of the former enemies over themselves. The following account is a painful reminder of this fact. It is told by a Vietnam veteran from Baltimore:

> One day I'm down on Oliver and Milton Avenue. Go into this grocery store. In my neighborhood. This Vietn'ese owns the store. He says, 'I know you?' I say, 'You know me from where?' 'You Vietnam?' 'Yeah, I was in Vietnam.' 'When you Vietnam?' ''68, '69.' 'Yeah, me know you An Khe. You be An Khe?' 'Yeah, I was in An Khe.' 'Yeah, me know you. You Montagnard Man.' Ain't that some shit? I'm buying groceries from him. I ain't been in that store since. I'm still pissed off. He's got a business, good home, drivin' cars. And I'm still strugglin'. I'm not angry 'cause he Vietn'ese. I don't have nothing against the Vietn'ese. Nothing', not a damn thing. I am angry with America. When the Vietn'ese first came here, they were talkin' 'bout the new niggers. But they don't treat them like niggers. They treat them like people. If they had gave me some money to start my life over again,

I'd been in a hell of a better situation than I am right now. We went to war to serve the country in what we thought was its best interest. Then America puts them above us. It's a crime. It's a crime against us.[25]

5. In Quest of a New Patriotism

The descriptive analysis of black Americans' participation in each major war clearly shows that their patriotism has been taken for granted. This has been possible because they have understood their participation in war as opportunity for upward mobility in the society. Militarism has been seen as a means of alleviating the suffering caused by racism and the denial of opportunity. Poor black males enter into war with the false premise that they can earn, through sacred sacrifice in combat, what others receive by virtue of having been born in the nation. This points to a social cleavage between those who believe they must achieve their rights to be Americans and those who understand themselves to be the recipients of ascribed rights of American citizenry. This cleavage of consciousness requires that the oppressed and oppressors serve the country out of different theological and ethical motivations. The oppressed believe that they, by fighting, can win their selfhood as well as the favor of their God and country; the oppressors, by fighting, believe they are expressing their gratitude to their God and country for being who they are. The former dream of becoming what they have never been allowed to be; the latter defend the right to remain what they think nobody different from themselves has the right to be. What is involved here is the issue of servile duty versus that of false gratitude. Those who are doomed to prove their right to be will ever be victims of servile duty. On the contrary, those who think that because of their ethnicity they are the only ones who have inherited the right to be American are victims of a demoniac kind of gratitude. Oppressors who subscribe to such a notion cheapen the idea of the grace of national citizenship. The oppressed who subscribe to the notion of servile duty to the nation's military case make themselves impossible candidates for the grace of national citizenship.

Modern war demands that the oppressed redefine their understanding of patriotism. They must see that an uncritical understanding of the wars-and-rumors-of-wars prophecy is woefully inadequate for dealing with a superpower that understands war as a game of controlled violence between national superpowers. The oppressed must see that they are used in those violent encounters merely as the means to an unrighteous end. The oppressed can only arrive at a new posture of patriotism by critically assessing the correlation between militarism, materialism, and racism. Martin L. King, Jr., did so in a way that was consistent with our biblical heritage. Any quest of a new patriotism on the part of the oppressed will require that they critique our presuppositions regarding the relationship between our duty to God and nation. King summons us to catch a vision of God that would demand that we include even our national enemies. To those blacks who criticized him for confusing the issue of civil rights with foreign policy, King asked:

> Did they not realize that the good news was meant for all men? Did they not forget that His ministry was in obedience to the One who loved His enemies so fully that He died for them? What can I say to the Vietcong or to Castro or to Mao as a faithful minister of this One? Can I threaten them with death or must I share with them my life?[26]

Such a vision of God will give the oppressed a new perspective of the theological and moral quandary produced by the relation between war, poverty and peace.

A Critique: An Unresolved Quandary

While their enthusiastic participation in wars has not made them fully American in the sight of the majority of white Americans, it has created a consciousness of Americanism among black Americans that is irreversible. The irreversibility must be seen in the fact that war sacrifices are given religious status by the majority of Americans. Black Americans, perhaps, have been too quick to buy into America's theological and moral presuppositions about the nation's engagements in war. Their leadership has been slow to affirm the correlation between peace, poverty, and war. King spoke of a demonic correlation between militarism, racism, and classism. He critically recognized that the superpowers used militarism for the express purpose of exploiting the underclass, primarily comprised of the darker population of the world. War, King observed, was antithetical to the morals of the civilized world. Prominent civil rights leaders have been reluctant to declare a connective link between race, class, and militarism for fear that they would sabotage the chances for making racial progress at home. Black educators have neglected to make black Americans' participation in the nation's wars a unit of critical inquiry in the college curriculums. And no major studies have been done by black theologians of the theological and ethical issues war poses.

Notes

1. Cf. Robert W. Kates, "Presence of War, not Lack of Food, Is Fueling the Famines around the Globe," *Atlanta Constitution*, April 22, 1988, p. 21A.

2. "Statements of an Anonymous New Orleans Black" in *Freedom: A Documentary History of Emancipation: Series II, the Black Military Experience*, eds. Ira Berlin, Joseph P. Reidy, and Leslie S. Rowland (New York: Cambridge University Press, 1982), p. 153.

3. Ibid., p. 154.

4. "Negro Fighters for Freedom and Unity, 1863–1865" in Herbert Aptheker, *Documentary History of the Negro People in the United States*, vol. 1 (New York: Citadel Press, 1951), p. 481.

5. Ibid., p. 490.

6. W.E.B. DuBois, *Black Reconstruction* (New York: Atheneum, 1969), p. 124.

7. Ibid.

8. Philip J. Drotning, *Black Heros in Our Nation's History: A Tribute to Those Who Helped Shape America* (New York: Washington Square Press, 1969), pp. 173f.

9. Hubert H. Harrison, cited in Arthur E. Barbeau and Florette Henri, *The Unknown Soldiers: Black American Troops in World War I* (Philadelphia: Temple University Press, 1974), p. 21.

10. W.E.B. DuBois, cited in *The Unknown Soldiers*, pp. 33f.

11. Ibid.

12. William L. Trudy, *A Soldier's Diary* (Chicago: [no publisher], 1930), pp. 36f. (entry of November 5, 1917).

13. Emmett J. Scott, *Scott's Official History of the American Negro in the World War* (1919; reprint, Salem, NH: Ayer Co. Pubs., 1969).

14. Aptheker, *Documentary History of the Negro People*, p. 164.

15. "Why the Negro Appeals to Violence" in *Literary Digest* 62 (August 9, 1919): 11.

16. DuBois, cited in *The Unknown Soldiers*, p. 179.

17. DuBois, *Black Reconstruction*, p. 125.

18. Joseph Dominic Capeci, Jr., "The Harlem Riot of 1943," Ph.D. diss. (University of California, Irvine), pp. 53, 312f.

19. Horace R. Cayton, quoted in Herbert Shapiro, *White Violence and Black Response: From Reconstruction to Montgomery* (Amherst, MA: University of Massachusetts Press, 1988), p. 342.

20. Ibid., p. 340.

21. Wallace Terry, *Bloods: An Oral History of the Vietnam War by Black Veterans* (New York: Random House, 1984), pp. 245f.

22. Ibid.

23. Ibid., p. 123.

24. Ibid., pp. 262f.

25. Ibid., pp. 263f.

26. In John J. Ansbro, *Martin Luther King, Jr.: The Making of a Mind* (Maryknoll, NY: Orbis Books, 1982), p. 261.

Chapter 13

The Indian Question
and Liberation Theology

GONZALO CASTILLO-CARDENAS

Since the nature of "the Indian question" is not self-evident to everyone let me try to clarify my own understanding of the problem with the help of two anecdotes that are indelibly stamped in my memory. The first one has to do with a massacre of Indians that took place in Colombia in 1968. Some *vaqueros* (cowboys) of the ranch known as "La Rubiera," working for an absentee landowner of the Eastern Plains, committed a calculated murder of sixteen Indians of the Cuiva tribe, including men, women, and children. The careful preparation of the action and the means employed added to the heinous nature of the crime. The *vaqueros* of the area have traditionally considered the Indians a threat because of their habit of coming back to the hacienda lands and helping themselves to what they need including sometimes heads of cattle. The *vaqueros* could not understand the fact that the open lands their employer considered his own were in fact part of the ancestral hunting grounds of the Cuiva tribe, whose members have the traditional practice of rotating the use of the soil by seasonal migrations and returns.[1]

Thus, the cowboys carefully planned an effective way to teach the Indians a lesson and solve the problem once and for all. According to the plan, they made a concerted effort over a period of months to show kindness and goodwill toward the Indians, providing them on several occasions with food and utensils, until finally one day they went up the river to the Indian villages inviting them to an open air dinner (*un sancocho*) around the main hacienda house. Although surprised, the Indians accepted the invitation and on the appointed day started coming down, one by one. They did not find the *vaqueros,* but their women were busy in the kitchen preparing the "banquet" and tables were set around the house, under the shade of the

140

trees. As confidence grew more Indians arrived, and the food began coming out of the kitchen to the tables. As the guests started to eat, the cowboys, who had been hiding, appeared suddenly with revolvers and knives and turned the banquet into a bloodbath. One child who managed to escape told the story to a priest and eventually the crime was discovered. A government committee found the remains mixed with dog bones buried near the house in a common grave.

The criminals were caught and brought to trial in the frontier city of Villavicencio in 1970. The climactic moment of the trial came when the defense attorney with a penchant for the spectacular brought in a large and heavy trunk and, placing it in the midst of the courtroom, said: "In this trunk I have the full proof of the innocence of the accused." What he produced thereafter was a number of large tomes of history, records, and documents which showed, according to him, that the Colombian history is filled with important people who at one time or another have killed Indians: generals, presidents of the country, heroes of the war of independence and even bishops and priests who killed Indians in the past. Therefore, he concluded, the cowboys were on trial not because they had killed a few Indians but because they were poor and illiterate. He went on to question the defendants one by one and all answered in the same fashion: "We did not know that killing Indians was a crime." The implication was that Indians had always been considered part of "the wild," the untamed and dangerous nature surrounding the human and civilized society, and that taming or killing them was part of the civilizing process, not a crime.

The second anecdote refers to an incident of Indian protest which I personally witnessed in 1971, in the small town of Ortega, Colombia. The Indian peasants of the area are nationally known for their struggles to maintain their lands since ancient times. One Sunday morning the Yaima family and other Indian peasants confronted the mayor, refusing to pay land taxes. Their reason was quite clear: As Indians they were protected by the special legislation on Indians which excludes them from many civil rights but also exempts them from paying land taxes. A heated argument ensued in which the mayor tried to convince the peasants that the "special legislation" did not apply to them because it was obvious that they were already "civilized," not Indians. They spoke only Spanish, they wore regular clothes, they belonged to the Catholic faith, and some among them even knew how to read and write! But the peasants, to my surprise, denied vehemently that any or all of these things had destroyed their Indian identity. At some point in the discussion one of the Yaimas yelled to the mayor, "We are not civilized; we are not civilized!" I had never seen anything like this before—people who vehemently denied the charge of being "civilized" and who took pride in distinguishing themselves from "civilization."

Through the years the Indians' own prophets and sages have interpreted "Western civilization" as unnatural and immoral. Civilization is artificial and violent: It destroys the earth as well as human life, it requires conquest and oppression to achieve its goals, and it inevitably leads to devastation and death. For the Indians this is the lesson of experience: "My race has been hated, cheated, persecuted, trampled under foot and robbed by non-Indian men [i.e., civilized men] ever since October 12, 1492."[2] White historians and chroniclers have also reported with surprise that "Indians fled from civilization."[3] Indian spiritual leaders have often indicated that, even though civilization may have some positive sides, it also seems to carry within it a *supay* (i.e., a demon) characterized by a strange compulsion to have more and more, to appropriate and expropriate the other, and to use the other as a means or instrument of its own acquisitive project. Some have also pointed out that this "demon" destroys not only the Indians but the civilized people as well: "When the white man does not have all of these things [i.e., abundant food and goods] he detests and curses his lot and becomes like the rotten trunk of a tree lying on the field, eaten by worms."[4]

Failing to appreciate the human dependence on the land, Western civilization has treated it as a disposable thing, as something external and alien. By turning the land into private property and by commercializing it, civilization has profaned the holy spirit inherent in the earth and also in the human being. These are some of the reasons why Indians see in "civilization" a death threat and in the Indian conversion to these practices the worst possible sin: "Indians who sell their land are like Judas Iscariot who sold our Lord."[5]

Christian prophets have also called attention to these facts since the earliest years of "The Conquest." Bartolomé de Las Casas, perhaps the greatest of all, reported in 1542 to the King the massacres and other crimes, "never before seen or heard of," inflicted by the Christians (i.e., the civilized) upon the innocent Indians "against all reason and justice." He also perceived the mechanism of perpetual misery and dependence that was being set in motion: "The Indians produce what is necessary for a day with a modicum of work, and eat moderately what is sufficient to sustain their lean bodies, while the Christians gobble up in a day what the Indians produce to feed a family of ten for an entire month."[6] No wonder Indians who had survived the initial thrust of civilization, reported Las Casas, were "dying little by little" in the institutions imported from Europe. It is therefore the premise of this chapter that Western civilization as we know it, especially in its consumerist form, holds no hope either for the present or for the future of the Indian. The solution of "the Indian question" therefore requires alternative spiritualities and alternative projects of historical development characterized by an ethos of solidarity and mutuality. The hope for the Indian lies in a change of consciousness, a cultural transformation on the part of dominant societies, including a fundamental religious and theological change that needs to accompany a new historical project for Latin American societies.

A Challenge to Liberation Theology

Historically, religion has played a powerful political role in Latin America. Either in alliance with the state, or in opposition to specific regimes, or as an independent agency of social and political activity, the church has been a factor in public life. One of the most effective and pervasive forms of political influence has been through the church's legitimation or denial of specific ideologies. The sociology of religion has documented extensively this ideological role, with its correlative implication that for major changes to take place the contribution of theological and other forms of religious ideology is a crucial one. This is particularly true regarding the old question of the humanity of the Indians as compared with the humanity of Western Christian peoples. At the formal level this question was resolved already in the sixteenth century in favor of the equality and freedom of the Indian. But in practice the theories of natural inferiority, "barbarian" status and suspicions of heresy prevailed, with the effective support of the Church. The Church's record on this point has been on the whole negative, both on the Catholic and Protestant sides. And it is not necessary to insist on it here since it has been exposed and denounced many times.[7] Dehumanizing ideologies have contributed decisively to the cultural and physical devastation inflicted on the Indian peoples of the continent. They have in effect cast a sentence of death upon the Indian race as a collectivity. Ethnocide and genocide have been practiced throughout the centuries and continue even today.[8] However, there is the astounding historical fact that the Indian people have not disappeared, they have refused to die, and today a theology of liberation is tested in its capacity to generate counter ideologies that affirm in theory and practice the humanity of the Indians and their rightful place in the future of Latin America. Thus, an ethic of liberation is one that not only denounces the idolatry involved in the Western model of development but also issues a prophetic call addressed to the national societies and to the Church demanding actions of historical repentance that involve just and effective restitution; it is an ethic grounded in the realization of the presence and power of God in the survival of the Indian communities as "testimonial peoples."

Testimonial Peoples

Two decades ago Darcy Ribeiro, the Brazilian anthropologist, introduced the concept of "testimonial peoples" or "witness peoples" to describe "the plundered peoples of history." In Latin America he referred specifically to the survivors of ancient civilizations (Aztec, Maya, Inca, and Muisca) that had crumbled under the impact of European expansion and who thus "entered a centuries-long process of acculturation and ethnic reconstitution."[9] Testimonial peoples is thus an appropriate historical and cultural concept, but it is also a concept capable of a theological interpretation that Ribeiro did not intend but that should not be left out of consideration. It has to do with the presence and power of God revealed in the historical experience of a people. Both "people" and "witness" (or "testimony") are classical theological concepts that refer to the beneficiaries and bearers of God's salvific grace. In the Old Testament those terms were applied by the prophets to the people of Israel, and in the New Testament the evangelists and apostles applied the same terms to the Church. The use of those same concepts in relation to the Indian communities suggests that their very survival in the midst of a civilization that has condemned them to death makes them bearers of grace and witnesses to the power of life over death. In the early stages of "The Conquest," Las Casas himself suggested this theological insight. Contrary to Gines de Sepulveda and to the mainline theologies of the time, which viewed the Indians who resisted conversion as "possessed by the devil," Las Casas saw the image of God in the Indians and considered them free and equal to European Christians. However, because of their poverty and innocence, and the affliction and abuse to which they were being subjected, they became an epiphany of Christ, a historical manifestation of the incarnation: "I leave Christ our Lord in the Indies being whipped and abused not once but one million times in the lives of the afflicted Indians."[10]

The Remnants

The Andean prophet Manuel Quintin Lame refers to the Indian communities surviving for centuries inside the conquering society as "the remnants" (los restos). This is also a classic theological concept and Lame seemed to have used it advisedly both in its sociological sense as well as theologically. He applied it to those members of the Indian race who had survived the cataclysm of the conquest and found themselves trapped or buried "in the bowels of the earth" from whence one day they shall rise to confront the colossus of Western civilization.[11] The interpretation of the conquest as the crucifixion and death of the Indian is a dominant theme in the traditional Christologies of the Andes. Some scholars find the same theme among the Amazonian tribes.[12] These Christologies tend to identify Christ with the Indian people and to view the Indian experience after the conquest as Christ "suffering under Pontius Pilate." Thus, "the ancestral shamans who founded the native cultures (e.g., Wanadi, Kuwai, Yabieri, Bochica, Incarri) come close to being identified with Christ, either as ancient manifestations or as native counterparts. In this way, native cultures become carriers of divine revelations."[13]

If these native Christologies lend themselves to ideological manipulation, as divinization of defeat, suffering, and resignation, native prophets see them also as forms of political resistance, moral reproach, and signs of impending radical reversal. By making Christ the creator of native cultures these traditions help the communities resist the pressure to integrate into white civilization and to affirm their cultural identity.

The Conflict with "Judas Iscariot"

The surviving Indian communities witness to an experience of God that is enriched by a most peculiar characteristic: it is inseparable from the communal link to the earth, to the sun, to the wind, and to the waters. Specifically, it is linked to "the land": "The land has always been the Indians' joy. They are betrothed to the land. They feel that life comes from the land and returns to it. For this reason the Indians may be indifferent to anything else except to the possession of the land which their hands and breath cultivate with religious sentiment."[14] This beautiful testimony, almost poetic in nature, is the observation of a Peruvian Marxist who found the world of the Indian too large to fit the simplistic sociology of doctrinaire Marxists and who was able to see the metaphysical depth of the Indian spirit as well as the true ground for their legitimate protest against "civilization." By appropriating and commercializing the land, "Western civilization" has violated the sacred core of life and separated Indians as well as civilized people from the ground of being. A Christian experience of God that is responsive to the Indian witness is one that shows reverence toward nature, that "tends and cultivates the earth" as a religious duty, that understands the command to "replenish the earth" not only in populational terms, but also in terms of preservation, sustaining, and caring for God's creation.

Toward a New Historical Project

The Indian question has to do with the present, and—more fundamentally—with the future of Indian peoples in Latin America. The present is the product of the sad legacy of the past, but the future is already present in struggle and hope. In the dynamic perspective of liberation history and of liberating activity, the hope of the Indian has a definite goal: the radical reversal of the history of suffering that began in 1492, with the earliest encounter with Western civilization.

In terms of political ethics, the Indian question focuses attention on the nature of the relation that should and could exist between indigenous peoples, with their distinctive history and culture, and a popular *national* movement of radical change that seeks to restructure the national society on the basis of economic and social justice, popular democracy, and collective self-reliance.

Several premises and tasks are involved in this definition of the problem: (1) The nature of the Indian struggle is seen as having two distinct foci: On the one hand, it is a protest against certain features of Western civilization; on the other hand, it is the positive affirmation of the Indian right to life, that is to say, to a future with land, cultural identity, and self-determination. (2) The nature of the national project of liberation is seen as one of inclusivity, economic and social justice, popular democracy, and collective self-reliance. In this perspective the relation between Indian peoples (tribes, communities) and a national movement of liberation should be one of both solidarity and autonomy. That such a relation is possible is the premise and the program of the indigenous mobilization that has developed since the 1970s throughout Latin America.[15]

It is in this context that revolutionary initiatives, such as the one advanced in the new Constitution of Nicaragua and its *Ley de Autonomia*, should be evaluated. In Chapter VI, the Constitution reads:

> The [Indian] communities of the Atlantic Coast have the right to preserve and develop their cultural identities within the framework of national unity, to be granted their own forms of social organization, and to administer their local affairs according to their traditions. The State recognizes [the] communal forms of land ownership of the Communities. Equally, it recognizes their enjoyment, use and benefit of the waters and forests of the communal lands ... [and] the right to the free expression and preservation of their languages, art and culture. The development of their culture and values enrich the national culture. The State shall create special programs to enhance the exercise of these rights.[16]

This project, which corrects the initial blunders of the revolution, proposes a program of cultural freedom and autonomy for the Atlantic Coast of Nicaragua which may inaugurate a new future for the native peoples of that country. It may also become a model for other national approaches to "the Indian question."

Notes

1. Bernard Arcand, *The Urgent Situation of the Cuiva Indians of Colombia* (Copenhagen: International Work Group for Indigenous Affairs, Document No. 7, 1972).

2. Manuel Quintin Lame, "The Thoughts of the Indian Educated in the Colombian Forests" (*Los Pensamientos*) in Gonzalo Castillo-Cardenas, *Liberation Theology from Below: The Life and Thought of Manuel Quintin Lame* (Maryknoll, NY: Orbis Books, 1987), pp. 97–151 (para. 118).

3. John Hemming, *Amazon Frontier: The Defeat of the Brazilian Indians* (Cambridge, MA: Harvard University Press, 1987), p. 297.

4. Lame, "The Thoughts of the Indian," para. 146.

5. Castillo-Cardenas, *Liberation Theology*, p. 185.

6. Bartolome de Las Casas, *The Devastation of the Indies: A Brief Account* (New York: Seabury Press, 1974), pp. 42f.

7. V. D. Bonilla, *Servants of God or Masters of Men? The Story of a Capuchin*

Mission in Amazonia (New York: Penguin Books, 1972); Grupo de Barbados, *Indianidad y Descolonizacion en America Latina. Documentos de la Segunda Reunion de Barbados* (Mexico: Editorial Nueva Imagen, 1979); Gerardo Reichel-Dolmatoff, "El Misionero ante las Culturas Indigenas" in Robert Jualian, ed., *El Etnocido A Traves de las Americas* (Mexico: Siglo Veintiuno, 1976).

8. Robert Jaulin, ed., *El Etnocido A Traves de las Americas* (Mexico: Siglo Veintiuno, 1976).

9. Darcy Ribeiro, *The Americas and Civilization* (New York: Dutton & Co. Publishers, 1972), p. 96.

10. Bartolome de Las Casas, *History of the Indies*, trans. Andree Collard (New York: Harper & Row, 1971), pp. 264f.

11. Castillo-Cardenas, *Liberation Theology*, pp. 78f.

12. Tod E. Swanson, "Sufriendo Bajo Poncio Pilato: Cristo en las Tradicion Andina y Amazonica" (Unpublished manuscript: Valparaiso University, 1988).

13. Ibid.

14. Jose Carlos Mariategui, *Siete Ensayos* (Lima: Biblioteca Amauta, 1967), p. 28.

15. Grupo de Barbados, *Indianidad y Descolonizacion*; Yves Materned, *The Indian Awakening in Latin America* (New York: Friendship Press, 1980); Jaime Wheelcok-Roman, *Raices Indigenas de la Luch Anticolonialista en Nicaragua* (Mexico: Siglo Veintiuno, 1984).

16. *Constitution of the Republic of Nicaragua*, Chapter VI, Articles 89–90.

Chapter 14

Feminist Theology
as Political Theology:
Visions on the Margins

REBECCA CHOPP

To be on the margin is to be part of the whole but outside the main body. As black Americans living in a small Kentucky town, the railroad tracks were a daily reminder of our marginality. Across those tracks were paved streets, stores we could not enter, restaurants we could not eat in, and people we could not look directly in the face. Across those tracks was a world we could work in as maids, janitors, as prostitutes, as long as it was in a service capacity. We could enter that world but we could not live there. We had always to return to the margin, to cross the tracks, to shacks and abandoned houses on the edge of town.

There were laws to ensure our return. To not return was to risk being punished. Living as we did — on the edge — we developed a particular way of seeing reality. We looked both from the outside in and from the inside out. We focused our attention on the center as well as on the margin. We understood both. This mode of seeing reminded us of the existence of a whole universe, a main body made up of both margin and center. Our survival depended on an ongoing public awareness of the separation between margin and center and an ongoing private acknowledgement that we were a necessary, vital part of that whole.[1]

Bell Hooks

Perhaps this notion of margin and center, at least at first glance, names the relations of feminist theology and political theology. For political theology — and by that I mean the white, First-World theology done in Europe and North America as a critique of bourgeois culture and Christianity —

has been done by those in the center, with full and easy access to the positions and resources of power, knowledge, and influence. Feminism, by way of contrast, is a voice from the margins, that is, a way of viewing and speaking that must always know both the rules of the center and the workings of its margins. Feminism is, as compared to political theology, a different way of seeing reality.

Women have been and are in Christianity and in our culture placed on the margins, repressed and oppressed as less than and other than men through legislation, cultural habits, forms of subjectivity, and linguistic practices. Though a small number of women have been "let in" (note the benevolence of the phrase), feminist criticism increasingly insists that women have been let in either to be "like" men or to extend their marginal roles as caretaker and silent supporter in low-paying professions such as secretaries, nurses, clerks, teachers, and so on. I want to suggest that if we refuse to define feminism in terms of the center, as letting women in, and understand its power as a voice from the margins, as a different way of seeing reality, then we have in feminism a theology that provides not only a critique of bourgeois culture and Christianity, but resources and visions for transformation.

But before developing feminism as a theology from the margins we must elaborate more carefully the relations between political theology and feminist theology. First, for both political theology and feminist theology, the personal is the political. That is, both feminist theology and political theology contend that there is an important and intrinsic relation between the way individual consciousness, or subjectivity, is formed and the political orderings of society.[2] Johannes Baptist Metz, for instance, suggests in his *Faith in History and Society* that the focus for critique in bourgeois society had to be around "evolutionary consciousness," while feminist theologians, drawing on feminist psychoanalytic and political theories, contend that the very distinction between the public and private realms is itself a political distinction, a way of ordering subjectivity and politics for, as Jean Bethke Elshtain termed it, "public man, private woman."[3]

Second, as I mentioned previously, the locus of feminist theology is different than that of political theology. Political theology is a theology of and from the center, while feminist theology is a theology from the margins. Now, I do not want to contend that feminist theology is from the margins in the sense that Bell Hooks has described, for her description is that of a black feminist.[4] There is, after all, no one margin to the present society, but a wide variety of places of repression and oppression. One cannot stand on all the margins at once, though understanding one's marginality may make one open to the marginality, and thus the specificity and difference, of others. As a white woman, I am related both to the center and to the margin, and as a feminist theologian my voice is explicitly from the margin, viewing, as Hooks would say, both center and margin.

Third, both feminist theology and political theology, despite their different locations, agree that transformation, not merely correction, is required in our society. Recall, for instance, the apocalyptic words of Metz in *The Emergent Church*, speaking of the need for an anthropological revolution: "This revolution affects the whole societal construction of our reality, of our political and economic systems."[5] Yet political theology has failed, at least thus far in its development, to offer resources for this transformation, attempting instead a type of apocalyptic critique in which the iron cage society, as Max Weber called it, simply caves in on itself, saved perhaps only by a God interrupting history from the outside.[6] Feminist theology, on the other hand, discovers in its marginality sources, images, and visions of new ways of being human, of loving, of living, and finds God working in these sources, images, and visions to transform the "main body made up of both margin and center."

Finally, before we turn to our present situation, I would like to raise the question if it is not the case that political theology needs feminist theology in two senses. First, political theology needs feminist theology to deepen its critique and broaden its basis of analysis not only of consciousness and the effects of oppression, but also of the rules, patterns and structures of how society has operated. Latin American liberation theologians have accused political theologians of a certain abstractness in their work, an abstractness due, I think, not to bad intent, but to failure to carry their critique deep enough into the patterns and structures of oppression in society.[7] Feminist theology (and feminist theory) takes its critique to the basic patterning of language, subjectivity, and politics, to how we form and constitute our world through patterns determining our anthropology, history, reality. Second, political theology needs feminist theology in order to provide resources for transformation. Warnings of apocalyptic doom are important and necessary, but finally politics, subjectivity, language — all of our symbolic reality — must be transformed in the present situation. To have an anthropological revolution we must find resources for change, new images of being human, new ways of relating, new visions of reality; and this, as I will illustrate, is precisely the task and nature of feminist theology in our present situation.

Feminist theology and political theology both begin on an apocalyptic note: As we approach the end of the twentieth century we are in a time of great crisis.[8] How do we describe the world in which we live? Death, control, destruction, deviance, force, manipulation, murder? If there are history books in the future, of what will they speak; what events will they choose to symbolize this age? The progress of science that results in a Hiroshima? Or in the foreboding nuclear apocalypse that threatens to explode the fragile force of life, dust to dust, ashes to ashes? Will our great-grandchildren know our historical period as the era of the modern state, with its hatred of the Jew finally fully manifest in the Holocaust? What is the crisis of the present but the masses of the poor, the poor with human faces, human hands, human hearts, human stomachs that barely survive? What is the present situation but apartheid, economic injustice between First- and Third-World peoples, the denial of women's lives through systems of violent repression?

The first characteristic of the present era, therefore, is that of systemic, structural injustice, an injustice characterized by the division between haves and have-nots, the structural crisis of scientific technology that can annihilate us, the crisis of structural inequalities that rob persons of their hope. But the present must also be characterized by the violent breakdown of psychic identity. The world we live in, the world of middle-class culture, can be characterized by runaway rates of depression among women (but also increasingly among men), rising rates of suicide among our youth, the massive suffocation of the brightest and the most promising in the professions and in the ghettos to drugs. Our society seems lost to itself, adrift in a sea of psychic numbing. Its tremendous drive for its own success through material prosperity has turned on itself, becoming now the ugly demon of consumerism: the empty desires of our hearts we try to quiet through the consumption of one more piece of clothing, the latest automobile, the newest colors in furniture, the new age in music. These goods do not fill the empty desire of our hearts: We are a people in need, in need of something we cannot buy, we cannot work for, we cannot will into existence. This is a description of where we are, a harsh description but one nonetheless that must guide our reflection. Christian analysis begins with an analysis of sinful condition, and this is our condition: destruction of humanity both on the outside and the inside. But we must press further to arrive at an analysis, one that draws upon sociological, economic, psychoanalytical, and historical literature, that uncovers how our society has structured what it is to be human, what it is to be in history, what values are held as natural and normative.

Modernity, the period that sets itself apart from the medieval world, was created by an intense focus on "man."[9] Modernity labeled itself as a movement of the freedom of man, through the tools of science and philosophy throwing off the hegemonic chains of religious and feudal authorities in order to celebrate the identity of the autonomous self. The self, the locus of true freedom, reigned supreme: reason, industry, government, science and even religion all reflected the identity of the self. This autonomous self expressed himself through history since history was the space and time of expansion, control, and manipulation through the strength and mightiness of the autonomous self. The values of the freedom of this self were individual autonomy, self-preservation, power of control, the progress of production, and consumption in history. From the textbooks of the philosophers to the assumptions of small businessmen we see the same value, desire, and drive: be a self-made man.

Of course, this construct of man, of history, of values was built on the backs of the oppressed; the progress and success of modernity had an underbelly of deceit, treachery, and subjugation. The material successes of the First World increasingly came to rest on the oppressed masses of the Third World: The wealth of countries such as Great Britain and the United States was in relation to neo-colonial relations with countries in Asia, Africa and Latin America. This autonomous man, who needed no one or no thing, depended on the private women who bore his children, fixed his meals, and provided a home of rest and companionship. The success of man's scientific and technological achievements, brought about in culture with no sense of moral responsibility to the whole, led to the development of weapons that could put an end to the world and of technology that could produce life beyond our moral ability to make decisions. The progress of history and the amazing feats of modern man outstripped our ability to be responsible to life itself. The autonomous man has created a monster that suffocates all meaning for the individual, is cut off from all relations, and murders life itself in the oppression of the poor and the destructiveness of modern technology.

It is difficult for those of us in, as Metz calls it, bourgeois Christianity to know what to do or say, for modernity is not other than us. It is us and we are it: tied by the fate of modern Christianity to the same values of autonomy, progress, success, mastery, and control. When modernity announced its independence from the church, Christianity was initially threatened. But soon Christianity became formed into a modern guise and came to represent the best values of the autonomous individual. Moving inward, Christian experience represented the individual self before his God, expressed in individual, private morality. To be a good Christian is to look like a good leading citizen. God becomes the guarantor of progress as God's providential role in history assures the progressive realization of man's enlightenment; things are getting better and better. God thus also secures the self, allowing the self, prior to any historical realization, to be accepted, to be secure.

Since religion became such a private affair, a matter between a man and his God, the church lost its communal, collective nature and became primarily an institution where individuals come for the meeting of individual needs. Americans, by and large, believe that you do not need to go to church to be a good Christian, and vice versa, the church, even in its own official literature, is understood as an institution to meet the needs of its members, rather than to proclaim God to the whole society. Christianity looks like culture, provides resources for the workings of culture, and continues the basic values of modernity.

Thus, Christianity, at least as we know it, struggles desperately to find any resources to address the crisis of our world today. Christianity has difficulty addressing structural oppression, for its values, views, and resources are geared mainly to individual needs. But Christianity also fails to address the psychic crisis of the middle class because such ills share in common the basic assumption of modern Christianity: The point of human life is for the individual to build and produce individual success, happiness, and existential meaningfulness.

Yet we must be cautious with our apocalyptic critique, for this focus of Christianity and modernity on the individual, on history as an expression of self-fulfillment and on the values of meaningfulness, happiness, and success have been the very tools that have allowed groups of persons to raise questions about their own meaning, value, and humanness.[10] The claims of freedom, the quest for personhood, the values of meaningfulness and happiness have been appealed to by Latin American liberation theologians, blacks and women. Indeed, the vision of the Enlightenment has ricocheted back to the groups it ignored, providing them with ways of asking questions, of clinging to their freedom, of looking for new ways of being human. As has happened in other historical situations, in the midst of crisis lie the seeds of a new transformation.

Feminism, arising out of the crisis of modernity, provides resources for addressing the crisis. As far back as 1860, women were using the basic principles and terms of modernity about equality and full humanity to argue their case for equal education, full representation in political rule, reforms in marriage and family legislation and to oppose oppressive cultural practices. We can trace a brief history of feminism, especially in light of modern Christianity, in the following fashion:

Feminism first began as a corrective to society and Christianity, a corrective stating that given the basic principles of modernity women must have equal rights and privileges in society.[11] This form of feminism we can call liberal egalitarianism, and in many of the Protestant denominations it has resulted in the ordination of women as well as the increased participation of women in official leadership roles. Its premises are simple: Women, given the basic terms of modernity, have every right and responsibility to express themselves as "equal" human beings. Women are full human beings and thus must use history to express themselves and find meaning. Yet, as women began to be let into the system as full human beings, they were expected to act just like men, and the feminism question then took a particular turn: What do women bring? Do women, now contributing as equal human beings in the public realm, have particular gifts, uniqueness, talents? For many women, frustrated in the exhausting fight to gain equality, this led to a second approach, renouncing the system, celebrating women's uniqueness, and, in Christianity, advocating a move beyond the church as patriarchical. Yet this position of romantic separatism was inaccessible to most women, for it is extremely difficult if not impossible to remove oneself from the surrounding linguistic, cultural, economic and political systems. Indeed, as feminism matured into its third decade in the 1980s, it began to realize that its theoretical reflections must find new ways to address the reality of women in the late twentieth century.[12]

In this context, the third space of feminism is being born, a feminism that seeks to speak to the cultural reality of crisis by using the marginality of women to revision the whole. Here feminism is a reflection, based on women's experience, of what it is to be human, what values are to be stressed, how history—space and time—are to be understood. This is a reflection for women, but also for men, for it suggests that on the margins of our cultural and Christian reality, the margins of modernity, lie alternative visions of God and world, visions that stir with fire, visions that speak to the diseases and crises of modernity. This perspective seeks to address our cultural crisis by listening to the voices of women who offer different views of what it is to be human, and what values are to be privileged, views based on the journey of women and God that may help speak to what Hooks called "a main body made up of both margin and center."

There are three characteristics of women's marginality that I wish to draw upon to guide us in opposing the terms of humanity, history, and values in the modern order and finding an adequate vision to guide us into the future. I do not mean to suggest these are the only characteristics possible or necessary but merely to suggest that they can contribute—in the churches and the culture at large—to a relevant and powerful vision that can serve to guide us out of the present crisis into new ways of being and doing in history.

The first characteristic of women's marginality that I would like to draw upon is simply the determination of what it is to be human. Against the autonomous man of the Enlightenment, the one who must conquer history to be successful, women have lived their lives as human beings in mutuality, fostering nurturing relationships instead of seeking dominance. To be human for a woman has been intimate involvement with familial relationships and close friendships, for mutuality connotes a balance of relationships and caring. I do not want to suggest that women continue carrying the burden of mutuality in the private realm only, for its restriction to family and friends has made mutuality politically ineffective. I want to suggest that this traditional defining characteristic of women be given political expression, that it be privileged over the values of autonomy and dominance, that we discover and create a view of human personhood that stresses mutuality, indeed solidarity, with other human beings. In relation to this view of humanity, we can again speak of God not as the agent of our autonomy, not as the guarantor of our dominance, but as the God of mutual self-giving and harmony.[13] Our image of God is the focus of our central values. Speaking out of women's experience, can we not value the God of mutuality and solidarity?

The second view I would like to suggest is of women's space and time, a space and time I would like to suggest is characterized by space of adornment and embodiment of time and cycle and cosmos. It is important to remember that both Christian tradition (in the writings of Augustine for example) and modernity (in the writings of philosophers such as Kant) are concerned with space and time, for our views of space and time exemplify and express how we live in history. In modernity, women have been given the space of physicality, of embodiment, of being connected to earth, to house, to body. For women, this has to some extent been a source of great anguish, for we have been said to be less intellectual, less capable, less strong than men because we are closer to physical nature. But it is also a space of great importance today, for it provides us with a vision of embodiment, of living in relation to our bodies and to the earth, that is desperately needed in a day when physical existence and the earth itself are threatened with annihilation and destruction. To women has been given not only living in embodied space, but adorning space and celebrating the beautiful. At times this too has been a burden on women, as women have been told to look certain ways and to fix the home in certain ways. But it also suggests a value for us all, a value that we must perhaps transform to serve for all as an antidote to the ugliness of the present crisis. This is the space of celebrating the beautiful and adorning with beauty the physicality of God's creation. Worship is after all but an act of adornment, an act of celebrating the highest beauty.

Woman's time has not been marked by the theme of progress, improvement, the march of the better and better, as has man's time in modernity. Rather woman's time has been marked, especially in motherhood, by cycles of natural rhythm, the time of harmony with the earth and with God, the time of birth and new creation. Cosmic time is a time of giving birth, and like cyclical time, is seen as a time of God, a time of new beginning: In every birth, the world is created anew. I am not suggesting that motherhood is a value somehow unique to Christianity; rather I am suggesting that it is necessary for all of us to learn something about being in time from the act of motherhood: the radical justification implicit in being given life, the act of creating anew, the celebration of specificity in each unique birth, the acceptance of difference in each birth—the same, and yet always different. Against a vision of history where space and time are viewed as dominance, control, manipulation, we need to offer a vision of space as embodiment and beauty, of time as cycle and celebration. We need to understand history as the site of specificity and difference, of embodiment and of beauty, as the place where worship takes place, where we are justified to live and do not have to justify our space and time by conquering all that is within our path.

Finally, women's religious experience—what I would like to call woman's practical Christianity—can give us an alternative way to construe Christianity. Several decades of reflection on women and religious experience in Christianity indicate that women experience the Christian faith in ways different than men do, if man's experience is adequately represented in religious and theological literature. Women experience God not in terms of the wholly other, limited experiences, and existential crises, but in terms of day-to-day practical experiences of caring and nurturing their families, churches and communities. Women have had a place of residency with God in the day-to-day living out of family systems, caring for the wounded, giving

birth, and feeding souls and bodies.[14] Many women have found these practices deeply satisfying and in the midst of this day-to-day existence neither
need nor desire spiritual crisis experiences or eruptive interventions in their
lives by God. Women express their piety and knowledge of God in the
language of caring for and with, rather than the language of the *mysterium
tremendum* and the wholly other. The nexus of religious experiences is in
and through relationships: friends, families, memories of the dead. Could
the vision of Christianity today, a time desperate for caring, nurturing, and
relating, come from women's everyday walk with God? Could Christianity,
which has accommodated itself to securing the middle-class subject and to
reflecting the cultural values, experience its own conversion by learning
from a most unlikely source: the experience of women?

But does this vision from the margins really make any sense or have any
real relevance when we are talking about the need for total cultural transformation? Perhaps what we need is structural change, corrections to our
institutions, a refashioning of basic laws. With all of this, I would agree.
But any societal change, just as any individual change, will only come out
of new cultural values, new visions of what it is to be human. These are
the most fundamental questions of all. Correcting our institutions will not
cure the present crisis until we have new visions of humanity, God, freedom,
and history.[15] Structural change is important, and must continue while the
fire of the Spirit stirs our testimonies of freedom. But the genuinely new
can only be born out of new visions of human hope, faith, and love.

To speak politically and theologically, I have argued, begins with seeing
reality differently. In this, feminist theology not only sounds the apocalyptic
warning of political theology, but critically exposes the particular ordering
patterns and practices which have brought us to this present crisis. Yet,
from the margin, feminist theology also finds new visions, images, poems,
songs. For those long silenced—assigned the unimportant tasks of nurturing, beautifying, being with and for, adorning, relating, hoping and loving—
must now speak for the main body, made up of both margin and center.

Notes

1. Bell Hooks, *Feminist Theory: From Margin to Center* (Boston: South End
Press, 1984), p. ix.
2. While political theologians have drawn their resources for such criticism
from the Frankfurt School of ideology critique, feminist theology increasingly has
combined ideology critique with the resources of poststructuralism, especially
through the influence of French feminism. For two interpretations of ideology critique see David Held, *Introduction to Critical Theory: Horkheimer to Habermas*
(Berkeley and Los Angeles: University of California Press, 1980) and Paul Connerton, *The Tragedy of Enlightenment: An Essay on the Frankfurt School* (Cambridge:
Cambridge University Press, 1980). For interpretations of feminism and poststruc-
tualism see Toril Moi, *Textual/Sexual Politics: Feminist Literary Theory* (London and

New York: Methuen, 1985) and Christ Weedon, *Feminist Practice and Poststructuralist Theory* (Oxford: Basil Blackwell, 1987).

3. Johannes Baptist Metz, *Faith in History and Society: Toward a Practical Fundamental Theology*, trans. David Smith (New York: Crossroad, 1980); and Jean Bethke Elshtain, *Public Man, Private Woman: Women in Social and Political Thought* (Princeton: Princeton University Press, 1981).

4. Hooks contends that white women are part of the center, and blacks are the margin. I think this fails to understand the patterning and rules of the center and margin distinction. Surely, in biblical myths women and the margin are identical. For in these stories it is men who are the dominant figures in the religious community, the ones who represent the community and with whom God speaks. This same monotheistic ordering continues itself in modern Western society, though now through the distinction of the "public" realm and the "private" realm. See Julia Kristeva, "Chinese Women" and "Women's Time" in *The Kristeva Reader*, ed. Toril Moi (New York: Columbia University Press, 1986), pp. 138–59 and 187–213.

5. Johannes Baptist Metz, *The Emergent Church: The Future of Christianity in a Postbourgeois World*, trans. Peter Mann (New York: Crossroad, 1981), pp. 36–37.

6. See my *Praxis of Suffering: An Interpretation of Liberation and Political Theologies* (Maryknoll, NY: Orbis Books, 1986), pp. 144–48. German political theology, following the Frankfurt School, comes close to portraying society as an "iron cage," where little change and transformation can take place without a radical alternative vision. This is due, in part, to not paying enough attention to the ambiguities in culture which provide the resources of transformation, to relying on German idealism's appeals to consciousness for enlightenment and change, and to the lack of an adequate social theory incorporated into the theologies. See Connerton, *The Tragedy of Enlightenment*, pp. 107–39.

7. José Míguez Bonino illustrates this type of criticism in reference to the work of Jürgen Moltmann: "But is it possible to claim a solidarity with the poor and to hover above the right and left as if that choice did not have anything to do with the matter?" *Doing Theology in a Revolutionary Situation* (Philadelphia: Fortress Press, 1975), p. 148.

8. Rosemary Radford Ruether has been the leading feminist theologian to sound the social-cultural critique in the context of the interrelatedness of issues having to do with sexism, racism, environmental destruction, economic injustice, and so on. See her *To Change the World: Christology and Cultural Criticism* (New York: Crossroad, 1981) and *Sexism and God-Talk: Toward a Feminist Theology* (Boston: Beacon Press, 1983), esp. pp. 259–66.

9. Note that Metz's early work traced this turn to an anthropocentric universe in *Theology of the World*, trans. William Glen-Doepel (New York: Seabury, 1973).

10. In relation to feminism, see Zillah R. Eisenstein, *The Radical Future of Liberal Feminism* (Boston: Northeastern University Press, 1981).

11. Kristeva, *The Kristeva Reader*, pp. 193–95.

12. I am referring here to the second wave of feminism in the United States that developed in the 1960s. See Hester Eisenstein, *Contemporary Feminist Thought* (Boston: G. K. Hall & Co., 1983).

13. To date, the most thorough-going examination of the themes of mutuality and connectedness in feminist theology is Catherine Keller's *From a Broken Web: Separation, Sexism and Self* (Boston: Beacon Press, 1986).

14. See, for instance, Mud Flower Collective, *God's Fierce Whimsy: Christian Feminism and Theological Education* (New York: Pilgrim Press, 1985), p. 65.

15. Julia Kristeva made this point succinctly: "In the twentieth century, after suffering through fascism and revisionism, we should have learned that there can be no socio-political transformation without a transformation of subjects: in other words, in our relationship to social constraints, to pleasure, and more deeply, to language." From the interview "psychoanalysis and politics," in *Tel quel*, Autumn 1974, and reprinted (trans. Marilyn A. August) in *New French Feminisms: An Anthology*, ed. Elaine Marks and Isabelle de Courtivon (New York: Schocken Books, 1981), p. 91.

Chapter 15

Notes on the Nature and Destiny of Sin, or How a Niebuhrian Process Theology of Liberation Is Possible

DELWIN BROWN

The claim of this essay is that there are no substantive differences between liberation theology, process theology, and Niebuhrian Christian realism regarding the possibility of radical social transformation.

This claim, if it can be substantiated, is important for more than merely academic reasons; it is *politically* important as well. Christians are unsure about what they may reasonably hope and work for in the struggle for justice and peace. These three theologies are among the leading influences in American Christianity, itself a major religious factor affecting, for good and ill, the global search for a better world. If these theologies can together affirm the realism of the quest for a radically better future, theirs could be a significant alliance. With one voice they could make a statement about the possibility of social change that few today seem to believe and all today need to hear.

"Liberation theology," as understood in this essay, is characterized by a central proposition and at least three or more derivative doctrines. Centrally it holds that salvation is inclusive and indivisible, embracing all the dimensions of life and not simply the realm of the spirit. In relation to history, it maintains that the qualitative advance of the salvific process is genuinely possible, and that this progress is possible in part because of human action. In relation to politics it insists that theology is partisan in the sense that Christians, as Christians, make particular political choices, even though no such choice can be simply equated with Christianity as such. In relation to sociology, specifically the sociology of knowledge, liberation theology holds that all thinking is perspectival and that authentically Christian thinking and theologizing must take place in solidarity with the poor and the oppressed.

"Process theology" refers to Christian theologies of a particular type, namely, those that use the conceptual framework of a process philosophy, such as A. N. Whitehead's, in the effort to give adequate, systematic expression to the faith of Christians. Process theology's ruling obligation, then, is to be faithfully Christian. Moreover, process theology contends that processive/relational categories are distinctively congenial to and supportive of Christian sensibilities. Hence this form of Christian theology reflects the two basic convictions of all process thought, namely, that becoming is more fundamental to reality than is being, and that relatedness is more basic than independence and absoluteness. These convictions also apply to God. Like all else, God is said to be in some real sense both becoming and relational.

By "Christian realism" we shall mean, simply, Reinhold Niebuhr's theological anthropology. Niebuhr's anthropology locates the human self at the juncture of nature and spirit, participating in both.[1] As a creature of nature, the self is "involved in the necessities and contingencies of nature." As a spirit, it transcends this context and is thus able to contemplate new possibilities, considering their promise and peril and contributing to their selective realization.

I. Thinking from Niebuhr to Whitehead

The anthropology Niebuhr espoused was not uniquely his own. Niebuhr's distinctiveness was the insight with which he utilized an ancient view of selfhood to illuminate and critique the political structures and processes of his day. In the situation he addressed, the problems of power, not powerlessness, were pronounced. Niebuhr spoke to a church, nation, and world mesmerized by and misguided about power's potential. Thus he focused on the aggressive personality, the self that exaggerates its participation in spirit to the neglect of its rootage in nature. By demonstrating the *limits* of human aspiration and achievement, and the destruction that follows when they are forgotten, Niebuhr sought to justify tolerance and compromise. His was a political theology of limitation.

Nothing in Niebuhr's anthropology, however, prohibits an equal concern with the problems of powerlessness, the destructiveness of the passive personality, and a concomitant political theology of aspiration. The self that is both spirit and nature sins no less, in Niebuhr's systematic view, by forgetting the one than the other. Denying the limits appropriate to being human is the sin of pride. But denying the possibilities appropriate to being human is also sin—as Niebuhr termed it, the sin of sensuality or sloth. While Niebuhr failed to emphasize this point, evil enters human life not only as pride's absolutizing of partial values, but also as sloth's indifference to potential values however partial they may be. Both, though rooted in the will, take on structural dimensions that finally envelop and enervate the will. Both may be and are hidden from the self by the self in that maze of self-deceptive strategies that Niebuhr himself so nicely elucidated. Both, in short, become demonic. To a church or world yielding to pride, exaggerating its potential, the Niebuhrian must speak of limitation. However, to a church or world yielding to what Christian tradition has called sloth, exaggerating its impotence against forces of oppression, the same Niebuhrian must speak of liberation.

Niebuhr's critique of pride was theological. Against pride he spoke of a God whose transcendence over all human achievements relativizes them all. The Niebuhrian critique of sloth or powerlessness, which thinks of itself *less* than it ought to think, must be similarly theological. And what kind of deity would unmask the pretense that we are nothing more than, and that we are captive of, the social and natural forces that form the context of our lives? The answer is a deity not itself bound to the status quo, a deity who pursues some historical possibilities rather than others, a God who rejects indifference, seeking instead to change the world. If, as Niebuhr once said, the demon of pride can "be exorcised . . . only by the worship of a God who transcends all partial . . . values,"[2] then it follows that the demon of passivity can be exorcised only by the worship of a God who is partisan. Thus, the latter God is no less required by Niebuhr's anthropology than is the former. In this sense, the God of Gutierrez is Niebuhr's God in a passive world.

It is instructive to ask why Niebuhr himself failed to emphasize the theology and politics of liberation implicit in the anthropological center of his own thought. I believe the chief impediment to a liberationist Niebuhr was Niebuhr's own concept of God and the God/world relationship. While his anthropology calls for a partisan God no less than a God transcendent, his theology and his particular (implicit) metaphysics cannot provide such a deity. If Niebuhr's God can "take sides," this is true only as God is within him/herself; God cannot take sides *in history* because Niebuhr's world is a closed system of causes and effects.

This becomes most apparent in Niebuhr's concept of grace. The primary emphasis in the Pauline view of grace, Niebuhr writes, is upon "grace as 'justification,' as the assurance of divine forgiveness." And this doctrine, Niebuhr adds, contains "the whole Christian conception of God's relation to human history."[3] Divine grace is also power for Niebuhr, but it is a power within the forgiven self as an effect of that forgiveness. It is manifest as the breaking of the "vicious circle of self-centeredness." But the resultant "new self" is one of "intention" and not of "actual achievement," or if the latter, it is an achievement in principle and not in fact. The dialectic evidently does not include actual realization, not even dialectically: "the Christ in us is not a possession," he says, "but a hope."[4]

Some years ago Paul Lehmann observed that Niebuhr's anthropology presupposes his Christology.[5] Given the fact that Christology hinges on a doctrine of God, this discussion only underscores Lehmann's point and notes its corollary. If Niebuhr's theology grounds his anthropology, it also sets its limits. His anthropology implicitly rebelled against the restraints of his doctrine of God, but the latter necessarily retained the upper hand. Whatever Niebuhr might have wished to say about divine grace as transformative power, whatever the neglected side of his anthropology might have encouraged, entitled, or even required him to say, Niebuhr could not say, because his implicit metaphysical system lacked a conception of God and the God/world relationship that would permit such talk. Thus, Niebuhr only replaced the closed-world optimism of nineteenth-century liberalism, which found substantive progress to be inevitable, with another closed universe, that of the "realist," for whom inevitability still reigns—the inevitable absence of any net growth of good.

What is required, if we are to give full due to both sides of Niebuhr's anthropology, is an alternative understanding of God. A conceptuality is needed which allows us to speak, consistently and coherently, of a deity who at once transcends every historical achievement, as judge over all, but who also "takes sides" within the historical process, as the partisan of some achievements rather than others. As transcendent judge, God would challenge every arrogant pretense that even our best achievements are more than *provisional* goods—to be sought and cherished for what they are, but also to be criticized and surpassed for what they are not. As immanent partisan, God would shatter every resigned pretense that our best historical achievements are less than provisional *goods*—to be scrutinized for their limitations and eventually superseded, but, in the interim, to be valued and defended for what they are. The dual nature of sin, in Niebuhr's analysis, requires the dual nature of God.

It is at this point that process theology contributes to the discussion. The process view of God allows for both sides of the Niebuhrian anthropology. Process theology does this by providing the conception of a God who both stands over, and yet is partisan within, the temporal process of nature and history. In the present context the relevant aspects of this view of God can only be summarized.

As primordial, God is the ideal envisagement of the infinitude of possible values in hierarchical patterns of order. Thus God is the inexhaustible repository of patterns of potential achievement. No one pattern can possibly embody all potential values, for all values are not compossible. In other words, no one pattern can ever be unsurpassable. Therefore, God as primordial (or abstract) transcends every conceivable historical achievement.

As consequent (or concrete) God is the preferential weaving of relevant ideals into the process of historical reality. Thus God is partisan, because all relevant ideas are not equal in their potential value. God is partisan, first, in the sense of *being for* some possible actualizations, i.e., being an agent within history. But God is also partisan in the sense of being for *some* possible achievements, i.e., being an advocate for certain alternatives rather than others. As Whitehead put it, God is that in the universe which works for right.[6]

To summarize, God as primordial is the transcendent Judge who, as surpassor of all partial values, "exorcises" (Niebuhr's term) the demon of pride. God as consequent is the immanent Partisan who, as champion of particular values in particular contexts, exorcises the demon of indifference and passivity. The process view of God, I am suggesting, provides a theological basis for the full development of a Niebuhrian anthropology. In doing so it opens the way to a Niebuhrian theology of possibility, a theology of liberation.

II. From Niebuhr to Whitehead to Liberation

We now must ask whether the Niebuhrian process theology of liberation said to be possible is consonant with the theology of liberation as characterized at the outset of this chapter. The central notion of liberation theology, I said at the outset, is that of the inclusiveness of salvation. That process theology shares such a vision is probably indisputable. Indeed, if anything, a process understanding of salvation, stemming as it does from a relational metaphysics, may be an even more explicitly inclusive vision than that of Latin American liberation theology; certainly it includes nature as well as the fullness of humans and their histories in its purview. For process theology, too, salvation "embraces all the dimensions of existence and brings them to their fullness."[7]

If we understand Christian realism in the terms of this essay, a comprehensive understanding of salvation can also characterize Christian realism. Existentialism's separation of nature and history was more or less assumed in Niebuhr's own work, but there is no evidence that his work requires it. Actually, the Niebuhrian and Whiteheadian views of the self are remarkably similar.[8] If anthropology is taken to be the heart of Niebuhr's thought, even as it is applied to sociopolitical processes in the form of Christian realism, that anthropology would not seem to be compromised by its insertion into a more explicitly relational conceptual scheme, such as that of process thought.

The more difficult question is whether Christian realism and process thought can accommodate the liberation claim that theology must be done in solidarity with the poor and oppressed. One could imagine versions of this claim that would not be acceptable. But this doctrine of the liberation theologians seems fundamentally to be the judgment that all thinking is perspectival, and the conviction that the definitive perspective of Christian thinking is the situation of those who are oppressed.

That thinking is perspectival is no less clearly a cardinal doctrine of Niebuhr and process thought. This being the case, the Christian realist and the Christian process theologian might well embrace the conviction that Christian thinking ought to be done primarily in terms of one particular perspective, that of the oppressed. Recognizing that all knowledge is perspectival, the Niebuhrian or the Whiteheadian might well maintain that in our time the "essential" Christian perspective—the viewpoint that must not be excluded and thus must now be made central—is the perspective of those who are in bondage.[9] In that sense, too, a Niebuhrian process theology of liberation is possible.

It remains only to discuss what liberation theologians hold to be possible in history, namely, personal and social transformation, or what liberation theologians themselves often speak of as "the emergence of a new humanity." Can Niebuhrian and process theologians affirm this possibility?

Process theologians *must* acknowledge the emergence of a new humanity, partly through human agency, as a genuine historical possibility. The Whiteheadian conception of the plasticity of nature and human nature prohibits entirely any notion of permanently fixed structures, good or ill, personal or collective—so much so that if Christian faith could be shown to be clearly and fully *in*compatible with any hope for qualitative advance in history, then a Christian process theology would be impossible. Like anyone else, the process thinker might personally be dubious about the realization of any particular prospect at any particular time, but there is an undercurrent of creativity within the process system which, if not forgotten, keeps that dubiety from becoming dogmatic. Moreover, if the Christian process theologian holds with the theologian of liberation that hope for historical transformation is central to the Christian vision, then his or her conviction as a Christian will no doubt energize what could conceivably be hope in a "mere" possibility. In short, Christian process theology, like Christian liberation theology, affirms the possibility of the real, qualitative growth of good with history.

But what of Christian realism? Can it, too, hope for a net growth of good? One possible response is fairly simple: (1) Christian realism is at heart Niebuhr's anthropology, (2) Niebuhr's anthropology can be placed in the framework of a processive view of God and the world, (3) this process view affirms the historical hope of liberation theology, and therefore (4) Christian realism may also share that hope. But is this response adequate?

III. A Concluding Unperfectionistic Postscript

If we understand Christian realism in the sense of this essay, the above argument seems to be more or less right. In fact, however, Niebuhr was more than a theologian, he was also a prophet, and Christian realism was more than a theological standpoint, it was also (strange as this may sound today) a prophetic stance. Prophets venture beyond the boundaries of systematic entailments; they hazard guesses about what is the case when neither systems nor the common opinions of their day are prepared to endorse their judgments.

Niebuhr's central prophetic insight had to do with the inevitable blindness of virtue. By "virtue" Niebuhr meant, principally, purity of motive. What he claimed, roughly, is that we can never reliably measure virtue, that when we attempt to do so we inevitably overestimate our own and underestimate that of others (particularly our adversaries), and that these miscalculations inevitably insinuate themselves into our various structures and systems—social, political, and the like—to culminate in an arrogance that becomes demonic, from which always comes destruction. Even if his analysis of virtue and its vices is not simply an extrapolation from some system, Niebuhr's perspicacity on this issue is uniquely prepared for by the spirit/pride side of Niebuhr's Pauline anthropology. Indeed, this insight into virtue's seductive devices might well be the special legacy of Pauline Christianity. Wherever this insight takes hold, all talk of a "new humanity" which is premised upon some known or knowable advance *in virtue* must emphatically be rejected.

But liberation theology may be understood in part as the re-Judaization of Christianity; as such, it reminds us that the question of justice is not identical with or secondary to the question of virtue. If the more introspective orientation of the spirit/pride dimension of Niebuhr's anthropology is particularly apropos to an assessment of private virtue and its proper limitations, the nature/sloth part of the same anthropology is especially suggestive for an understanding of public justice and its real possibilities. The Pauline emphasis upon the subjective dimensions of selfhood might have been entirely adequate so long as Christianity remained in a symbiotic (or parasitic) relationship with, and thus continued to be complemented by, Judaism. But the loss of its Jewish grounding historically requires that Christianity recover elements of Judaism theologically if Christianity is to regain the practical balance of the Pauline anthropology in its early setting. Liberation theology should be viewed as precisely that recovery.

So interpreted, nothing liberation theology wishes to say about the possible achievement of objective structures of *justice* is inconsistent with what Niebuhr calls us to remember about the subjective structures of *virtue*. Growth in virtue is not measurable and the effort to measure virtue is inevitably destructive. Assuming a partisan God and a malleable world, transformation in the realm of virtue must be acknowledged as a possibility. But that does not gainsay Niebuhr's judgment that such advance, if and when it happens, is unknowable, and that all efforts to know it are self-defeating.

Liberation theology, like Judaism, insists that it is otherwise with justice. And advance in justice implies a beneficial transformation of social structures, whatever the mixed motives and deceitful strategies that linger within them. Such an advance is a genuine good, bringing the created order to greater fulfillment. And a net growth in justice is really possible if, as

Niebuhr insisted, a knowable growth in virtue is not. Niebuhr's most stinging criticisms were directed against those utopians who envisioned a perfection of human nature or the achievement of social structures that transcend the contradictions of history. Neither is an expectation of liberation theology.

In assessing the prospect for social transformation, liberation theology, like Judaism, may suggest that we should be less concerned with inner purity and more concerned with the establishment of "living" or self-critical institutions of justice. It is perhaps significant that Judaism, taking this approach, could have remained so hopeful throughout a history so marred by its own oppression. Whatever the ebb and flow of personal virtue, the establishment of qualitatively better political and social systems remains for Judaism a genuine possibility. Framing the issue in those terms, Judaism has been able to hold that social transformation is possible, that our capacity for achieving a net growth of public good is in fact limitless. This is also the claim of liberation theology. It is, in a sense, utopian. Understood in this sense, Christian process theology and Christian realism can be utopian, too.

Notes

1. Cf. Reinhold Niebuhr, *The Nature and Destiny of Man*, vol. 1 (New York: Scribner's, 1941), pp. 181f.

2. Quoted in Dennis P. McCann, *Christian Realism and Liberation Theology* (Maryknoll, NY: Orbis Books, 1981), p. 31.

3. Niebuhr, *Nature and Destiny*, vol. 2, pp. 103f.

4. Ibid., pp. 110, 114, 125.

5. Paul Lehmann, "The Christology of Reinhold Niebuhr" in *Reinhold Niebuhr: His Religious, Social and Political Thought*, ed. Charles W. Kegley and Robert W. Bretall (New York: Macmillan, 1956), p. 254.

6. For a theological development of this view of God, see Delwin Brown, *To Set at Liberty* (Maryknoll, NY: Orbis Books, 1981), chapter 3.

7. Gustavo Gutiérrez, *The Theology of Liberation* (Maryknoll, NY: Orbis Books, 1973), p. 153.

8. David Griffin, "Whitehead and Niebuhr on God, Man and the World" in *Journal of Religion* 53/2 (April 1973): 156–59.

9. Delwin Brown, "Thinking of the God of the Poor: Questions for Liberation Theology from Process Thought" (forthcoming, *Journal of the American Academy of Religion*, 1989).

Chapter 16

What Would Bonhoeffer Say to Christian Peacemakers Today?

G. CLARKE CHAPMAN

It may be hard to imagine Dietrich Bonhoeffer as a "peace activist" in our sense of the term. Another label, "pacifist," was one which he applied to himself by 1932, and continued to do so as late as mid-1939.[1] But ought either term be generalized to include the remainder of his tragically shortened life?

A brisk discussion on just that issue arose in the 1970s in the English Language Section of the International Bonhoeffer Society. It began with the superb analysis by Larry Rasmussen, published in his *Dietrich Bonhoeffer: Reality and Resistance*, and its thesis that "Dietrich Bonhoeffer's resistance activity was his Christology enacted with utter seriousness."[2] Indeed, I would expand it to say that all his peacemaking activity was such an enactment, as an interplay of ethics with the rich complexity of his Christology.

Rasmussen then traces Bonhoeffer's lifelong pilgrimage on questions of peace and violence through several stages: Lutheran just-war thought in 1929, followed by selective conscientious objection, then a more categorical pacifism, selective conscientious participation in war (with the burden of proof on whomever would take up arms), and finally, in the 1940s, an agonizing participation in the conspiracy.[3] Having defined the pacifist as "one who always views the use of violent coercion as an evil and who rules out war even as a necessary evil," Rasmussen goes on to ascribe to the later Bonhoeffer a defection from such principles: "All the twisting possible cannot make the author of *The Cost of Discipleship* a volunteer for assassinating even Adolf Hitler."[4] He attributes this revision to Bonhoeffer's eventual turn away from a certain "asceticism" (i.e., perfectionist disdain for political compromise) and from "parasiticism" (i.e., a two-realms dependence by nonviolent purists on state coercion for their own safety). Dale Brown objects to these two terms as pejorative, preferring instead "witness to life" and a provisional "interdependence" of the old and new social orders. But Brown concedes Rasmussen's conclusion of a shift in Bonhoeffer's thought.

The problem, however, with emphasizing such a shift is that Bonhoeffer himself seems to contradict it. Writing from his Tegel prison cell and reflecting especially on his 1939 decision to return to Germany from the safety of the United States in order to share the struggles of his people, he stated flatly, "I'm firmly convinced—however strange it may seem—that my life has followed a straight and unbroken course, at any rate in its outward conduct."[5] Eberhard Bethge, Bonhoeffer's friend and biographer, likewise rejects Rasmussen's view, "as if Dietrich had moved from a conviction of non-violence to a conviction of using violence; for me this does not at all express what was going on. . . . Dietrich did not come from pacifism to be a murderer of Adolf Hitler. He encountered [instead] that the murderer had to be stopped."[6] To stand by, inactive, during the slaughter of Jews is to be an accomplice. Rejecting Rasmussen's interpretation as misled by a "luxurious individualism," Bethge holds that Bonhoeffer was consistent to the end: "I think he would have said: Of course I'm still in your terms 'pacifist,' even in doing this (participating in the conspiracy) and I took the guilt, I took all the consequences of not being on the successful side and being killed for it."

However, there is a cost to Bethge's spirited defense of his friend's consistency. That price is a diminished notion of pacifism, a prejudgment which invites the very charges of asceticism, parasiticism, as well as individualism. Such a pallid view can only serve to reinforce the conventional wisdom that dismisses pacifism as soft-headed, an idealism effective only when the enemy is gentlemanly (such as the British in India). But against the uncivilized or the unscrupulous, we are told, a resort to violence is the sole "realism."

Is there an alternate means to defend Bonhoeffer's "straight and unbroken course"? Dena Davis believes there is. Less of the "twisting" that troubles Rasmussen is needed, she points out, if one takes as central Bonhoeffer's serious interest in Gandhi.[7] The effect would be to infuse pacifism with a greater flexibility, a robust dynamism. Thereby pacifism could properly encompass the several phases of Bonhoeffer's "Christology enacted with utter seriousness" under the changing circumstances of his life.

Bonhoeffer first wrote of his great interest in Gandhi in 1928. By 1934 he was making plans for a study leave in India, to learn directly the spiritual discipline of *satyagraha*, self-sacrificial "truth/soul force." Unfortunately this dream was never realized; he was instead called to organize a seminary for the confessing church. But this did not end the theological influence of Gandhian ideas on Bonhoeffer's hopes. Davis suggests three striking parallels in their thought. First, both conceived of nonviolent resistance as a

positive, holistic force in the active pursuit of justice. Pacifism is not passivity that tries to distance itself from contamination or compromise. Neither neutrality nor acquiescence in evil are worthy of *satyagraha;* even
violent action would be preferable. "To do nothing for fear of doing violence is cowardice, in Gandhi's view, and un-Christian obsession with one's
own moral purity, in Bonhoeffer's." Second, for both persons, faith requires
being there "for others." Bonhoeffer voluntarily returned to Germany in
1939, and Gandhi reached out to the untouchables. The sacred is not sealed
off from the public realm, but is displayed and enacted in it. Discipleship
means "the hermit's cell is rejected for the prison cell."[8] Third, accordingly,
voluntary suffering and a willing self-sacrifice are intrinsic to the disciple's
existence for others. For Bonhoeffer this means sharing God's suffering,
standing with Christ in a hostile world, and for Gandhi this means the
vindication of truth by accepting injury rather than inflicting it on the opponent.

Granted, there are significant differences between the two men. Gandhi
was himself a member of the oppressed group he championed, while Bonhoeffer was not, so Gandhi had greater latitude in altering tactics or even
postponing a campaign. Also Gandhi was doubly blessed with long personal
experience in pacifist activism as well as the sociocultural roots for its support. Bonhoeffer had neither. Nevertheless, Davis says, what they share in
common—a positive and sacrificial peace-with-justice activism—sets the
tone for Bonhoeffer's lifelong pilgrimage. Already in his year in New York
City (1930-31) and among black Christians there, his avowed pacifism was
linked to a keen sense of social justice. This same conjunction, under the
blood-soaked urgency and the severely reduced options available under the
Third Reich, led quite naturally to Bonhoeffer's involvement in the conspiracy—even to the point of tyrannicide.

I believe Davis is correct in viewing this development in wider perspective than Rasmussen's sharp contrast between a categorical pacifism of *The
Cost of Discipleship* (1937) and the later conspiracy. Instead, says Davis, it
is *The Cost of Discipleship* period that is the anomaly, a temporary lapse of
the social activist element of his ethic occasioned by the narrow concerns
of the church struggle. But both before and after that segment of his career,
Bonhoeffer saw nonviolence as inseparable from active resistance in the
name of justice.

This is the extent of the debate on Bonhoeffer's "pacifism." Certainly
his own fundamental theology was complex and underwent some evolution—and all the more so because of his incarnational approach and the
dramatic progression of events during his adult life. Let us concede also
that whether and to what extent Bonhoeffer should be called a "pacifist"
is unresolvable, for the label itself is susceptible to up to twenty-eight meanings.[9] I prefer instead the word *peacemaker*—a term hardly less ambiguous,
but one which conveys better Bonhoeffer's holistic concern for responsibility and justice.

So what is the next step? How may we derive some guidance about what Bonhoeffer would say today to Christian peacemakers? I begin with three comments. First of all, there is no substitute for a careful study of his mature theology in its richness and nuances. It is not permissible to snatch a few quotable sentences out of context, whether from the challenging idealism of *The Cost of Discipleship* or the more somber tones of his prison letters. We must struggle instead to catch his basic vision of Christocentric existence.

What is of ultimate importance [in ethics] is . . . that the reality of God should show itself everywhere to be the ultimate reality. . . . Henceforward one can speak neither of God nor of the world without speaking of Jesus Christ. All concepts of reality which do not take account of Him are abstractions. . . . In Christ we are offered the possibility of partaking in the reality of God and in the reality of the world, but not in one without the other.[10]

Second, we must be true to our own time and place by seeking to understand the situation in which we are placed. This means immersion in a serious, multi-disciplinary study of modern society, but also and always in light of the new reality, the form of Christ in our midst. Third, to give some focus to these two formidable assignments, it would be wise to single out for special attention that segment of Bonhoeffer's life which most nearly matches our situation. Not that any two historical contexts can ever coincide, or that we ought to follow slavishly any theological mentor. But we share a hope that Bonhoeffer may nevertheless offer guidance today to faithful peacemakers. The remainder of this chapter will address this third task, the selection of a focus.

The problem is, which period of his career to choose? For instance, one might select "Bonhoeffer, the political resister" of the late thirties and early forties, in unexpected alliance with German military leaders who represented not the church but instead the ideals of Western civilization. What brought them together was not faith, but a common opposition to monstrous evil. In the case of such enormity, a theologian's role and even duty could be portrayed as reluctant collaboration with necessary violence for the sake of a higher good. Might this be the pattern that best resembles our modern situation?

For our brothers and sisters in the Third World, oppressed by entrenched and brutal power, this does indeed have relevance. Not surprisingly, Bonhoeffer the conspirator is an attractive figure for liberation theologians of Latin America and other regions burdened by neocolonial legacies, where options for democratic struggles and reform have been foreclosed by police-state repression. Liberationists would highlight such themes as the critique of religion in a world come of age, cooperation with secular allies as a penultimate path to the ultimate, a compression of modern piety into prayer and righteous action, a social ontology that supports an ethic of being-for-others, a defense of human maturity against all dehumanizing dependencies, and the deed of free responsibility which in extreme cases might involve complicity in violence.[11] While these themes are all rooted in Bonhoeffer's lifelong theology, it is evident that the above formulations are tailored to guide victims of a totalitarian state. In the last two decades, for instance, in South Africa and the struggle against apartheid, a keen interest in Bonhoeffer has arisen.[12]

For some others living in the industrialized First World, however, there is another and less defensible version of this argument. An image of Bonhoeffer the eventual conspirator could be contorted to one of Bonhoeffer the reluctant Cold Warrior. His turn to conspiracy in planning *limited* violence, namely tyrannicide in a police state, may be transposed to complicity in threatening *limitless* violence, the global balance of terror between two nuclear superpowers. Such a shift is aided by the commonplace assumption (noted above) that once injustice crosses a certain threshold, nonviolent idealists must exchange their naiveté for "realism." Diabolical enemies, it is claimed, "only understand brute force," and, as the lesser evil, such force is the only responsible choice. Thus might Bonhoeffer be enlisted nowadays to support nuclear deterrence, the credible threat of devastating retaliation—and implicitly as well as the whole arsenal of Cold War tactics.

This, I say, is less excusable than the Third World liberationist application of Bonhoeffer. Not only does it stretch his Christocentric theology beyond the breaking point, but it falsifies the historical analogy of that evil which is to be opposed. Even if one grants that at least one of the superpowers is a police state with crimes comparable to those of the Nazis, the Cold War is not a credible parallel to the contained ferocity of living inside Hitler's Germany. The situation of the early 1940s was not just a potential but an actual holocaust—administered efficiently by entrenched party control and reinforced by wartime conditions. By contrast in our day the evil is much more diffuse—geopolitically, ideologically, and stretching indefinitely into a future of nuclear stalemate. It is a far leap from Bonhoeffer's acceptance of solidarity with indigenous evil "here," in order to overcome it, to the scapegoating rhetoric about an Evil Empire over "there."

What seems to unite both Cold Warriors and Third World liberationists is their common appropriation of the late Bonhoeffer and his decision of responsibility in approving a particular act of armed violence. The chief danger in both is that of romanticizing this sacrificial deed of ill-fated courage into a precedent, a heroic display of Wagnerian proportions, which would legitimate the role of violence as ultimate arbiter in a fallen world. To the contrary, Bonhoeffer saw his role in the conspiracy in its particularity as no more than a measured and prayerful response to an exceptional moment with desperately narrowed options. To generalize beyond that is to risk seduction by spirits alien to a world taking form in Christ. In the case of the Third World there may indeed be occasions of such extremity, although that is not for us in the First World to judge. In any event, liberation theologians certainly do not glorify violence and rarely condone or even discuss it as a theme.

The case of North America is quite different. Here violence is routinely glamorized—in mass entertainments such as film and TV, in our frontier heritage and folklore, and in the very metaphors undergirding everyday language. This cultural addiction has captivated religion as well. The militant rhetoric of New Right preachers is only an exaggeration of mainstream Christianity here, which has long embraced self-righteous individualism and the "manly" virtues. Such a brew of Messianic nationalism, injured innocence, and crusading confidence hardly deserves any promotion by Bonhoeffer's example. To the contrary, it far more resembles the very ideology he opposed—eventually with his life's blood.

To recall our question: Which period of Bonhoeffer's career should be our prime focus? The answer for us in the affluent and industrialized West, I maintain, is not Bonhoeffer the political conspirator of the 1940s. Rather it should be Bonhoeffer the peacemaker of the early thirties.

The parallels of that earlier decade to our own, while partial, are also sobering. It was a time of neither war nor peace. War clouds were gathering, punctuated by brief incursions and surrogate bloodshed. At home parliamentary democracy was being undermined by social and economic unrest, racial hatred, street violence, and covert uses of power. The church was polarized but not yet hopelessly compromised and silenced. In short, unprecedented social evil was not yet a reality, against which only conspiracy could act. Instead it was an ominous and unfolding possibility, against which one should mobilize.

Therefore let Christian peacemakers today turn their attention to the Bonhoeffer of 1932 to 1934. His duties then as a youth secretary of the World Alliance of Churches gave him wide ecumenical contacts, and he used them in calling the churches to a peace witness. His speeches and writings of this period are well summarized elsewhere,[13] and space here does not permit. But we recall his insistence that the church's lack of trust in forgiveness of sins is the source both of its timidity in advocating peace and its excuses that we never seem to have enough facts for a specific moral judgment. Peace, he contended, must be the concrete command of the Gospel for this hour. Not that international peace is an end in itself, but it is a means (an "order of preservation") toward the end, namely justice and an openness to faith in Christ. The very struggle for national security is itself insecurity, assuring endless countermeasures.

> There is no way to peace along the way of safety. For peace must be dared. . . . To demand guarantees is to mistrust, and this mistrust in turn brings forth war. . . . The hour is late. The world is choked with weapons. . . . For what are we waiting? . . . We want to give the world

a whole word, not a half word—a courageous word, a Christian word. We want to pray that this word may be given us today.[14]

The word needed in those critical years of struggle for the soul of the German church was a new confessing of faith. Bonhoeffer believed the time of *status confessionis* had arrived. Granted, his use of this portentous phrase was not concerning peace advocacy as such, but the Jewish question and specifically the Aryan clauses.[15] But anti-Semitism was but one component of the broader seduction of the church by an alien spirit. That spirit was "totalism," an absolutist ideology necessarily incompatible with the Lordship of Christ.

Totalism, as defined by psycho-historian Robert Jay Lifton, is a misguided response to the decay of traditional symbol systems that earlier had shielded humankind from death anxiety. Totalism manipulates both language and persons in the service of some genocidal principle. It is a pseudoscientific attempt to enforce purity from contamination, suppress dissent, and gain absolute control over life and death.[16] The terror of death is averted by transforming it into a worship of death—which in turn is imposed on "others," outsiders and victims. Lifton describes fascism, with its scapegoating blood lust and death imagery, as a prime example of totalism.

Small wonder that Bonhoeffer saw this threat as a historic moment of *status confessionis*, i.e., an exceptional crisis which the church can survive only by rediscovering its identity and confessing anew its faith. Nazism demanded that singular and holistic loyalty which rightfully belongs to Christ alone. Militarism of course was part of that idolatrous passion. So Bonhoeffer's peace advocacy should be viewed in light of his opposition to the supreme totalism of his day, a threat which called for nothing less than a renewed confession of faith and a redefined church.

What then would Bonhoeffer say today to Christian peacemakers? He would, I believe, denounce once again the totalism that endangers peace. That is, he would brush aside the tactical, the political, and perhaps even the moral arguments about the Bomb which are common today. Instead he would push decisively to the theological core of the matter: the idolatry that befuddles minds, the new form of totalism which displaces Christ. For us, in this time and place, it is not fascism that is the issue. Nor, arguably, is it even Communism. Instead the totalism we confront is "nuclearism," which Lifton defines as "the passionate embrace of nuclear weapons as a solution to death anxiety and a way of restoring a lost sense of immortality. Nuclearism is a secular religion, a total ideology in which 'grace' and even 'salvation'—the mastery of death and evil—are achieved through the power of a new technological deity."[17]

The issue above all is a theological one: What (or better, Who) is the final reality, in its wholeness and ultimacy? Elsewhere I have argued at length that not only is nuclearism today a thriving and functional religion, but the virulent heresy of our time.[18] This totalism arises from the boundless effects of the Bomb and our morbid fascination with mass destruction. Its idolatry rivals that of Nazism. Yet the church has hardly come to grips with the Bomb on a theological level. Rather it limits itself to piecemeal and inconclusive critiques of nuclear weapons on the moral level.

But we know Bonhoeffer to be a "theologian of reality."[19] He insisted the world has been restructured by the presence of God within it, in the form of Jesus Christ, and so the Christian life is one of formation around and in response to this new reality. His description of the fourfold structure of the responsible life includes "correspondence to reality,"[20] that is, to the profoundly Christocentric reality of the world which is embodied in, yet transcendent to, everyday "facts." This vision of "the real," therefore, simply cannot be harmonized with totalism of any sort, whether Nazi or nuclearist.

Here then is Bonhoeffer's prime contribution to peacemaking today. The peace movement will continue to be ineffective so long as it remains on the level of political or moral discourse, ignoring the deeply religious fascinations and fears commanded by nuclearism. A demonic totalism will persist, immune to every argument, until it can be exorcised by a church renewed in its confession of faith in the One who came among us, forming the structure of reality and calling us to responsibility. It is from this vantage point that we can understand peace, not as a problem, but as God's command. "We want to pray that this word may be given us today."

Notes

1. See Eberhard Bethge, *Dietrich Bonhoeffer: Theologian, Christian, Contemporary* (London: Collins, 1970), p. 155. For the best summary of the textual evidence on this subject, see Dale W. Brown, "Bonhoeffer and Pacifism," *Manchester College Bulletin of the Peace Studies Institute* 11:1 (June 1981): 32–43.

2. Larry Rasmussen, *Dietrich Bonhoeffer: Reality and Resistance* (Nashville: Abingdon Press, 1972), p. 15.

3. Rasmussen, *Dietrich Bonhoeffer*, pp. 95–116; see Brown, p. 38f.

4. Rasmussen, *Dietrich Bonhoeffer*, p. 120; see pp. 120–24.

5. Dietrich Bonhoeffer, "11 April 1944" in *Letters and Papers from Prison*, enlarged edition, edited by Eberhard Bethge (New York: Macmillan, 1972), p. 272.

6. Eberhard Bethge, in *Newsletter* #12 (April 1978), International Bonhoeffer Society for Archive and Research, English Language Section, pp. 6–7.

7. Dena Davis, "Gandhi and Bonhoeffer," *Manchester College Bulletin of the Peace Studies Institute* 11:1 (June 1981): 44–49.

8. Ibid, p. 46.

9. See John H. Yoder, *Nevertheless* (Scottdale, PA: Herald Press, 1976).

10. Dietrich Bonhoeffer, *Ethics*, edited by Eberhard Bethge (New York: Macmillan, 1965), pp. 188, 194f.

11. See G. Clarke Chapmann Jr., "Bonhoeffer: Resource for Liberation Theology," *Union Seminary Quarterly Review* 36:4 (Summer 1981): 225–42; and Julio de Santa Ana, "The Influence of Bonhoeffer on the Theology of Liberation," *The Ecumenical Review* 28:2 (April 1976): 188–97.

12. See the several important writings of John W. deGruchy on South Africa, available through Wm. B. Eerdmans Publishing Co., and especially his *Bonhoeffer and South Africa: Theology in Dialogue* (Grand Rapids, MI: Eerdmans, 1984). Also Eberhard Bethge, *Bonhoeffer: Exile and Martyr*, ed. John W. deGruchy (New York: Seabury, 1975). In this book, deGruchy remarks that it is Bonhoeffer's earlier writings that seem more relevant to the South African situation (p. 41).

13. See Brown, Davis, and Rasmussen. Also see F. Burton Nelson, "The Relationship of Jean Lasserre to Dietrich Bonhoeffer's Peace Concerns in the Struggle of the Church and Culture," *Union Seminary Quarterly Review* 40:1–2 (1985): 71–84; Keith W. Clements, *A Patriotism for Today: Dialogue with Dietrich Bonhoeffer* (Bristol, England: Bristol Baptist College, 1984), especially pp. 116–26.

14. Bonhoeffer, "The Church and the Peoples of the World" in *No Rusty Swords*, Fontana edition (London: Collins, 1970), pp. 286f.; see "A Theological Basis for the World Alliance," *No Rusty Swords*, pp. 153–69; Bethge, *Dietrich Bonhoeffer*, pp. 158–60, 167.

15. See his correspondence with Barth, *No Rusty Swords* (Fontana edition), pp. 226–28, and the declaration he and Martin Niemöller sent out, pp. 244f.

16. Robert J. Lifton, *The Broken Connection: On Death and the Continuity of Life* (New York: Basic Books, Harper & Row, 1983), pp. 293–334, especially pp. 297–301.

17. Ibid., p. 369.

18. G. Clarke Chapman, Jr., *Facing the Nuclear Heresy: A Call for Reformation* (Elgin, IL: Brethren Press, 1986).

19. This is the subtitle of Andre Dumas' book, *Dietrich Bonhoeffer* (New York: Macmillan, 1971); see Bonhoeffer, *Ethics*, pp. 188–213.

20. Bonhoeffer, *Ethics*, pp. 227–35.

Chapter 17

Military Realities and Teaching the Laws of War

JOHN H. YODER

The following is an effort to summarize the learnings derived from teaching university courses on "The Legality and Morality of War," working initially with a colonel, a professor of law, and a philosopher as team-teaching colleagues.[1] That experience puts to the test some assumptions basic to the credibility of our nation as a morally committed community. Can future military decision makers be taught? Can the principles underlying right legal and moral decisions be taught?

Numerous challenges have been addressed from alternative moral and philosophical perspectives to the so-called *just-war tradition*, but the heart of the matter for present purposes is the question of internal pragmatic coherence: Can the tradition in fact work as an instrument of real political/moral decision? Can it lead a decision maker, whether a political leader or a field commander, to respect those values which ought to limit their defense of their own interests?

For present purposes it is immaterial whether we describe the just-war tradition as a classical, religiously buttressed moral system or as a modern network of provisions of treaties and positive law. Both ends of that spectrum, from the "moral" to the "legal," coincide in defending the intrinsic human dignity of all parties with whom one has to do, *including the adversary*. The Christian says it in terms of the love of enemy, whose dignity may be jeopardized only under numerous specified conditions. The secular rule of law says it in terms of the rights of the adversary not to be harmed, which may only be overridden by due process and in conformity with the rules. For the philosopher the two formulations are significantly different; not for the adversary, whom both formulations if respected will defend against our unjustifiable violence.

The *prima facie* effect of this principle is thus to reject violence in social and political relations. When violence cannot be avoided completely, then the indispensable fallback shape of the same principles is the bona fide application of a firm set of previously defined restraints.

The legal form of the just-war theory has been in principle the stated commitment of the United States at least since the adoption (in 1863) of General Orders 100, "Lieber's Code."[2] But is that commitment operational? Teaching the substance of the traditional system to future officers (and their civilian peers) has rendered visible the weak points of this system. Here I note *five* of them.

First, what happens when the just-war criteria cannot be met? If it becomes evident that a war cannot be won by fighting in conformity with the rules *in bello*, or that it was entered upon counter to the rules *ad bellum*, the system in both its legal and its moral forms calls the responsible party to sue for peace.[3] There is however in the American mentality little room for thinking about surrender.[4] On the contrary, an aura of mystical heroism surrounds going down with the ship. Thus, the possibility of honestly respecting the bottom threshold is vitiated.

Second, there is an evident tension in the use of the term "necessity." As this term is defined in the Lieber Code[5] and in the 1956 *Army Field Manual* 27-10,[6] it is a *limiting* concept operative only *within* the other rules *in bello*. Even weapons, strategies, tactics that are otherwise legitimate according to the rules shall only be used when indispensable to a justified end. In its more current usage, however, as is well argued by Telford Taylor[7] and Richard Wasserstrom,[8] the term "necessity" has come to be used as another word for "utility." In lay terms, "don't break the rules unless you *really* have to," whereby the meaning of "really" is left to the discretion of the individual decision maker in a pinch. Thus to let a party to the conflict determine when he can be dispensed from the rules is to end the rule of law.

Third, if an unjust command is issued (which should never happen, but can in fact happen on any level), the just-war tradition calls any individual who knows that fact to refuse to obey. Nuremburg gave this moral obligation formal legal reinforcement. American civilian thought in the 1960s developed the concept of "selective conscientious objection" to make almost the same point. In actual articulation the concept was new for many of those who came upon it[9] although its logic had always been there.[10] "Selective objection" is probably a confusing term for it. It is not whimsical or intuitive. It does not appeal to "conscience" in any subjective sense. It could be called "legal objection," since the ground for refusing to serve is the illegality of what one is asked to do.[11] The moral logic of the concept is irrefutable. Yet the effectiveness of a military command system is predicated upon readiness to obey orders, assuming a basic trust in the moral reliability of the command structure.[12] Military educators and those who assign staff would rather have a person withdraw from the service as a conscientious objector (although he is not in fact strictly that) than have him continue to serve while retaining the right to determine in particular settings whether the orders he is given are just. Or his moral independence may be penalized by administrative transfer or denial of promotion.

Fourth, the effective implementation of the just-war system would call for wide and deep education both of the public and of military personnel. It should cover both the letter of the rules and their philosophical-religious underpinnings. That such education must happen is the very serious concern of some military educators,[13] but there does not seem to be the public auditing that would assure that it is going on widely.

Fifth, the most convincing and most simple appeal that threatens the rights of prisoners or the innocent would appear not to be the imperative of winning the battle or the war at all costs. Most students who envision themselves in future command roles believe that they could be realistically modest about the chances of victory. What they cannot envision is risking the lives of the persons under their command. Whereas both law and morality affirm the special jeopardy of military personnel as part of the meaning of their special role and status, the cultural common sense of our people tends to reverse that, thinking that if they risk their lives in battle, combatants should be free to have less respect for the lives of prisoners and other noncombatants than for their own.

In labeling the above five factors as the primary pitfalls in the way of teaching the restraints of the system, I have chosen to set aside some other factors which also matter and which would have belonged within a fuller treatment. These are no less significant as moral challenges, but they are not peculiar to the realm of our concern: (1) The factor of "team spirit," whereby members of a group defend one another against outside scrutiny and the rights of others. It is clearly important, and has been destructive (note the My Lai coverup), yet it can be countered and is being worked on in military education. (2) The absence of regular institutional sanctions, or social support for such sanctions, in case of infractions (note the Nixon intervention to undercut the My Lai prosecution). (3) The present ambivalence about how much authority military educators have to acknowledge open questions and to foster educationally effective open discussion in the hundreds of schools in the land where education in these matters would have to be done.

My present concern is with internal realism when facing the pedagogical task. In the wider perspective of "religion and politics," a few wider questions could also be raised: It could be argued that this difficulty of implementation betrays a conceptual flaw within the logic of the just-war theory at its best, which would belie the claim of the just-war tradition to reconcile pragmatic realism and moral accountability. It could be argued that, while the just-war theory "at its best" is of some use as an ideal projection, its effective application to provide restraint at the points named above is incompatible with the values that dominate American culture, or with the values of those kinds of persons who get into positions of decisive responsibility in American political and military decision making. It could be argued that, while the just-war theory is *ideally* compatible with stated national values, it is not compatible with the pragmatic prerequisites of effective structures and styles of communication and command.

From any of the above it might follow that someone who on general theological/philosophical grounds holds the just-war tradition to be valid might be called to a political stance rejecting modern military planning, *not only* (with the Catholic bishops) at the point of the nuclear threat but because the military enterprise as a whole, as presently structured, falls short of being able to insure implementation of the just-war disciplines.[14]

Notes

1. Theology 381 (also for a time listed as Philosophy 249) was offered at Notre Dame twelve times, from fall 1978 to fall 1987. Professor Robert Rodes (Law), Lt. Col. Henry J. Gordon, and philosophers James Sterma and Milton Wachsberg shared in its design. It now figures as a regular offering under the responsibility of my colleague, Professor Drew Christiansen, S.J. Dr. King Pfeiffer (Capt., USN, retired) described the experience in "An Interdisciplinary Course on the Legality and Morality of War" in *International Studies Notes* 9:4 (Winter 1982): 12–14.

2. What is usually called "Lieber's Code": *General Orders No. 100: Instructions for the Government of Armies of the United States in the Field*, April 24, 1963, is best available in Richard Shelly Hartigan, *Lieber's Code and the Law of War* (Chicago: Precedent, 1983). It is well interpreted by James Childress, "Francis Lieber's Interpretation of the Laws of War," published in *The American Journal of Jurisprudence*, Vol. 21 (1976), pp. 34–70; and in his book *Moral Responsibility in Conflicts* (Baton Rouge: Louisiana State University Press, 1982), pp. 95–163.

3. The logical imperative of surrender in this situation was stated by the most eminent and competent moral theologians of the postwar generation; cf. my summary in "Surrender: A Moral Imperative" in *The Review of Politics* 48/4 (Fall 1986): 576ff.; earlier more briefly in my *When War Is Unjust* (Minneapolis: Augsburg Press, 1984), pp. 64ff.

4. John Courtney Murray reported in his "Morality and Modern War," *Theological Studies*, Vol. 20 (1959), pp. 49–61, that the U.S. Congress has in fact legislatively forbidden any military contingency planning that would take account of the possibility of not winning.

5. "Military necessity, as understood by modern civilized nations, consists in the necessity of those measures which are indispensable for securing the ends of war, *and which are lawful* according to the modern law and usages of war." Lieber, Art. 14 (my italics).

6. "The law of war . . . requires that belligerents refrain from employing any kind or degree of violence which is not actually necessary for military purposes and that they conduct hostilities with regard for the principles of humanity and chivalry. The prohibitory effect of the law of war is not minimized by 'military necessity' which has been defined as the principle which justifies those measures not forbidden by international law which are indispensable for securing the complete submission

of the enemy as soon as possible. Military necessity has been generally rejected as a defense for acts forbidden by the customary and conventional laws of war inasmuch as the latter have been developed and framed with consideration for the concept of military necessity." *Department of the Army Field Manual FM 27-10*, 1956, pp. 3ff.

7. Telford Taylor, "War Crimes," in *War, Morality, and the Military Profession*, ed. Malham M. Wakin (Boulder, CO: Westview, 1979), pp. 242–26.

8. Richard Wasserstrom, "The Laws of War" in *War, Morality, and the Military Profession*, especially pp. 454ff.

9. A text on "Conscientious Objection to Particular Wars; The Movement of 1965–75 and its PreHistory" is available for handling costs from my office at 348 Decio Hall, Notre Dame, IN 46556.

10. Cf. the statements of Martin Luther in my *When War Is Unjust*, pp. 87ff.

11. Prof. Christiansen (cf. n. 1 above) prefers the adjective "legal" to "selective." It renders better the logical point at stake.

12. This kind of basic trust that the command structure in general will not go wrong would seem to assume a view of human nature which the ethicist would quality as "pre-Niebuhrian." It presupposes an affirmative answer to the just-war question of "legitimate authority."

13. Col. Malham M. Wakin of the Air Force Academy (cf. n. 7 above) and the Joint Services Conference on Professional Ethics, which he helped to found and helps to lead, represents this concern. Cf. Col. W. Hays Parks, "Teaching the Law of War," *The Army Lawyer* (June 1987): 4–10.

14. The Parks article (n. 13) demonstrates encouraging intentions and initiatives from the Pentagon on the level of stated educational goals. It is not clear how well the goals are met, how compliance in field decision settings is monitored, or how the civil citizenry can be a part of the process.

Chapter 18

The Universality of God
and the Particularity of Peace

JAMES E. WILL

Mystery and Complexity

To know Jesus as the Christ is to receive through him what only God can give—a power so creative that it brings creatures in all of their complexity and conflict to completion. It is to experience in and through him, and the communities that derive from him, what all personal therapies and social revolutions seek, and sometimes approximate, but never fully achieve. Yet we hardly know what we mean when we frame so comprehensive a thought. How can incomplete persons in an unfinished history know what the fulfillment of their personal and social lives might be? And if we ever experience so creative a power, can we recognize and name it? Could the symbols or concepts we use to name and understand it ever be adequate for its characterization?

Millions of human beings affirm Jesus as mediating the power of God. Given the variety of our human needs, however, it is inevitable that such ultimate power will be comprehended under many metaphors: to the hungry, Christ is bread; to the homeless, refuge; to the oppressed, liberation; to the culturally privileged, truth, beauty and community; to the sick, healing; and to the dying, resurrection.

Peace as a Meaning of Salvation

Our personal and social relativities especially affect the long tradition that has sought to understand salvation in terms of "peace," whether the *shalom* of Israel in the Hebrew Scriptures (Psalms 125:5; 128:6); the *eirene* of Christ in the New Testament (Col. 3:15); the *pax* of St. Augustine in the

Roman Empire (*The City of God,* XIX, 12); the confession of Allah as "the All-holy, the All-peace" (Qu'ran 59:23); or the benedictions pronounced as the completion of almost every Christian liturgy.

It is not surprising that this symbol achieved larger currency during periods of greater danger and insecurity. The Hebrew prophets expressed their most powerful visions of *shalom* during the eighth and seventh centuries B.C.E., when Israel faced devastation and deportation by the Assyrian and Babylonian empires. The evangelists of the New Testament witnessed to Jesus mediating an *eirene* that their "world could not give" just when Rome was destroying Jerusalem because of the zealot revolt. And St. Augustine focused on *pax* as Rome itself was falling to the Goths, bringing centuries of the *pax Romana* to an end. He wrote at that perilous time in a way that many Christians since have found fits all times:

> Whoever gives moderate attention to human affairs and to our common nature will recognize that even as there is no one who does not wish to be joyful, neither is there anyone who does not wish to have peace.[1]

Peace may function in the Judeo-Christian tradition as so comprehensive a symbol because its meaning is rooted in the concept of wholeness. The prophetic vision of *shalom* foresaw a society where the needs of every person would be satisfied in a covenant between God and persons and nature. The *personal* peace of everyone "under his vine and under his fig tree" is joined with the *social* peace of nations not learning war any more (Micah 4:3, 4), and the *natural* peace of the wolf dwelling with the lamb (Isaiah 11:6). This comprehensive meaning of peace came to its climax in II Isaiah's vision of the suffering love that "made us whole" (Isaiah 53:5), where the word properly translated as "whole" is *shalom.* The proper meaning of *shalom* implies personal and social wholeness. This biblical meaning of peace, however, is often the dialectical opposite of the actual historical and personal reality which the Bible also portrays. The breakdown of tribal peace in Israel's early history is portrayed in Genesis, when Joseph is sold into Egyptian slavery because his brothers no longer could "speak shalom" to him (Genesis 37:4). The dissolution of national peace after a brief epoch of Davidic glory is told in the long history of national decline and defeat following the division of the kingdom, because of the extravagance of King Solomon and the injustice of King Reheboam (1 Kings 7-12).

Human Limits and God's Peace

The human failure to achieve either the peace of personal integrity or social harmony is vividly recounted again and again in the Judeo-Christian Scriptures. Christians, nevertheless, have sought to express the meaning of Jesus for over twenty centuries in the affirmation that "he is our peace"

(Ephesians 2:14). Given our human need, it is no wonder that we have looked to Christ for this great gift; but by the same token, it is also to be understood that they, and we, have often misinterpreted the peace we have received in highly particularistic ways, distorted by the alienations and conflicts of our particular contexts.

Our human limits in expressing Christ's peace may be seen even in their earliest expression in the New Testament, as in the way that the resolution of the long-standing conflict between the Jews and the Greeks was formulated. Jews had known deep conflict with Greeks since the Seleucids, after the conquests of Alexander the Great, had sought to impose Greek culture and religion upon them, even to the extreme of compelling the worship of Zeus in the Jerusalem temple dedicated to YHWH. The Hasmoneans/Maccabeans had fought a long, and finally victorious, war to liberate them from this oppression. Nevertheless, Greek culture was rich and in many ways attractive, so that hellenistic Jews knew the struggle between Hebraic faith and Greek culture in their very souls. It is no wonder that first-century Christians received and interpreted the peace of Christ as overcoming this deep division. Paul could exult with the church in Galatia, "There is neither Jew nor Greek . . . for you are all one in Christ Jesus" (Galatians 3:28). And the Christians in Ephesus saw the basis for their social peace in Christ:

> For he is our peace, who has made us both one, and has broken down the dividing wall of hostility, by abolishing in his flesh the law of commandments and ordinances, that he might create in himself one new man in place of the two, so making peace (Ephesians 2:14, 15).

Yet this very way of understanding their peace, so attractive especially to hellenistic Jews living in the diaspora, bore the seeds of a continuing, and even heightened, conflict with the Jews, and Jewish Christians, who understood their everlasting covenant with God to be mediated through their law (the Torah). How could "abolishing" the Torah of YHWH—as expressed in Ephesians above and elsewhere (cf. Galatians 2:16, passim)—contribute to ultimate peace between Jews and Greeks? How could the universal peace brought by a Jewish Jesus be created on the basis of so conflictual a stance toward the religious foundation of his and their Jewish brothers and sisters?

The "Common Declaration" of Professor Pinchas Lapide, an Orthodox Israeli Jew, and Professor Jürgen Moltmann, a Protestant theologian of the University of Tübingen, after their dialogue in West Germany in 1978, puts this issue so poignantly that no Christian should any longer be able to evade it:

> The tragedy of Christian-Jewish relations lies above all in the fact that Jesus of Nazareth, who should have been "our peace" (Eph. 2:14)—

a bridge of reconciliation between Israel and the world of the nations—has become a trench of hostility. . . . When the teacher and the (later) teaching, the preacher and the praxis separate from one another so terribly, when the good news of the Christians could become the sad news of the Jews, we should pluck up our courage so as to place before us the basic questions: . . . Where is it really the Lord, the Eternal One our God, who separates us in all that which for so long has split and alienated Christians and Jews? And where is it we, with our handiwork and our human thoughts, who set up barriers and hinder a rapprochement?[2]

The Inevitability of Ideology

The divisiveness of our history is enough to convince many Christian thinkers that there is an inevitable ideological factor in any of our understandings of Jesus as the Christ.[3] That is, there is a factor, even if often unconscious, of self-interest and group-interest in the complex of feelings, attitudes, evaluations, and ideas that affect every theological formulation of Jesus' meaning for human salvation. And when "peace" is the symbol used to appropriate and express our salvation, this ideological factor is often heightened and always more dangerous. The contemporary German theologian, Wolfhart Pannenberg, has therefore concluded:

> . . . a separation between Christology and soteriology is not possible, because in general the soteriological interest, the interest in salvation, in the *beneficia Christi,* is what causes us to ask about the figure of Jesus. . . . However, the danger that is involved in this connection between Christology and soteriology has emerged at the same time: Has one really spoken there about Jesus himself at all? . . . Do not the desires of men only become projected upon the figure of Jesus, personified in him? . . . The danger that Christology will be *constructed* out of the soteriological interest ought to be clear.[4]

The Christian theological ethicist, Gibson Winter, has also addressed this concern by examining whether it may be transcended by using the modern methodology of social science. He examined the work of sociologists like Talcott Parsons and C. Wright Mills to identify the scientific aspects that may be common to a variety of objective considerations of society. He had to conclude, however, that ideology was inevitable even in the work of social scientists:

> They follow to differing degrees the procedures of the empirical sciences, and they attempt, so far as possible, to give a reliable interpretation of their findings. So far as these scientists suffer ideological

strains, and all to varying degrees undergo such strain, this is perhaps the human condition.[5]

Ideology is an inevitable dimension of our human condition, because we are finite, social, incomplete, and estranged selves. There is no objective, scientific methodology that enables us fully to escape this condition. So when we think theologically about issues of ultimate concern like salvation and peace, we hardly dare hope entirely to escape the self- and group-interests that inevitably affect our thought.

The ideological strain in all thought, including theology, may be more readily accepted as inevitable when we understand that we are social selves, constituted in part by the relationships we have intimately experienced. The security and stimulus provided by a family is the necessary context for our personal growth and individuation. The varying degrees of tension, rejection, and even abuse in these intimate relations, however, are the climate of anxiety in which our personal distortions and estrangement also emerge and develop. Deep patterns of affirmation and rejection of self and others, of moving toward or away or against other persons, of basic trust and distrust, hope and despair, developed in early intimate relationships, continue to affect feeling, thought, and action long after we have moved into larger spheres of relationships in our world. We may transcend these early patterns through personal growth in later creative contexts, but the continuity of unconscious and conscious memories in our personal histories allows for no complete transcendence. The child remains parent to the adult in us all.[6]

For this reason, the "honoring of father and mother" in the Mosaic sixth commandment does not only have moral significance; it also has a deeper theological meaning, directly related to the earlier Mosaic commandments that specify our relation to God our Creator. God concretely creates us through the biological and social processes we experience in relation to our parents. It is thus impossible to worship our Creator without honoring the relational context in which we have been created. No matter what personal inadequacies or distortions we may later think traceable to deficiencies in the way we have been parented, our family is still the primary context of grace through which we have been given our existence. Using a paraphrase of an affirmation sometimes made soteriologically about the church, we may assert ontologically that no one can have God for his or her "Abba" ("father" in Jesus' terms) who does not have the family for his or her mother.

The dependence upon culture for personal fulfillment in the context of contemporary nationalism explains the inevitable ideological strain even in our theological sense of "peace." The peace of personal integration requires some sense of harmony with the social wholes of family and society in which we have come to being. As social selves, we cannot know or even approximate any wholeness of being and personal peace apart from coming to terms with the concrete context to which we are internally related. No matter what degree of spiritual transcendence over family and society is later realized, every self-transcendent person remains continuous with the self initially created within a national culture. Our experience and expression of "peace" will inevitably remain relative to the national culture through which we have partially been given our being. Thus, national particularity will inevitably characterize even our most universal affirmations of peace.

Many "nationalists," of course, have no difficulty recognizing and affirming this reality. They expect peace only within national borders, which must be drawn and protected precisely for the sake of peace. To the extent that they see peace dependent upon factors beyond their national borders, it must be secured by diplomatically, or, if necessary, militarily extending the economic and political power of their state. In this nationalistic view, war is a possible instrument of peace, as the extension of national diplomacy by other means. From a nationalist perspective, any threat to one's state is an enemy of peace, and any means finally necessary to the removal or neutralization of this threat is in the service of peace.

Enmity Is the Enemy of Universal Peace

Any nationalistic understanding of peace, however, is profoundly incoherent with belief in the universal God. All monotheistic faith moves beyond nationalism toward concern for universal peace. Despite all contrary ideological tendencies, the peace of God in the love of Christ directs Christians toward more universal community.

The character of Christian commitment to universal peace has its clearest expression in the memory of Jesus' most distinctive teaching, preserved in the "Q" source of Matthew's and Luke's gospels: "Love your enemies and pray for those who persecute you" (Matthew 5:44; Luke 6:35). The threat to any particular peace is in some sense *enemy*; but the threat to universal peace is *enmity* itself. Universal peace may be achieved and sustained only by transforming all enmity. It is precisely the love of all enemies that finally vanquishes enmity.

God's universal gracious relation to the whole creation is the theological context in which Jesus set his teaching of the love of enemies:

> Love your enemies and pray for those who persecute you, so that you may be children of your Abba who is in heaven; for he makes his sun rise on the evil and on the good, and sends rain on the just and on the unjust. . . . You, therefore, must be perfect, as your heavenly Abba is perfect (Matthew 5:44-48; cf. Luke 6:35, 36).

The notion of perfection here attributed to God and demanded of Christians is closely related to the biblical sense of *shalom.* Our particular human loves must finally be transformed by experience of God's universal love, which embraces the whole and makes it whole. The universal gracious love of God knows no limit set by human enmity. The limitation, negativity, and estrangement created in particularistic human relationships are transcended by God, who calls us to transcend them in God.[7]

The revelation of God in Jesus Christ has usually been interpreted theologically with the theme of "salvation history" that runs through the Bible. But this teaching of universal love of enemies illustrates that much of Jesus' message must also be interpreted within the blessing tradition, grounded in belief in God as the Creator, which also runs through the Hebrew and Christian Scriptures.[8] God's redemptive activity, whether interpreted through the covenant with Israel or the new covenant through Jesus Christ as salvation history, must finally be understood within the context of God's creation and universal blessing of all humanity.

Divine Wisdom as the Basis for Universal Peace

In the Bible's universal wisdom motif, grounded in faith in one God as universal Creator, enmity is the evil to be overcome. The teaching in Hebrew wisdom literature is that the enemy is to be met with care and concern: "If your enemy is hungry, give him bread to eat; and if he is thirsty, give him water to drink" (Proverbs 25:21). Persons who share in God's universal creativity do not seek to vanquish the enemy, but to transform enmity, so that God's image may be actualized in the wisdom of all human beings.

The portrayal and interpretation of Jesus in the New Testament, especially in the Q tradition, establishes a close connection between its picture of Jesus and the idea of Wisdom found in the late Hebraic wisdom tradition. Some of the New Testament's most ancient hymns use this notion of preexistent Wisdom to interpret the meaning of Jesus. Hebrews 1:2-4, Philippians 2:6-11, Colossians 1:15-20, and most clearly the prologue of the gospel of John express Jesus' divine significance by symbols derived from this tradition:

> In the beginning was the Word, and the Word was with God, and the Word was God. He was in the beginning with God; all things were made through him, and without him was not anything made that was made. . . . And the Word became flesh and dwelt among us, full of grace and truth; we have beheld his glory, glory as of the only Son from the Father (John 1:1-3, 14).

Thus Christians came to affirm, and continue to affirm, that it was the divine Logos in Jesus who gives us universal peace. Apart from the relation he mediates with the universal God, we cannot know any ultimate peace in our human history. Yet the ideological strains in the national/cultural particularities of our human existence make our reception of universal peace problematic, as became evident from the very beginning. Even the way in which it was received and expressed in the earliest apostolic communities shows this ideological distortion, as we already have noted in the arguments about the salvific meaning of the Jewish Torah. The inertia of their Jewish, Greek and Roman histories resisted any more universal meaning. Habit, anxiety, and defensiveness distorted, and continue to distort, our human reception of the incarnation of God's universal gracious Logos.

This problematic of universal peace and historical particularity puts before us the very elements with which every theologian has had to work in understanding Christology. The issue always has been whether and how a fully particular person and, in Jesus' case, a fully Jewish man might "incarnate" the universal wisdom and peace of God. Because Christians experience Jesus as having done so, the further question is to what degree his Jewish and hellenistic disciples could receive and communicate this revelation of universal peace in our Scripture without ideological distortion. The same issue continues down to our day: Can European or Russian or American or Asian or African Christians hope to receive the gift of universal peace from the Christ mediated through our Scripture and interpreted within the traditions of our churches?

Dialectical Panentheism: The Incarnate Logos as Critical Transformation

The way toward non-ideological reception of Christ's universal peace, in my judgment, runs ecumenically from Chalcedonian understandings of Christ's divine-human unity through the contemporary reformulations of the Logos Christology that always has been its basis. Only when we understand that there is one Creator at work through one Logos in the whole creation to bring it to communion through one Spirit will we be drawn toward universal community in our finite communities without succumbing to the sinful dynamic of their alter egoisms. It was precisely because the author of Colossians experienced the Logos of creation in Jesus that he could interpret the resurrected Christ as reconciling all things in universal peace:

> For in him all the fullness of God was pleased to dwell, and through
> him to reconcile to himself all things, whether on earth or in heaven,
> making peace by the blood of his cross (Colossians 1:19, 20).

Wolfhart Pannenberg's and especially John Cobb's understanding of the Logos as "creative transformation" universally incarnated in a dynamic world process provides an adequate christological perspective to guide our struggle for universal peace.[9] When the church follows the non-dualistic criteria of Chalcedon, every liberating and reconciling impulse Christians receive through Jesus will be mediated in the sociopolitical processes where we seek peace.

Cobb's panentheistic Christology, however, because it fails to include any salvific meaning of the cross for resolving the conflicts of human history, must be deepened by the "dialectical panentheism" of Jürgen Moltmann.[10] The creative transformation accomplished through the Logos' incarnation in Jesus finally required his death and resurrection. Dialectical panentheism affirms that the conflicts we experience in history are taken into the suffering love of God and transformed into forgiveness and new possibility. This concept also enables us to understand that the only peace we shall know through the power and pathos of God is a dialectical peace that requires and enables our participation in historical struggle. The full meaning and joy of this struggle for peace with justice may best be interpreted, as Moltmann and Leonardo Boff do, in terms of participating in the trinitarian life of God:

> The mystery of the Trinity is reflected in human community, which lives by truth, keeps seeking more truth, finds its nourishment in love, and works constantly for social relations based on greater love and brotherhood.[11]

To participate spiritually and politically in transforming the conflictual social reality of which we are a part, however, runs the risk of ideologically compromising the church's identity with the Logos' incarnation in Jesus. The "always already" of the church's ecumenical catholicity is always limited by the "not yet" of our continuing social fragmentation. This requires giving at least preliminary privilege to any who have been oppressed or marginalized, so that the church may continue to be creatively transformed toward increasing catholicity. Only thus may we move toward universal peace through participation in the power and pathos of God.

Notes

1. St. Augustine, *The City of God*, XIX, 12.
2. Pinchas Lapide and Jürgen Moltmann, *Jewish Monotheism and Christian Trinitarian Doctrine*, trans. Leonard Swidler (Philadelphia: Fortress Press, 1981), p. 91. Cf. the comprehensive research and the irenic conclusions of Robert Jewett, "The Law and Coexistence of Jesus and Gentiles in Romans," *Interpretation* XXXIX, No. 4 (October 1985): 341–56.
3. Gibson Winter, *Scientific and Ethical Perspectives on Social Process* (New York: Macmillan, 1966), p. 54.
4. Wolfhart Pannenberg, *Jesus, God and Man* (Philadelphia: Westminster Press, 1968), pp. 47f.
5. Winter, *Scientific and Ethical Perspectives*, p. 54.
6. The work of Erik H. Erikson is especially instructive here; cf. especially *Identity and the Life Cycle* (New York: W. W. Norton & Co., 1959, 1980).

7. For an insightful and provocative interpretation of this theme in relation to contemporary experience, I know nothing better than Prof. James A. Sanders' lecture on "The New History: Joseph, Our Brother," interpreting Genesis 37:1–11 and Matthew 5:43–48, delivered to and published by the Ministers and Missionaries Benefit Board, The American Baptist Convention, 1968.

8. This certainly was my experience in studying theology when neo-orthodox interpretations were dominant, especially with Reinhold Niebuhr. For insight to the wisdom/blessing motif that is equally intrinsic to Scripture, cf. Clauss Westermann, *What Does the Old Testament Say About God?* (Atlanta: John Knox Press, 1979); and Walter Brueggemann, *In Man We Trust: The Neglected Side of Biblical Faith* (Richmond: John Knox Press, 1972).

9. John B. Cobb, Jr., *Christ in a Pluralistic Age* (Philadelphia: Westminster Press, 1975), p. 75.

10. Jürgen Moltmann, *The Crucified God*, trans. R. A. Wilson and John Bowden (New York: Harper & Row, 1974), p. 277.

11. Leonardo Boff, *Liberating Grace*, trans. John Drury (Maryknoll, NY: Orbis Books, 1979), p. 211.

Contributors

Kurt Biedenkopf. Member of the West German Parliament (*Bundestag*). Former General Secretary of the Christian Democratic Party. Professor of Business Law and former Rector of the University of Bochum. Author of *Theses for Energy Policy, Progress in Freedom* and *Outlines of a Political Strategy*.

Delwin Brown. Harvey H. Potthoff Professor of Christian Theology, Iliff School of Theology, Denver, Colorado, and a foremost representative of Process Theology. Author of *To Set at Liberty: Christian Faith and Human Freedom*.

Jimmy Carter. Thirty-ninth President of the United States, who regards his peace initiative in the Middle East as one of the most important contributions of his presidency. Author of *Why Not the Best?, A Government as Good as Its People, Keeping the Faith* and *The Blood of Abraham: Insights into the Middle East*.

Gonzalo Castillo-Cardenas. Associate Professor in Church and Society and Third-World Studies at Pittsburgh Theological Seminary, Pittsburgh, Pennsylvania. A native of Colombia, before coming to the United States he was involved in the Church and Society Movement (ISAL) in Latin America and popular education among Indian and peasant communities in Colombia. Author of *Liberation Theology from Below*.

G. Clarke Chapman. Professor of Religion at Moravian College, Bethlehem, Pennsylvania, and chairperson of the Lehigh Valley Interfaith Peace Resource Center. Author of *Facing the Nuclear Heresy: A Call to Reformation*.

Rebecca Chopp. Associate Professor of Systematic Theology, Candler School of Theology, Emory University, Atlanta, Georgia. An editor-at-large of the *Christian Century*, and co-editor of *Religious Studies Review*. Author of *The Praxis of Suffering* and *The Power to Speak: Feminism, Language and God*.

Riggins R. Earl, Jr. Associate Professor of Christian Ethics, Interdenominational Theological Center, Atlanta, Georgia. Author of *To You Who*

Teach in the Black Church and *Dialectics of Slave Liberation: Foundations of Black Theology and Ethics*.

Marc H. Ellis. Associate Professor and Director, Peace and Justice Program and Summer Institute for Justice and Peace, Maryknoll School of Theology, Maryknoll, New York. Author of *Peter Maurin: Prophet in the Twentieth Century*, *Faithfulness in an Age of Holocaust* and *Toward a Jewish Theology of Liberation*.

Gabriel Fackre. Abbot Professor of Christian Theology, Andover-Newton Theological School, Newton Centre, Massachusetts. Author of *The Christian Story* (2 vols.) and *The Religious Right and the Christian Faith*.

Manuel Antonio Garretón. Member, Central Committee, Socialist Party of Chile. Professor of Sociology, Latin American Faculty of the Social Sciences (FLACSO), Santiago, Chile. Visiting Professor, Kellogg Institute, University of Notre Dame, South Bend, Indiana. Author of *National Integration and Marginalization*, *The Political Process in Chile* and *Dictatorship and Democracy*.

Gordon Harland. Professor, Department of Religion, University of Manitoba, Winnipeg, Canada. Author of *The Thought of Reinhold Niebuhr* and *Christian Faith and Society*.

Dennis P. McCann. Associate Professor, Religious Studies, DePaul University, Chicago, Illinois. Co-Director, Center for the Study of Values in Modern Society; Chairperson, Board of Directors, World Without War Council Midwest. Author of *New Experiment in Democracy: The Challenge for American Catholicism* and *Christian Realism and Liberation Theology*.

José Míguez Bonino. Former Dean and Professor of Systematic Theology, Institute of Advanced Theological Studies (ISEDET), Buenos Aires, Argentina. Woodruff Visiting Professor, Emory University, Atlanta, Georgia. Former President of the World Council of Churches and member of the Faith and Order Commission. Author of *Doing Theology in a Revolutionary Situation*, *Christians and Marxists* and *Toward a Christian Political Ethics*.

Jürgen Moltmann. Professor of Systematic Theology, University of Tübingen, West Germany. Woodruff Visiting Professor, Emory University, Atlanta, Georgia. Member of the Faith and Order Commission, World Council of Churches and of the Department of Theology, World Alliance of Reformed Churches. Active in the Jewish-Christian Dialogue and the Marxist-Christian Dialogue. Editor of the journal *Evangelische Theologie*. Author of *The Theology of Hope*, *The Crucified God*, *The Church in the Power* *of the Spirit, The Future of Creation, On Human Dignity, The Trinity and the Kingdom,* and *God in Creation.*

Theodore Runyon. Professor of Systematic Theology, Candler School of Theology, Emory University, Atlanta, Georgia. Editor of *Hope for the Church: Moltmann in Dialogue with Practical Theology, Sanctification and Liberation: Liberation Theologies in Light of the Wesleyan Tradition,* and *Wesleyan Theology Today.*

Theodore R. Weber. Professor of Social Ethics, Candler School of Theology, Emory University, Atlanta, Georgia. President of the North American Society of Christian Ethics, he is an authority on just-war theory. Author of *Biblical Faith and Ethical Revolution, Modern War and the Pursuit of Peace* and *Foreign Policy Is Your Business.*

James E. Will. Pfeiffer Professor of Systematic Theology and Director, Peace Institute, Garrett-Evangelical Theological Seminary, Evanston, Illinois. Author of *The Moral Rejection of Nuclear Deterrence, Must Walls Divide?* and *A Christology of Peace.*

John H. Yoder. Professor of Theology, University of Notre Dame, South Bend, Indiana. Fellow, Institute of International Peace Studies. Author of *The Politics of Jesus, The Priestly Kingdom: Social Ethics as Gospel* and *When War Is Unjust.*

Andrew Young. Mayor of Atlanta, Georgia. Former U.S. Ambassador to the United Nations, U.S. Congressman from Georgia, Executive Director of the Southern Christian Leadership Conference, and a close associate of Martin Luther King, Jr.

Index

DATE DUE
